# Reporting from the Front

# Reporting from the Front

## The Media and the Military

JUDITH SYLVESTER
AND SUZANNE HUFFMAN

ROWMAN & LITTLEFIELD PUBLISHERS, INC.
*Lanham • Boulder • New York • Toronto • Oxford*

ROWMAN & LITTLEFIELD PUBLISHERS, INC.

Published in the United States of America
by Rowman & Littlefield Publishers, Inc.
A wholly owned subsidary of The Rowman & Littlefield Publishing Group, Inc.
4501 Forbes Boulevard, Suite 200, Lanham, MD 20706
www.rowmanlittlefield.com

P.O. Box 317, Oxford OX2 9RU, UK

British Library Cataloguing in Publication Information Available

**Library of Congress Cataloging-in-Publication Data**

Sylvester, Judith L., 1952–
  Reporting from the front : the media and the military / Judith
Sylvester and Suzanne Huffman
    p. cm.
  Includes index.
  ISBN 0-7425-3059-0 (alk. paper) — ISBN 0-7425-3060-4 (pbk. : alk. paper)
  1. Iraq War, 2003—Press coverage.   2. Iraq War, 2003—Journalists.
  3. War—Press coverage—United States.   I. Huffman, Suzanne.   II. Title
DS79.76.S954 2005
070.4'4995670443—dc

                                                                    2005011766

Printed in the United States of America

⊗™ The paper used in this publication meets the minimum requirements of American
National Standard for Information Sciences—Permanence of Paper for Printed Library
Materials, ANSI/NISO Z39.48-1992.

To all the journalists who died in battle
and to all the American soldiers who died on Iraqi soil.
—Judith Sylvester

To my father, who served in the U.S. Army,
and to my brother, who served in the U.S. Air Force.
—Suzanne Huffman

# CONTENTS

# ACKNOWLEDGMENTS

To colleagues at Lousiana State University and Texas Christian University who offered encouragement and support; and to Janelle and Jennifer Sylvester and Nadine Smith, who were inspirations.

Special thanks to the public relations specialists at the Associated Press, CNN, National Public Radio, CBS, and the Pentagon who arranged interviews and provided facts and figures; and to the A. H. Belo Corporation, for encouragement and assistance in numerous ways.

Journalist in the Palestine Hotel had front row seats as a group of Iraqis attempted to pull down one of Saddam Hussein's statues shortly after American troops arrived in Baghdad. When the Iraqis failed to topple the image, U.S. Marines moved in and provided assistance. On April 9, 2003, AP Photographer of the Year (2003) Jerome Delay recorded the scene as Cpl. Edward Chin from New York, of the 3rd Battalion, 4th Marines Regiment, wrapped the Stars and Stripes across Saddam's face. However, soldiers had been ordered not to display the American flag; so within minutes, the Iraqi flag replaced Old Glory and the statue fell. Jerome Delay and NPR Anne Garrels describe the scene on pages 207–8. (AP Photo/Jerome Delay)

# Introduction

# INTRODUCTION

Freedom of the press has been a vital component of United States governance since the First Amendment to the Constitution was adopted in 1791, a few years after the individual states that became the United States declared themselves in 1776 to be a separate nation. The First Amendment states: "Congress shall make no law respecting an establishment of religion, or prohibiting the free exercise thereof; or abridging the freedom of speech, or of the press; or the right of the people peaceably to assemble, and to petition the government for a redress of grievances." How, in reality, the freedom of the press in particular is expressed and exercised can be controversial when it concerns the coverage of war and other military and national security matters.

The American colonists had objected to the monarch's control of the press in Britain and in the colonies. The idea of a democracy is that the government derives its just powers from the consent of the governed. In reality, citizens must be fully informed to give that consent. About thirty newspapers operated in the American colonies by 1765. The first daily paper began in 1784. These papers were of two general types—they were political, or they were commercial. In 1848, the Associated Press (AP) cooperative was founded as a way for newspapers to cut costs by sharing stories. This arrangement introduced a more "objective" tone to news reporting, at a time when stories were becoming more widely and quickly distributed because they could be transmitted over the newly invented telegraph. In 1851, the *New York Times* was founded and would grow into what many would call the nation's "newspaper of record."

In the 1860s, when photography was new, Mathew Brady brought a sense of photographic documentation to his recording of the U.S. Civil War. Brady and his camera team followed the armies and photographed every phase of the war—including battlefields, ruins, officers, men, artillery, corpses, ships, and railroads—and Americans saw the photos weeks and months later in public exhibitions. Nothing like them had ever been seen in America before. The art of engraving photographs for reproduction had not yet been invented when Brady and his team of photographers were working. The majority of the seven thousand negatives taken by Brady and his camera team are preserved in the National Archives and in the Library of Congress for civilians and historians to see to this day when they contemplate the carnage of that conflict. Readers of newspapers and magazines of that era had to rely on the work of artists and illustrators using pen and ink to see what the fighting looked like. For these artists, being a spectator was nearly as dangerous as being a participant.

In the 1890s, prior to the Spanish–American War, rival New York City publishers William Randolph Hearst and Joseph Pulitzer began fighting a newspaper circulation war with sensationalistic coverage that may have inflamed the military situation. To sell more newspapers, Hearst had his writers "make up" stories about Spanish soldiers' committing atrocities in Cuba and about Americans in peril there. One of Hearst's employees in Cuba cabled him, "Everything is quiet. There is no trouble here. There will be no war." Hearst cabled back, "You supply the pictures. I'll supply the war." He then did. By reading the headlines, one may remember the sinking of the battleship *Maine* in Cuba's harbor but may not remember that it might have been only an accident.

During World War I, from 1914 until 1918, Americans read about the European battlefront in national magazines and in hometown and national newspapers. Some saw brief newsreel film coverage narrated by Lowell Thomas when they went to the movies on the weekends. The romanticized dispatches Thomas produced about Lawrence of Arabia in particular not only became brilliant propaganda but also grew into one of the most enduring myths of the war.

Media industries grew and expanded during the early twentieth century. The number of newspapers and magazines grew as did their circulation areas and readership. Radio and television were developed and quickly became popular American household fixtures. The craft and practice of journalism also grew and developed during these years. Journalism schools and programs were established, and ever greater numbers of students enrolled to learn how to write and record "the first draft of history."

To millions of Americans waiting on the home front as World War II unfolded, Ernie Pyle's newspaper column offered a foxhole view of the struggle. He reported on the life, and sometimes death, of the average soldier. Pyle was traveling with a group of infantrymen on a small island just west of Okinawa in April 1945, when he was killed by a sniper's machine-gun bullets. By the time Pyle died, his readership was worldwide, and his column appeared in hundreds of daily and weekly newspapers. He did not report so much on the war of "maps and logistics" as on the war of "the homesick and weary common man." He reported from Britain, North Africa, Sicily, Italy, and France as well as from the Pacific theater. Although

Pyle's columns covered almost every branch of the service, he saved his highest praise and devotion for the regular foot soldier. He wrote, "I love the infantry because they are the underdogs. They are the mud-rain-frost-and-wind boys. They have no comforts, and they even learn to live without the necessities. And in the end they are the guys that wars can't be won without."

Broadcaster Edward R. Murrow also covered Europe during World War II. He worked for CBS Radio, and his voice became familiar to millions of Americans listening in at home. Murrow gave an eyewitness report on Adolf Hitler's seizure of Austria in 1938, and in 1944 he rode a C-47 loaded with Allied paratroopers to a drop zone in Holland, recording his audio dispatches aboard the plane. One of his many memorable scripts recounts the 1945 liberation of the Buchenwald concentration camp in Germany. He wrote, "As I walked down to the end of the barracks, there was applause from the men too weak to get out of bed. It sounded like the hand clapping of babies; they were so weak."

As a correspondent for the wire service United Press International (UPI), Walter Cronkite covered several battles of World War II, including the D-Day invasion of Normandy, in June of 1944, in which thousands of American, British, and German soldiers were killed. While there was unlimited access to the battlefront, Cronkite and his fellow journalists submitted everything they wrote to military censors, who decided if and when the copy would be released. Technological advances, such as the trans-Atlantic cable and radio, increased the speed with which dispatches could be received and printed or broadcast. Media competition also moved in a different direction, with journalists from a number of news organizations competing for stories and "scoops."

Many in that generation will always remember Alfred Eisenstaedt's classic *Life* magazine photograph of a sailor kissing a nurse in New York's Times Square to celebrate with relief and jubilation the end of that long war. That photographic image became part of the nation's collective consciousness, as did a number of popular songs. Receiving widespread radio play were songs with lyrics ranging from "There'll be bluebirds over the white cliffs of Dover, someday when the world is free" to "Praise the Lord and pass the ammunition and we'll all be free."

By the 1960s and 1970s, television was a presence in most U.S. homes, and military leaders would later blame television news coverage in particular for eroding public support for military action in Vietnam. Nightly news film of carnage on the battlefield created a stark contrast to official military pronouncements that the United States was winning that conflict. Bob Schieffer covered the Vietnam conflict, as did scores of other broadcast and print reporters and photographers, by writing the stories of local soldiers for his hometown Texas newspaper. Schieffer sees parallels between the kind of reporting he sought to produce and the embedded journalists' reports of the Iraq War. However, uncensored reporting resulted in a distrust between the military and the media that continued until the embed program began.

Marlene Sanders and Liz Trotta also covered Vietnam, becoming among the first American women to work as war correspondents "in the field." At that time, foreign desk editors in some news organizations thought women in war zones would be too sensitive. They were right, in a way. That sensitivity produced some of the most moving reports, thanks to the determination and professionalism of the small group of female correspondents who covered the Vietnam War. They had to overcome the so-called Westmoreland edict, in which the top U.S. commander, General William C. Westmoreland, aimed to ban female reporters from combat zones. Photographer Dicky Chapelle, a woman of infinite courage who was covering a marine operation when a land mine exploded, died covering that conflict. The North Vietnamese captured UPI's Kate Webb and held her for a harrowing period. Radio freelancer Jurate Kazickas still carries within her person some shrapnel from the shell that wounded her. These women had to overcome a prevailing sexism and narrow-mindedness among mostly male editors and an entirely male military brass.

In 1991, when the United States government and President George H. W. Bush undertook the Persian Gulf War to drive Iraqi strongman Saddam Hussein out of Kuwait, the southern neighbor he had invaded, journalists were largely barred from on-the-scene coverage. They were limited to reporting on what government officials said and showed about what was happening on the battlefield. It became something of a videogame war in the public memory because many of the images were sterile gun-sight videos of bombs dropping on targeted buildings, bridges, and vehicles. In hindsight, U.S. officials may have regretted that there were few independent eyewitness accounts and photographs of what the officials viewed as the rapid success of that war. The expectation when the United States ended that war was that Saddam's own people would quickly drive him from power and overthrow his government. But that did not happen.

On September 11, 2001, nineteen Muslim men hijacked four U.S. commercial passenger planes and used them to attack the United States. The hijackers/ terrorists flew two of the planes into the World Trade Center towers in New York City, and the other one into the Pentagon, outside Washington, D.C.; one crashed into a field in Pennsylvania. The actions of these men were regarded as acts of war. Because news helicopters were in the air covering the rush-hour morning commute in New York City, some television viewers actually saw— live—the second plane crash into the tower and explode into jet-fueled flames. The plane that crashed in Pennsylvania was believed to be headed toward either the U.S. Capitol or the White House; but when passengers on board learned about the other hijacked planes (through cell-phone conversations with their families), they are believed to have stormed the cockpit, overpowered the hijackers, and taken the plane down into the field instead. In the days that followed September 11, President George W. Bush declared war on terrorists such as the hijackers and on any and all nations that harbor such terrorists.

In the fall of 2002, when the United States and President George W. Bush and the U.S. military began developing plans to forcibly remove Saddam Hussein from power in Iraq, both the news media and the Department of Defense began to develop plans to place, or "embed," U.S. and international journalists among the troops themselves, should war come. Aware of the enormous number of journalists who would be clamoring to cover the war, Pentagon planners began to think about how to organize journalists' placement and how to protect them from potential biological and enemy attack. The thinking was that this arrangement would give a clearer picture of what was actually happening on the battlefields, even though only parts of the larger battle plan would be covered by any one correspondent at any one point in time, coverage that Defense Secretary Donald Rumsfeld would later call seeing "not the war in Iraq" but "slices of the war in Iraq."

The publicly stated purpose of the United States' going to war with Iraq in 2003 was "regime change"—to rid that country of the brutal dictatorship of Saddam Hussein. U.S. president George W. Bush emphasized the urgency of this course of action on January 28, 2003, in his nationally televised state of the union address. Bush said, "The British government has learned that Saddam Hussein recently sought significant quantities of uranium from Africa." Bush also implied that Saddam had, or was developing, weapons of mass destruction—chemical, biological, and possibly nuclear—that he could unleash, or threaten to unleash, on the rest of the world. The U.S. government would partially justify this preemptive action based on a United Nations Security Council resolution requiring Saddam to fully disarm, although Bush undertook this specific action without United Nations authority. He did cite congressional approval, given following the September 11 attacks, to protect the United States from terrorists.

On the evening of March 17, 2003, in another televised address to the nation, Bush gave Saddam Hussein forty-eight hours to leave Iraq or be removed by force. Saddam did not leave. By then, most journalists also were in position in Kuwait or were in the process of embedding with their assigned troops. About to pay off were the months of positioning, the securing of satellite access, and the testing of equipment that was the most advanced any journalist had taken onto the battlefield.

On March 20, 2003, Baghdad time, the United States, in coalition with its allies—Great Britain in particular—officially began waging war with Iraq by dropping a dawn hail of missiles and bombs on Baghdad, the Iraqi capital, where Saddam was believed to be at that moment. At the same time, thousands of coalition ground forces began moving into Iraq, coming in from Kuwait. Nearly seven hundred embedded journalists were advancing with these troops. (This was the evening of Wednesday, March 19, 2003, in the U.S. eastern time zone, and network anchors relayed the news to Americans who were watching at home. There is an eight-hour time difference between Iraq and the U.S. East Coast, and the bombing actually started less than forty-eight hours after Bush's speech. Iraq is eight thousand miles away from the U.S. East Coast.)

As the days and weeks passed, television viewers would see coalition tanks and armored personnel carriers crawling north through the Iraqi desert in the night-time, in the daytime, and through blinding sandstorms as the embedded corre-spondents sent back real-time video and audio reports from the advancing units. Viewers would see cruise missiles being launched from warships and submarines. They would see bombs rain down on Iraqi targets, setting those targets ablaze. They would see images of American and British soldiers killed, wounded, and held as prisoners of war, images that television networks in other countries, most notably Al Jazeera in Qatar and state-owned networks in other Arab nations, broadcast to the world by satellite. Newspaper and magazine readers would see similar, "still" images on front pages and covers. Radio listeners would hear the sounds of bombs falling and buildings exploding as correspondents delivered their satellite telephone reports live from the battlefields.

On April 9, 2003, the leading edge of a force of approximately 140,000 U.S. forces moving slowly up from the south reached Baghdad. Civilians and soldiers attached ropes to a towering statue of Saddam Hussein, standing in front of the Palestine Hotel at which numerous foreign journalists were staying, and pulled it down to the ground. That image was transmitted worldwide and became part of the collective consciousness of the war.

Heavy military action in Iraq continued for six weeks, until May 1, 2003, when President Bush declared the "major" combat over. U.S. troops then became in-volved in a "peacekeeping" effort in Iraq as political leaders worked out the details of electing a new government in Iraq and a timetable for U.S. forces to leave the country and return control to the Iraqis.

Throughout the summer and fall of 2003, U.S. and coalition forces continued searching for Saddam Hussein, and they sought out numerous Baathist Party leaders for prosecution. To aid the ground troops in this effort, the United States issued a deck of playing cards with pictures of the fifty-two most wanted leaders of the former Iraqi regime. Saddam Hussein was pictured as the ace of spades, his son Qusay was the ace of clubs, and his son Uday was the ace of hearts. U.S. and coalition forces also continued to search, without success, for Saddam's supposed large cache of weapons of mass destruction.

In late July 2003, the U.S. military released graphic postmortem photos of Saddam Hussein's sons, Qusay and Uday, to prove that U.S. troops had killed them in a fierce shootout in the northern Iraqi city of Mosul early in the week of July 20. The photos were immediately broadcast on the Arab satellite net-works Al Jazeera and Al Arabiyya, networks that are seen daily by millions of Arabs across the Middle East. On December 14, 2003, former Iraqi dictator Sad-dam Hussein was pulled from a "spider hole" hideout next to a hut near his hometown of Tikrit, Iraq, and taken into custody by U.S. forces. Immediately becoming part of the collective consciousness was the image of his disheveled face while a military medic checked his mouth with a small flashlight and tongue depressor. The U.S. government took Saddam into custody and later declared him a prisoner of war.

Attacks on U.S. forces in Iraq continued through the end of 2003 and into 2004. In fact, more U.S. military personnel were killed in Iraq after May 1, 2003, when Bush declared an end to major combat, than during the actual invasion of the country. By January 2004, the death toll of American soldiers killed in Iraq had passed five hundred. At least thirteen journalists had been killed covering the war there. In Ron Suskind's *The Price of Loyalty* (2004), former treasury secretary Paul O'Neill suggested that the Bush administration began laying the groundwork for an invasion of Iraq months before the September 11, 2001, terrorist attacks on the United States.

Coverage of this war by the embedded journalists, much of it up-close and live, was unprecedented, although the embedded concept itself was not. But Americans and viewers worldwide had never seen anything like the 2003 real-time coverage in Iraq. How the journalists came to be embedded, how they were trained, and how they did their work in such dangerous conditions form the focus of this book: What was it like to be there? What was it like to write and photograph and report under those conditions? What is it like to now live with those memories and pictures? This is the story of how journalism "got done" in the early twenty-first-century battlefield, much of it in the words of the journalists who did the work, with retrospectives and comparisons by reporters who covered previous wars and conflicts.

# Retrospective

## WALTER CRONKITE
CBS ANCHOR/CORRESPONDENT EMERITUS

---

Walter Cronkite, the dean of television broadcasters, was a United Press (UP) war correspondent from 1941 shortly after the bombing of Pearl Harbor through the end of the war and the Nuremberg war-crime trials. As a correspondent, he covered nearly all the branches of the armed services. He was on the North Atlantic convoys immediately after the Pearl Harbor bombing, when there were still problems with German submarines cutting them off. Then, he made the landing in North Africa, after which he went to England to cover the air war, the only war going out of England at the time. He made flights with the Ninth Air Force over Germany and France. He covered the Battle of the Bulge and dropped with the Army Airborne into Holland. "So I got a broad experience as a war correspondent," he said.

During World War II, the U.S. government had nothing to do with correspondents' assignments. "We requested where we wanted to go, and then they made arrangements for us to go, usually. Very seldom were missions put off limits to us," he said. "All written copy was passed by censors. And I think that is the way it should be. We had total freedom at the front with no restrictions where we went. When we were with an army or a division we would get the same briefing that their officers got in the morning as to where the action was likely to be and what the plan was for the day, and we would just decide where we wanted to go."

Cronkite said that correspondents had at their disposal jeeps with government issue (GI) drivers who would get them as close to the action as possible. "We'd cover the action during the day—sometimes for a couple of days. We'd be sleeping in foxholes with the troops, but then we had to go back to headquarters to file our copy. We'd write up a piece and submit it to the intelligence officer for the unit." Cronkite said that if the officer didn't think the copy was too sensitive, he would okay it to be sent back to the chief censors in London. "They would approve it there and then release it for our wire service, United Press, to distribute. It worked very, very satisfactorily," he said. "I believe—in that system—censorship is necessary in those cases where they give us full freedom of the battlefront. They've obviously got to be sure that we are not releasing any military secrets in the copy that we file thereafter. I believe in censorship. It worked pretty well. It was very fair. We could appeal when they censored something [that would put the troops in danger]. And when they did censor something, they would put it on file, and as soon as the danger to their intelligence passed, they would release it. So we were able to report history at all times."

Cronkite said that the history of the battles, and the way men and women responded to it, was preserved. There was no question that the press observers would be able to print their stories—eventually, if not immediately. However, Cronkite doubts that the old system would work as well in this day of satellite television coverage. "In that case there would have to be a different sort of monitoring—what was reported and where it was reported from, I assume. Maybe the system they used in World War II was as close as you could come, but maybe it could use some improvement."

Although he didn't land on the beach with the troops, Cronkite was a D-Day observer. "I was overhead on D-Day, with a special mission of B-17s. For the first time, B-17s were being used at lower levels, to go after some German gun emplacements on the beach." Cronkite completed that historic mission and then returned to Normandy three days later.

Media were very different in 1945. "Of course there was no Internet, computers, or satellites. Television had not been perfected yet. But radio and print complemented each other very definitely. It was a little more difficult for radio to operate. Without satellites not all radio transmission went through. They were interrupted by atmospherics and other things. Far more reliable was print, which was carried by cable. They were carried by radio from the front to London and then were transmitted by cable from London to New York. That was a reliable form of communications."

The length of time required to get stories from the field onto the printed page varied. "It depended upon whether it was held up by censors or by communication problems, but if it was passed on the scene by the intelligence officer to London and transmitted by cable, today's story could be in tomorrow's morning papers. It certainly wasn't wide coverage in the way we saw television coverage during the Iraq War."

Cronkite said that there were many reporters on the scene who could have been considered the pioneers of war coverage. "There was no exclusivity among the reporters as to who was doing a good job and who wasn't doing a good job. There were some who weren't quite as good as others, but there were many who were very good, and who were much better than I."

However, competition among media companies was a factor. "We [UP] had a lot of tough competition with the Associated Press and the International News Service. We were out to beat them. When I decided which unit I was going to go with, I hoped the AP guy wouldn't decide to go to the same place so that we wouldn't have competing stories, and I would have an exclusive if there was good action out there to make it a good story. And of course many times, when there wasn't any immediate action, we'd dream up a feature story that we had in mind—a particular unit or a particular soldier perhaps or a particular community who had taken it on the chin, that sort of thing. So there were many opportunities for initiative to get his own type of reporting in."

Cronkite said that Ernie Pyle made a point of being with the forward troops at all times. "It was very daring of him; he was taking great risks and got caught [killed] at it. But his problem then was getting his copy back because he wrote it in a foxhole on a beaten up typewriter. He had to get some GI to get it back to headquarters for him. That was a case of where a very good reporter sets a kind of story that he is going to specialize on."

Most of those in the press corps covered all kinds of stories, such as the briefings at headquarters, especially at the Third Army headquarters at the Battle of the Bulge. "That story was really at headquarters—how that battle was going. For several days it was a frightening situation. The Germans might be able to get to Antwerp and cut the Allies in half. As that situation improved then, we had the story at Bastogne. The 101st Airborne was surrounded by German forces and cut off from the rest of the American forces. That was a major story for a few days. We would leave the Third Army headquarters in Luxemburg and go up close to the front where the Germans were. Of course we couldn't get through to our own troops, nobody could. But we could see what the German battle looked like."

Unlike the contact that reporters had with Iraqis, contact with the Germans, except for a few prisoners, was nonexistent. "I wasn't really conscious of it, but apparently the American and Allied forces kept prisoners separated from us. Occasionally we'd see them, of course, as they would be taken back toward the rear. But we were never given the opportunity to associate with them."

After the end of World War II, Cronkite was planning to go back to Europe as United Press general news manager for Europe. But the Korean War broke out, and Edward R. Murrow wanted him to go to Korea as a correspondent. So he swung over to CBS, but then the network expanded its television network and needed an anchorman, so they moved him into that rather than send him to Korea. Cronkite said that the reporting on the Korean War was quite similar to that of World War II. "It was the same pattern precisely. The correspondents went where they wanted to go. They hitchhiked to the nearest unit and joined them. They had to have war correspondent credentials, but then those credentials were a free pass to the front with any unit you wanted to go with. That included the air force, marines, navy, and everybody."

"In Vietnam it was even looser in that there was no mass operation, no major movement along the front. Everything was on patrols in this jungle and they had guerrilla warfare, which was a vastly different game. There you just heard of a group that was going out on patrol and you just hitched along with them. You got as far as they got, and then when they started hacking their way through the jungle, you hitched along with them. There was no communication at all from that operation until you got back. If you got back safely, you got back to Saigon and hammered out a story."

Cronkite said that some other correspondents, who were not committed to covering the battle themselves, simply covered army headquarters in Saigon and reported on its briefings. "It was that free coverage and that lack of censorship that suffered and the old army command from Vietnam, many of them blamed the press and television for losing the war for them. That canard was attacked by army intelligence and they came out with a report that said that it was not the fault of the press that we lost that war, but that did not change the minds of an awful lot of top officers."

Cronkite said that, as a result, the press has never since had the kind of freedom that it had in Vietnam, Korea, or during World War II. "The next few actions that we got involved in—Panama, Grenada—we were not permitted to be anywhere near them. The army did attempt, on the advice of several of us who sat with the secretary of defense, to work out a plan for pooled coverage of the next operation, which turned out to be Panama. They did send pooled reporters along with the invasion forces in Panama, but then they didn't permit them to cover the action. Meanwhile there were a lot of assigned reporters who were covering Panama outside the army, and they were reporting the stories freely. So that didn't work. Then for Grenada they didn't permit any coverage whatsoever. When reporters tried to get ashore in Grenada in some of their own boats, they were threatened with being shot at by the U.S. Navy. They had to back off."

Cronkite said that lack of freedom was still the case during the first Persian Gulf War. "There it was a major war and it was really criminal, I think, that the army did not permit any coverage of live action of any kind. They allegedly selected some pool reporters and then didn't let them accompany the troops in action or report anything. So the American people in one of the more sensitive commitments between the people and its government—that is sending young people to war—did not permit us to have any history or any reporting of how our troops performed in that war. We'll never have that history, because there were no news people along—only the military."

Television changed the way war is covered. "In Vietnam we were taking cameras along with the troops into action. They had to get back to Saigon to airship the film back to the United States. There was about a twenty-four-hour to thirty-six-hour delay. But still, people were getting on their evening newscasts very graphic action film almost every day."

He said that CBS grappled with how to handle these graphic pictures. "We were very sensitive to pictures themselves. We considerably limited those pictures that showed blood letting and missing members and things of that kind. Very rarely did we show that. We showed the action taking place but did not focus on the wounds themselves."

Cronkite does not see an escalation in gory visual coverage of the Iraq War. "It's not more graphic particularly because of the nature of the war itself. Most of the damage was being done to the Iraqis out of sight of our cameras. We were not taking that kind of casualties. And also the nature of the assignments was such that the army, of course, assigned the reporters to different units and spread them around so that all units have some coverage. The result in that was that a few of the reporters and camera people were lucky enough to see some action. But a lot of them were not. Because the company that sent them had spent a lot of money and made a big investment, they wanted to show their people on camera, so there was an awful lot of coverage that was not very interesting or at all important. It was that necessity of putting on the air correspondents who were with units who didn't do anything. In World War II if that were the case, we'd just move to the units that were in action. We didn't have to ask anybody's permission."

Biological weapons, particularly gas, were not as much of an issue in World War II as they had been in World War I. "They had used mustard gas and others in World War I, and there was an acknowledgment that this might happen again, although in the meantime between the two wars nearly all the combatants agreed they were not going to develop all this poison for warfare. Although gas masks were available, I don't recall anyone carrying them around with them.

"During World War II there was some specified training, for instance, for those of us who went with the airborne. We practiced parachute jumping from a tower—not jumping freely from an airplane—and landings on enemy shores for D-Day. You would try to wade to shore to get there safely. There were some specialized units that would give correspondents who wanted to go with them some training. But there wasn't much of that. For the air operation, flying in the B-17 flying fortresses, they gave us a six-day course in high altitude first aid—how to survive at high altitudes in case you lose oxygen and things like that. There was a little drill in how to behave if you had to parachute down and were captured by the enemy. But that was primitive sort of stuff really."

Cronkite noted that training was different for the Iraq War. "Most of them were carrying some very special equipment against germ warfare, against gas warfare and that kind of thing. They all had special armor that they wore. That was something quite different from World War II, when neither the soldiers nor the correspondents had any armor of any kind. We went into battle in our birthday suits practically. So there was a different preparation for a different kind of war."

During World War II, the military felt no obligation to protect journalists. "That wasn't part of the game. It was understood that correspondents who elected to go along with the troops faced the same danger as the troops, and there was no special effort to protect them or take care of them at all. They were along with the troops and were in the foxholes with the troops."

Cronkite thought the Iraq War coverage was "quite well done by those correspondents who were lucky enough to be with units that were in action. We got some pretty graphic pictures and some slight feelings about what the war was about. But this was a vastly different kind of war. Many correspondents were with units that did nothing. They didn't ever have a major firefight. They moved along very successfully, and they had accidents and lost some people, but without a firefight there wasn't anything to photograph. So it was spotty coverage, very spotty. It was not the correspondents' fault; it was the nature of the assignment."

For his long career, which ended with his retirement from CBS in 1981, Cronkite earned the title of "most trusted journalist in America." He covered every important story during the second half of the twentieth century, including the assassination of President John F. Kennedy and the first steps taken on the moon. Today he has returned to his roots and now writes a newspaper column. He wrote about his career in his book *A Reporter's Life*.

## BOB SCHIEFFER

CBS News Correspondent, Washington, D.C.

As a young reporter for the *Fort Worth Star-Telegram*, Bob Schieffer—now CBS News chief Washington correspondent and moderator of *Face the Nation*—spent more than four months in Vietnam, arriving in 1965. His main preparation for the job was reading Graham Greene's *The Quiet American*, which revolves around the experiences of an American in Vietnam during the French era. His assignment was to track down young soldiers who were from Texas, especially Fort Worth, and write feature stories about them.

"We ran ads in the paper saying 'Bob Schieffer is in Vietnam, and he's looking for your sons and daughters. Write him a letter,'" he said. "I was just overwhelmed with letters. I had a little mailbox in the AP office, and I would say over four months I probably got one thousand letters from people telling me where their kids were. I would literally line these letters up by location, and I'd go out into the field and stay a week or ten days, find these kids, and then I would come back to Saigon and write enough stories to last for about a week or ten days and then go back to the field."

He said that although he did get a few scoops along the way, he was mainly writing features that were not time sensitive. "These were stories about kids, and working as I was for a regional paper, I could really stay under the radar as far as the Pentagon was concerned because by the time my stuff showed up in the paper, it might be a week or so after it happened. I was writing stories about what it was like to be a soldier and how these kids were doing."

He still recalls the details of some of his encounters with young, homesick soldiers in the field. "I'll never forget, once, I was way out in the middle of nowhere, in the northern part of Vietnam in the Danang sector where the Marines were. I walked up to this kid, a marine, who was in full battle gear. He had on his body armor, his helmet, carrying his weapon. I said, 'I'm Bob Schieffer from the *Star-Telegram*, and your mom asked me to come and see how you were.' The kid broke into sobs—this big, tough marine, who was nineteen years old. He was so glad to see somebody from home, and he was so lonesome. It's not often you feel you can make a difference in someone's life, and most of the time when I would see these kids, it just made their day a little happier. It just made at least one day pass a little faster for them. I still think about that. Of all the things I've done in journalism, that remains the single most rewarding part of my career."

There was no embedding during the Vietnam era and very little control over reporters by the military. "Vietnam was maybe the last and maybe the only war in American history where there was no censorship. In World War II correspondents were assigned to units much as they were during this recent war, but everything they wrote had to be submitted to the censors who were traveling with that unit for clearance," he said. "In Vietnam there was no censorship."

Schieffer said that the lack of censorship was initially due to the military's not wanting the operation to appear to be an American war. The official line was that these were American troops who were in Vietnam to help the Vietnamese. "Once you take that line, then you can't say, 'But we're in charge of everything.' So, there was no censorship."

However, the military commanders would sometimes exert control by limiting transportation into areas where the news might be bad. "In theory, reporters had to get permission from the U.S. military command headquartered in Saigon to travel outside Saigon. If I wanted to travel to Danang, they would call flight operation and find a transport plane going there that afternoon and make a place for me. But when there was a battle where the news was not the way they wanted, it was very difficult to get transportation for that particular place. It was clear that they tried to block it off by putting a control on the transportation. But what most of the reporters realized after they'd been there a while and established relationships was that you could go around the central command and get to wherever you wanted to go."

Whether he was at the Ton Son Nhut airbase in Saigon or elsewhere in the country, Schieffer would go to flight operations and ask the officer in charge if they had anything going to Danang or to wherever he wanted to go. "If they did, I'd just go talk to the pilots and say, 'How about a ride?' Normally, they would give you one."

Schieffer learned that if he was willing to share the war with the people who were fighting it, they were happy to have reporters around. "The further you got from headquarters and the closer you got to the fighting, the more forthright the soldiers would be, the more helpful they would be. If you were willing to go where they were and run the risk of getting shot and if you were willing to sleep on the ground the way they were, you just established a camaraderie with them, and they would take you into their confidence. They would help you all they could."

So Schieffer would locate helicopter units and just hitch a ride. "They would do what they called 'water runs' where they would take water and food out to the guys who were dug in the foxholes out on the perimeters. I would just go with them, and then I would get off and visit with the people."

Filing his stories was far different from the "instant coverage" of the Iraq War. "It is almost quaint the way I did it. I would go out in the field. I would interview people and fill up my notebook. I was taking photos with the old standard Nikon thirty-five millimeter. Then I would go back to Saigon, where I would literally take my film to a drug store to be processed and get contact prints. I would take those contacts and draw circles in red crayon around the ones I wanted the *Star-Telegram* to use. Then I would just sit down at the typewriter, and I would write for about two days." Schieffer would try to send as many as ten to twelve stories at a time. "We had a morning and evening paper, so I wrote one piece for the morning paper, one for the evening paper, and then a Sunday takeout with pictures. Then I simply put them in letters and mailed them. I always sent at least two copies, and I wouldn't put all the stories in one envelope. Obviously, some of them were lost. But most of the time they got through."

Other news organizations used different methods to file stories. For example, the Associated Press reporters sent stories by wire, and television was experimenting with satellite technology. Television reporters were relying on what was essentially movie film but had no facilities to process it in Vietnam. "So if it was a story that they didn't think was that urgent, they would bundle it up. The correspondent would write and record the script and do a stand-up. Then they would literally ship it back by airline. There was airline service into Saigon on Ton Son Nhut airbase. They generally would send it to Los Angeles." He said that if the story were more important, they would process the film and assemble the piece in Los Angeles and then send it by either satellite or telephone line to New York.

However, if the story were time sensitive, the networks would go together, charter a plane—most likely a 707, a four-engine jet—and take the film to either Tokyo or Hong Kong; and then process, edit, and assemble the story there. "But in those days, the situation was such that the correspondent who covered the story would not know how his film came out. He was with the cameraman, of course, but he had no way of knowing if the pictures were any good. So care had to be taken in how the stories were written. Sometimes you would write alternative versions that you would record so that the editors and producers who were putting it together would have options if the shots didn't come out the way you expected. It was extremely difficult." Schieffer said that even when film was taken to Hong Kong or Tokyo, at least twelve hours and usually twenty-four hours would elapse between when the story happened and when people back in the States saw it.

Unlike many of the journalists covering the most recent Iraq War, Schieffer had no preparatory training. "I was twenty-seven years old and thought I was bulletproof—which was probably a good thing. It never occurred to me I couldn't do it, and after I got there I wasn't about to let those kids who were ten years younger than me think they could do something I couldn't do."

Schieffer said that when he was in Saigon, he went to restaurants; but when he was in the field, he shared rations with the solders for a very practical reason—there was no place else to eat. In his four-and-half months in the field, Schieffer estimates he went on thirty-five ground operations with marines and other American military. He also accompanied the air force on dangerous missions.

Schieffer honed his photography skills while in Vietnam. "I traveled around with photographer Eddie Adams, who won a Pulitzer. We'd go out together because he didn't really like to go out with the AP writers much, because he didn't want them telling him what to do. But I'd go along, and he taught me how to take pictures. I would catch cutlines [photo captions] for him. We traveled around together a lot, and he taught me the basics." He learned enough of "the basics" to later make it through two rounds of interviews with *Life* magazine, hoping to make it back to Vietnam. But a series of circumstances steered him into a career in broadcasting.

"After coming back from Vietnam, the local television station invited me to come out and talk about the war on the noon talk show. Afterward they offered me a job for twenty dollars a week more than I made at the newspaper. I literally didn't think there was that much money in the world. I took it because I needed the money."

He eventually moved to Washington, D.C., because he had decided he wanted to work for a national news organization. "I got to Vietnam, and I realized that I was as good a reporter as the other guys who were there. I just didn't have the circulation that they had. I wanted to work for a big newspaper—the *Washington Post*, the *New York Times*—and I sent out resumes and clips, and it came to nothing." He landed a job with a Metromedia station in Washington, D.C. "They were supposed to become the fourth network, but the financing fell through, and they didn't. But that is what brought me here," he said.

A fortuitous mix-up, at least for Schieffer, landed him at CBS. "I walked through the door one day without an appointment. I was mistaken for someone who had an appointment and got in to see the bureau chief. I always try to tell students not to get discouraged when they are trying to get a job because I tried for five years and then just walked in and got hired because they happened to need somebody." Whom did he displace? Robert (Bob) Hagar, the aviation correspondent for NBC.

In Schieffer's view, the Vietnam War and the Iraq War have some rather unpleasant parallels. One is the concern about the use of chemical weapons. Ironically, it was the U.S. military that used a chemical agent in Vietnam. A member of the dioxin family, Agent Orange is an herbicide that was sprayed into jungle areas in an attempt to destroy enemy cover. Although it was not intended to be used as a biological weapon, exposure to it was later linked to cancer, Hodgkin's disease, and birth defects in children and grandchildren. Unlike U.S. troops and journalists in Iraq, who had chemical suits and detectors for protection, those serving in Vietnam had no such advantage. "We did not know about Agent Orange at all," Schieffer said.

However, a second parallel is more apparent. "We were quite aware of terrorism. What is kind of tragic about what is happening in Iraq right now is that it is very much like Vietnam, in the sense that some of these kids [soldiers] would be out in the field, and they wouldn't hear a shot fired in anger for two or three weeks. Then they would get leave and come to Saigon and be sitting in a restaurant when some child would walk by and throw a hand grenade into the restaurant. There was always the specter of terrorism, and you always had to be on the alert for that. But you are seeing the same kind of situation now in Iraq, although the government has denied that."

Schieffer said that the question asked during the Vietnam War was, Are we winning? "In fact, that is the wrong question. When you are winning, you know you're winning. If you have to ask, you are probably losing." He says that the right question is, Is it worth the cost? "The American people concluded it was not worth the cost. We could still be in Vietnam, but how much would that have cost?"

The Vietnam experience led to a wariness between the press and the military that has lingered, even among reporters and soldiers who were too young to have been there. "In the military it became part of this lore that it was the fault of the press that the war turned badly. It wasn't," he insists. "The American people lost confidence and turned on the war because of the casualties. As the casualties began to mount in these towns, people began to ask, 'Is this worth what it is costing us?'"

Schieffer pointed out that he is part of the last generation of reporters who grew up in an era when there was a draft. "We either went in the army, were drafted, or were in the ROTC [Reserve Officers' Training Corps]. Some people tried to evade the draft. But everyone either was in the military or knew someone who was in the military. That has been going on since World War II. People had connections with the military."

That connection was lost with the all-volunteer army, but Schieffer believes the embed program has taught soldiers and journalists valuable lessons. "I think putting reporters with the military gave the reporters a better chance of coming to know the military, and I dare say it gave the military a chance to have a better understanding of what the press does. So I think it was good for both sides."

The program also gave reporters a chance to do reporting as Schieffer did in Vietnam. "Embedded reporters could write about and talk about people from their area. News is what's closest to city hall. If you live in Dallas, and you're seeing a story about a kid from Dallas, then it's a better story than if it is about a kid from New York, all other things being equal. I think that was a very smart thing for the Pentagon to do."

Schieffer credits Secretary of Defense Donald Rumsfeld with encouraging the development of the embed program. He said that Rumsfeld told him that the "uniform military" resisted the program. But Rumsfeld foresaw a need for American reporting. "He said that once American troops got to Baghdad, the Iraqis would use every kind of propaganda trick that they could to debunk whatever was happening there; and, in fact, that is exactly what happened." Schieffer pointed to the Iraqi information minister Mohammed Saeed al-Sahaf—mockingly referred to as "Baghdad Bob" and "Comical Ali"—who made ludicrous statements about the American march toward Baghdad. "They put him on one side of the screen and put what American cameras were showing on the other side of the screen. Don Rumsfeld, he was absolutely right about that. It was a very shrewd thing to do."

Schieffer said that Rumsfeld had not anticipated the extent to which reporters were able to tell the stories of American soldiers. "I think that the most important thing that happened is—and I think this is good, although you could argue it one way or the other—that it gave a whole new generation of American reporters a new appreciation of the American military and the difficult job they have to do."

Schieffer is aware of the criticism directed toward the embed program. "Other people say it puts reporters too close to the military and dulls objectivity. But my answer to that is, 'How can you know too much about a story?'" He sees little difference between the embeds and the typical beat reporters. "When I was coming up, beats were the core of every good newspaper. When you are out covering a beat and you do a story that is wrong, you are going to hear about it the next day because you have to go back and deal with the same people that you dealt with the day before and the day before that."

Schieffer has little respect for the journalists he calls "sharpshooters," reporters who "parachute into a story, do the story, and move on." He thinks they are less credible than the embedded reporter, who is covering the same people every day. "The embed is going to be kind of careful about how he reports; he is going to make sure he gets it right. That doesn't mean you aren't going to do a story they [the military commanders] don't like, but when you're doing a story that is a tough story, you are going to go get their side of it because the next day they are going to ask, 'Goddamn it, why didn't you come see what I had to say about this?'"

Schieffer thought that there were some very tough stories that could have been sensationalized with less-responsible reporting. He used as an example the deadly incident when American soldiers opened fire on civilians who tried to speed through a roadblock. "Had reporters not been on the scene, I don't think you would have gotten balanced coverage. It would have been very easy to get a sensational headline like 'Trigger-Happy U.S. GIs Slaughter Iraqis.' So I think it was a very good program on several levels."

Schieffer thinks Secretary Rumsfeld did the right thing in releasing the photographs of the dead bodies of Saddam Hussein's sons, Qusay and Uday. "I think you had to do it. I think it is very important. The people in Iraq have lived with lies, with a government who doesn't tell the truth. It is very difficult to convince them those guys are dead, and I think we had to do everything we could do." He also thinks that is it important to make "a really big deal" of paying the reward money offered for the capture of members of Saddam's family. "We have to let the Iraqis know that we are serious about that—that the money really is there, because in this case you are not dealing with religious nuts like Osama bin Laden, you are dealing with criminals—these people are criminals. Anybody who has ever been on the police beat knows that you don't catch criminals with clues or all that, like in mystery stories. You catch them when one of them rats on the other one."

He thinks the media were justified in showing graphic photos to the American public. "You tell the kids not to watch the TV on this one. I'm against gruesomeness, but I also believe that in a war you have to show the bodies every once in a while so people understand how awful it is. The example I cite is, you find people who watch the movie *The Longest Day*, and they all had the desire to be there on D-Day; but if you show those people *Saving Private Ryan*, nobody wants to be there, and they realize how difficult that war was and what those people were up against. We can't sanitize it. So obviously, you don't show gruesomeness to sensationalize it, but I think you have to give people a picture of what is going on. There is a downside, but I think in the long run it is better for the media to do it. You are performing a public service. I think you are saving lives."

In response to whether U.S. credibility is weak in Iraq, Schieffer said, "I don't think it is a question of U.S. credibility. I think it is that you are operating in a land where nobody can be sure anybody is telling the truth. People who have been ruled by Saddam Hussein—how in the hell are they supposed to know what is true? They sure haven't been told the truth in a long time. I don't think there is any argument about that. And I'll tell you something else. We don't owe Qusay and Uday anything. These people are thugs."

Schieffer likes how *Washington Post* television critic Tom Shales likened the release of the pictures to how the people of Oz couldn't believe the wicked witch was really dead; he remembered that the munchkin coroner had to reassure them that the witch was not just merely dead, but truly and sincerely dead.

Schieffer thinks the U.S. government overplayed its hand regarding weapons of mass destruction. "There is no question that they hyped it. In retrospect, it is quite clear that they were trying to make it appear that the threat of Saddam Hussein was more urgent than it was. I think he was a threat. I think it was a good idea. I think the world is better off without him. But there is no question that they juiced it up a little bit, and that is not good. It is not good in the long run. It is not good when this administration goes up to try to deal with Congress. It's not good if we have to ask people to go with us to Korea. They hurt themselves more than they helped themselves by trying to pile on evidence that wasn't there."

Did the huge financial commitment on the part of the military and the media make war inevitable? "I hope they weren't susceptible to this, but you have to ask the question, especially with the cable people, Did they fan the flames of war to boost ratings? I hope not. I don't think so, but I can understand why people would ask that question."

Schieffer said that another serious question is, Did the government go after Saddam Hussein because they couldn't find Osama bin Laden? "That is a very serious question."

Schieffer sees Afghanistan as a completely different military–media situation. "You had the special operations people running that operation, and they work in secret. That is what they are designed to do, and that's what they do. My guess is that they would not be very comfortable having a bunch of press with them. My guess is that toward the end you had more reporters there than you did special operations people. You can't have a large herd of reporters going around with six or eight military people."

According to Schieffer, the twenty-four-hour news cycle also pushes journalism to the edge at times, such as when the U.S. Supreme Court justices issued their opinion in regard to the 2000 presidential election. "The night I was standing out in front of the Supreme Court waiting for that decision was the coldest, loneliest night of my life. In the old days we probably would have looked at it and probably concluded what it meant and then gone on the air with it. But because everyone was anticipating a major story—and you don't get a much bigger story than that—we went on the air before the report came out because if the viewer is out there flipping around on the channel and he knows there is a big story coming, he wants to know about it. If he flips over to the CBS channel, and you are not on the air saying, 'Folks, we are going to have this for you as soon as we get it,' he's going to flip to someplace else. He is going to keep looking until he finds somebody on the air. Once he goes past your channel, he is not ever going to go back."

Schieffer provides more details about covering war and many other important stories in his book *This Just In: What I Couldn't Tell You on TV.*

## JOE GALLOWAY

SPECIAL CONSULTANT TO KNIGHT RIDDER NEWSPAPERS, WASHINGTON, D.C.

Joe Galloway has earned the title "legendary" among foreign correspondents. His career began in Vietnam and extended through most of the major conflicts in the last half of the twentieth century. He coauthored a book, *We Were Soldiers Once . . . and Young,* which was made into a Mel Gibson film. The United States Army, in May 1998, decorated him with a Bronze Star with *V,* for valor in combat, for rescuing wounded American soldiers under heavy enemy fire. "Mine was the only Bronze Star with *V* medal the army awarded to any civilian in the entire Vietnam War. One was awarded to a Red Cross worker in the Korean War. I wear that lapel pin every day, in memory of seventy of my journalist friends who gave their lives trying to tell the truth in Vietnam. I wear that pin in memory of Spec 4 Jimmy D. Nakayama of Rigby, Idaho, who died two days after I carried him out of a napalm fire."

Galloway did four tours as a war correspondent in Vietnam: 1965–1966, 1971, 1973, and 1975. He covered the India–Pakistan war of 1971; the Sri Lanka guerrilla uprising of 1971; and the Indonesian takeover of East Timor in 1976. Then, in 1990–1991, he covered Operations Desert Shield and Desert Storm, in the Persian Gulf War. His last outing was the Haiti incursion. "I did not go forward for this latest Iraq War. I was hired by Knight Ridder to train their young reporters going out to cover their first war and to write analysis pieces from Washington."

Perhaps no journalist better illustrates the difficulty in separating reporting duties from military duties under combat conditions than does Galloway. He didn't seek to carry a weapon, but a weapon was often thrust on him by field commanders who thought journalists should take orders as the soldiers under their command did.

"In over two-and-a-half years covering the war in Vietnam, on only two occasions did I feel obliged to use a weapon. In both cases I believed that it was necessary for my own survival and the survival of those around me. I make no apologies to anyone for that. I would do it again if the circumstances were the same," he said. "It was not my job. But an old friend, Ms. Dickey Chapelle, who was herself killed in Vietnam, told me early on: 'You have got to survive to get the story out; if you get killed, you have failed.' I was determined not to be killed in that war or any war. And, yes, in several battles, including the LZ Xray battle, which I wrote my book about, I carried wounded American soldiers, and I carried water to those wounded soldiers.

"In my career as a war correspondent, I worked for United Press International, a worldwide news agency, which at that time had client newspapers, radio stations, and TV stations everywhere. We had no hometown, though we always tried to get the hometowns of every soldier interviewed, so his hometown paper could play it up. In the Gulf War and Haiti, I worked for *U.S. News & World Report*, a national news magazine. Same deal.

"I can tell you that the hometown newspapers and radio and TV media *wanted* to go to war with units from their coverage area. Makes sense. Their families remain in that town. That makes the stories much more personal, much more poignant, and much more susceptible to being covered from both ends—in combat and in the home area with the families. This isn't bad journalism; this is *good* journalism. This is *smart* journalism. And, no, I don't think this makes a reporter less objective or afraid to report something the military high command might not like," Galloway said. "You know, it is possible to love soldiers and marines for who they are and what they do—a low-paid, dirty, dangerous, and largely unappreciated job—and still do your job as an objective honest reporter. In fact, if you do love soldiers, you are more likely to raise absolute hell if you find someone in command doing something that puts those soldiers at an unnecessary risk of being hurt or killed. You are more likely, not less likely, to rip the lips off those who throw away the lives of your friends by stupidity or poor performance or failure to do the planning right."

His counsel to the reporters of Knight Ridder as they prepared to cover the Iraq War was, "Do not be afraid to be a human being first and a reporter second. There are times when it is all right to reach out and lend the wounded a hand or reach down to help a wounded civilian. It does not make one somehow less of a reporter or a less-ethical reporter. Hard lines are usually drawn by people who have no personal experience of war and combat. Am I a less-honest reporter because I have held a dying young man in my arms and watched the life drain out of his eyes, even as I lied to him and told him, 'You are going to be all right, son. Hang on. You are going to make it'? These debates are conducted by people who don't really know and never will."

In regard to his own involvement, Galloway is clear about his views. "I am not ashamed of what I did. I am proud of what I did. And I would do it again. And again. And again. I would be ashamed of any colleague who would not do the same thing, given those circumstances. Would you just stand there and wave your light meter and give Jimmy Nakayama a bit more aperture on the Nikon? Listen to him scream from the terrible burns and see if you could interrupt to find out his hometown?

"In Vietnam there was a good deal less sensitivity on everyone's part, military and media, about photographing wounded soldiers. It took a fair amount of time for your film to make it back to Saigon to be processed, printed, captioned, and then radiophotoed to Tokyo or Paris for relay to New York. Time for the army to send a telegram to a family back home advising them of their loved one being hurt. I was always careful not to show the faces of dead American soldiers. A matter of respect. A matter of not wanting that man's wife or mother or child to see him as he had died, dirty, bloody, thirsty, torn apart, or burned horribly. I have some photographs I took of the poncho-wrapped American dead in the Ia Drang. Even though the faces were covered, I never sold those pictures. I have never posted them on my website. I can hardly bear to look at them, dozens of them lying wrapped in those green rubber ponchos, their booted feet askew."

Galloway said that the military–media relationship is best viewed as a pendulum. He agrees with Cronkite and Schieffer that at the end of the Vietnam War some in the military blamed the media for "losing the war." "We didn't, but those who chose to kill the messenger continued to say we did. Relations went into a death spiral." He ticked off several examples that illustrate this point:

Grenada—no media allowed onshore till the war was over.

Panama—national ready pool activated and sent south, then locked in a hangar on the airbase till the war was over.

Persian Gulf—first ten pools of ten media each; then, on eve of war, expanded to fifteen pools of ten each, each with its own military officer minder who had, and exercised the power of, censorship. The outcome was an unmitigated disaster for the military.

However, the pendulum began to swing back:

Bosnia—sees the first few reporters deployed with American units, and the term *embedded* came into use.

Kosovo—ditto.

Haiti—an even larger use of media embeds.

Iraq—seven hundred media embedded across the full spectrum of American units involved in the war.

"The media embed program—something that I have promoted, along with full, open media coverage, in speeches to military audiences ever since the last

Gulf War—worked very well indeed. And, yes, it was quite necessary. The last Gulf War was a disaster for both the military and the media. The pool system did not work. The American public got no real view of what was going on on the ground. The army, when it was over, found it did not have a single inch of film of the great tank battles in the Kuwait desert."

He termed the embed program a "win-win situation." "The military won because for the first time since Vietnam the American public got a clear view of what young soldiers and marines really do in combat; the media won because for the first time since Vietnam it got relatively unfettered access to frontline combat. Some form of embedding and even more open coverage should definitely be used every time American troops are committed to combat."

Technology has definitely affected war coverage. "For reasons of more open access and infinitely better communications technology, the Iraq War played live, real time, on America's TV sets and on the front pages of newspapers. Vietnam was wide open to free media coverage, but the communications were almost as bad as World War II: pigeons to ferry film and photos back to Saigon. Reporters screaming over the antiquated military phone system that went through half a dozen manual switchboards. 'Hello, Puma Switch. Get me Lion Switch. Hello, Lion Switch, get me Tiger Switch. Hello, Tiger Switch, get me PTT. Hello, PTT, get me 57324. *(busy signal)* Oh shit! Hello Puma Switch. Hello, Puma! PUMA!' You could spend six or so hours screaming at the top of your lungs to get five hundred words dictated to Saigon."

Galloway said that Knight Ridder Newspapers sent to Iraq thirty-two embedded reporters and photographers, one combat sketch artist, and seventeen unilaterals. All of them went out equipped with satellite telephones and laptops so that their copy, photos, and sketches could be instantly transmitted to the Washington bureau where a team of the best editors from all over the Knight Ridder group was assembled to process the individual reports into main leads, color leads, individual unit reports, and so forth. "The change in technology is breathtaking when compared to Vietnam or even the first Gulf War. But wars are covered in the same old way: with courageous reporters and photographers willing to risk their lives to tell and show the truth from the front lines of combat."

War correspondents have many motivations; but, according to Galloway, "Quite simply, it is the biggest story of the day, day in and day out, for the duration of the war—if Americans are involved. Any good reporter can cover war. It is a simple and compelling story involving life and death, blood and suffering, winning or losing. War strips away so much of the camouflage and pretension of humans. You are left with the basic, raw emotions. Great stories."

# LOUIS A. DAY
## PUBLIC INFORMATION OFFICER WITH
## THE 199TH LIGHT INFANTRY BRIGADE, VIETNAM

Louis A. Day, a media law and ethics professor at the Manship School of Mass Communication, was a public information officer with the 199th Light Infantry Brigade headquartered at Long Binh in 1969–1970. Lieutenant Day arrived in Vietnam about a year after the Tet Offensive and spent his tour of duty assisting civilian journalists and writing for his own unit's newspaper.

Day's 199th Brigade unit had about six thousand soldiers and reported to a larger military headquarters. A division, however, might have ten thousand soldiers; companies, two hundred; and platoons, thirty. Public information officers were usually assigned at the brigade or division level. There also was a big public information office in Saigon that usually had a general running the operation. "The commander at our military public information unit was a captain," Day said. "But when you got to the army Vietnam level, usually general officers ran the operation."

Day said that logistically there was a major difference between Iraq and Vietnam. "Iraq was more of a traditional military operation in the sense that there was an identifiable enemy, and it was not a guerrilla war, at least in the beginning. So, even though it was a fast-moving and high-tech war, it was still in some aspects more traditional than the Vietnam War. In Vietnam, when reporters wanted to go out, they worked through a central headquarters in Saigon; and, by military regulations, they were entitled to travel, within reason, where they wanted to go."

In addition to being second in command at his public information unit, Day had two main media-related duties. "One was to actually arrange for visits by the civilian news media to our unit. Whenever we had a request, I made the arrangements," he said. "The other was that I actually covered news about our unit for our unit newspaper. I was a military correspondent, so I did a lot of writing and reporting."

He said that journalists generally found ways to reach unit headquarters, and their reception often depended on the views of the commanding officer. "Different commanders had different reactions to the press. Some welcomed them and made it very easy," Day said. "But we had a commander who didn't trust the media. He didn't mind them coming out, but if we got a last-minute request where he didn't have time to really prepare, he was very upset. Sometimes the executive officer would throw a fit, but then he would realize that he had no choice but to accommodate the visit."

The journalists who visited usually were treated hospitably. "They had a right to come out, and we did everything we could to accommodate them. Usually, there was one reporter every now and then, but occasionally, we would get two or three at a time together. But typically, it would be one at a time. There would, of course, be a technical crew—a camera crew and sound and so forth, so for a broadcast network operation we might have as many as four."

Day said that he handled requests from national media and smaller newspapers that had correspondents there. "The national media were interested in the larger picture, but local papers—and that included the *New York Daily News*—were more interested in writing profiles. There was one *Daily News* reporter who did nothing but hometown profiles on soldiers from New York City. He didn't want anyone that was not from New York City. Because the profiles were very popular, that is basically what he did. So these local reporters did, in fact, try to localize the war and to concentrate on those who where there from their hometowns."

Day said Vietnam was where he first encountered the notion of "the marketing of the news." He traveled to Saigon to visit all three network bureaus—ABC, CBS, NBC—to learn what kind of stories interested them. "CBS, in 1969, basically said, 'We still think the combat part of the war is the main story, so we are more interested in blood and guts than anything else. If you've got something else, we'll take a look at it, but we like combat contact stories.' NBC said, 'We want that too, but if you've got a good Vietnamization story, give it to us.'" Day explained that "Vietnamization" was the process by which the Americans were trying to pacify the country and teach the South Vietnamese to defend themselves once the Americans left. "There were some who didn't think this would ever happen, but there was a big push for Vietnamization. The government was big on this. They made us look like we were trying to extricate ourselves from Vietnam and let the South Vietnamese take over.

"ABC, on the other hand, said, 'We think the people back home are sick and tired of blood and guts. We are really interested in Vietnamization, and that's the kind of story we want to do. If you have a big story that needs to be covered, we're interested, but [we] basically want to focus on Vietnamization.'" Day said that raises an interesting question about whether the networks were responding to the government's Vietnamization propaganda or whether they decided this really was the story they wanted to cover. "I do know that from then on, NBC and ABC did focus on Vietnamization, at least to us. I can't speak for the other units, but I know when they came out to our unit, they seemed always interested in Vietnamization stories. It came across as 'this is what we can sell to our audience.' I heard a speech in Saigon by a UPI bureau chief. He talked about marketing of the news. He talked about what would sell back home. I got to thinking he may have been right."

Day was well aware of how the networks operated. "I don't know about the print people, but with the networks there was no satellite uplink. There were satellites during this time, but there were no satellite uplinks in Vietnam," he said. "So, they would put their film on a plane to Tokyo. They would uplink their stories from Tokyo back to New York, then edit it there. So there was delay." The military had to deal with this time lag. "Where it affected us," Day said, "was that they often would come out and tell us, 'Now we need to be back in Saigon by such and such a time.' So, we had to make sure we had the helicopter support, that we had the transportation in place, for them to get back."

This sticks in his mind because of one harrowing experience Day had getting an ABC correspondent back to Saigon to meet a deadline. "One of the ABC correspondents who came to my unit frequently was Frank Mariano. He was really a very fine reporter and a fine person. He'd been a chopper pilot at one time, so he knew something about the military," he said. "He was out on a base camp one night, and I thought he was going to spend the night there. But he said, 'I've got to get back to Saigon, and I need to get back tonight.' I wasn't too happy about that because we were in the middle of a monsoon." To make the situation worse, Day had the flu and was feeling terrible. "I called general headquarters and I said, 'We have a request from Frank Mariano to get back to Saigon tonight.' And the general apparently told his aide, 'We've got to get this man back. The only chopper we have is my chopper. We'll send it.' So, he sent the chopper down, and we boarded in the monsoon." The chopper was so full, with camera people and sound people and equipment, that the VIPs sat on the front seat of the chopper. Day sat on the floor with his back to the pilot and copilot. "So, we began flying. I noticed that Mariano kept looking at the control panel with a worried look on his face. I didn't know that he had been a pilot and that he knew what he was looking at," Day said. "It was terrible because of the weather, the worst trip I've ever had. So, we didn't make it to Saigon. We had to set down at our base camp at Long Binh." Day asked Mariano why he had been so worried while they were flying. "He said, 'Well, I used to fly these things, and we didn't have any instruments. We were flying blind.'"

Day still had to get Mariano back to Saigon. "It was getting to be midnight, and it was still eighteen miles to Saigon. We commandeered a truck, and we rounded up a number of weapons—a rocket launcher and fire power that none of us knew how to fire. But we got him back to Saigon." Day was under no orders to escort the television crew back to Saigon, but he believed it was his duty to do so. "Basically, we felt we had an obligation to get him back that night," he said.

Day said that since television reporters sent the raw footage back to New York, they really didn't know how it turned out until they would get copies of the completed stories back on a reel. "They didn't know if any of it ran or half of it ran or whatever. But there were other people [editors] involved in these stories, so you could see why sometimes they might not turn out as the reporter expected. Unlike print journalists, who wrote their copy and sent it in, television was a team operation. There were opportunities for distortions and omissions all along the line."

Day thinks that television was among the many factors that led to the military's blaming the media for the outcome of the war. "Lyndon Johnson was credited with saying that when Walter Cronkite abandoned the military point of view, the war was lost. I think there were a lot of contributing factors. Television news stories were a factor." He said that in the Vietnam era, some reporters became more cynical or at least more skeptical.

"I think there was some good reporting in Vietnam, and I think that journalism in that era took a beating. There were stories about reporters who sat in the bars at Saigon and wrote their accounts—it happened," he said. "One of the problems was, in fact, the desire of some reporters to get back to Saigon rather than staying out there and learning more about the story they were covering. We had a visit from a bureau chief at *Newsweek* who went back and wrote this comprehensive, in-depth account of what he had found, and he wasn't there long enough to find much of anything. So, even though there was good journalism, there was a lot of bad journalism."

In Day's view, the legacy of Vietnam was evident in the Gulf War. "In 1991, some of the people who were deciding whether the media were going to be allowed access to the battlefield had been in Vietnam, and they had been burned. They were determined that they were going to control what came out. I think in a sense it was a kind of reaction you could expect—an overreaction," Day said. "I think one thing that we lost in that coverage was any kind of counterpoint to the military's claim of the accuracy of the weapons they were using." He said that after a period, it became obvious that some weapons the military promoted as being accurate and reliable were not so reliable. He said that simply not having the final figures on the results of that campaign contributed, but if journalists had more access, information counter to what the military was putting out would have surfaced much earlier.

Day said that one of the disadvantages from the military's standpoint of having reporters embedded is that "if things go wrong, there are reporters right there to report it. If the cameras are rolling, it can look bad. On the other hand if the men are well aware of this—it's kind of like attorneys in court with cameras—they may be less inclined to do things, so it's a double-edged sword, really. It can be risky for the military, but on the other hand it can pay a huge dividend if you are really careful about what you do when the reporters are around."

Concerning the 2003 embed program, Day said, "At first I was worried because the military took a lot of criticism after this Gulf War about controlling coverage, that maybe they wanted to be seen as being more open and accommodating. Nevertheless, when you start embedding, there are risks. But somebody up there apparently made the judgment that the risks might be less than the benefits of having this coverage."

He thinks that when the military has to handle a large contingent of reporters, embedding does solve a lot of problems up front. "In fact, it is hard for me to imagine how they could have possibly taken the Vietnam approach in Iraq because the war was so fast moving—even the mail didn't catch up to some of these troops. In Vietnam, even if you were out in the field, you normally got your mail. So it was such a fast-moving war and so high tech that logistically it would have been very difficult for the military to accommodate the arrangements they had in Vietnam. It was a different kind of war."

## NEAL CONAN

Host, *Talk of the Nation*, Nation Public Radio, Washington, D.C.

Near the end of the 1991 Gulf War, reporters in Kuwait started to hear reports of a Shia rebellion centered in Iraq's big southern city, Basra. National Public Radio (NPR) correspondent Neal Conan ran into his old friend Chris Hedges who was reporting for the *New York Times*. Conan prevailed on Hedges to let him go across the border to check out the rumors.

"We drove from Kuwait City the next morning on the 'highway of death,' the road taken by the last, doomed Iraqi column to flee northward," Conan said. "Past that, we saw the astonishing pillars of flame and smoke gushing from a dozen oil wells and the charred corpses of Soviet-built tanks. There were small groups of Iraqi soldiers headed north, too, trudging home from the debacle in Kuwait, some armed, some not."

Because Hedges could speak Arabic, he would ask them what they knew of the situation in Basra. They also begged Vermont National Guard troops in the most advanced American tank for a couple of their prepackaged Meals, Ready-to-Eat. "One Iraqi we met after that said that his army had completely reestablished control of the city. After we thanked him and headed on our way, Chris remarked that, if he was right, we might find ourselves in trouble," Conan said.

As if on cue, a speeding jeep with armed soldiers drove alongside and gestured for them to pull over. "Soldiers leapt out and, without saying a word, put their AK-47s in our faces and pulled us out of our Land Rover, patted us down for weapons and threw us in the back of the jeep," he said.

The Iraqis were part of a regular army formation that was isolated south of Basra, out of touch with higher command. "We also learned that they were holding four other reporters—two Brazilians, an Uruguayan, and a Catalan—and, because we were suddenly six, or because there were now two Americans, or because one was from the *New York Times*, they decided they needed to send us up the chain of command. And we found the rebellion we'd been looking for."

With white trails of tracer bullets from automatic weapons whizzing overhead, the men were driven onto the campus of Basra University, which had been taken over by a Republican Guard division. "That evening, at sunset, we heard the unforgettable sound of mortar fire, incoming, and soon afterwards the concussive whumps of Iraqi howitzers, outgoing," Conan recalls.

The next day they joined a convoy of about 150 vehicles that, they were told, was headed to Baghdad. Because the bridges across the Euphrates had been blown, they waited in a village not far from biblical Ur for slack tide to steady the pontoon bridge that Iraqi engineers had thrown across the river. Just as they started to move across the bridge, gunfire erupted from the village. "Our 'minder,' Major Hassan, herded us down an alley to safety and exposed himself to fire to protect us. Half an hour later, when we were back in a now thoroughly confused convoy, more shots rang out, and, as we huddled in the back seat, Major Hassan blasted away with his AK out the right front window and handed us his ammunition pouch and empty magazine to reload."

The worst was over. They made it to an army camp on the south side of the Euphrates, where they remained until they were flown by helicopter to Baghdad a couple of days later. There, they were joined by a much larger group of reporters, most of them French, who'd been picked up trying to crash the cease-fire talks at Safwan.

"After being locked into rooms in the Hotel Diana by the secret police, we rejoiced the next afternoon when one of our colleagues heard on shortwave radio that Iraqi authorities admitted that we were in their hands. We might still be tried for anything between trespassing and espionage, but this meant they could no longer just take us out back and shoot us," Conan said. "As it turned out, we were delivered into the gentle care of the International Committee of the Red Cross, who piled us into a bus the next morning and drove us to safety in Jordan."

In addition to his harrowing experience, Conan recalls a number of other aspects of covering the 1991 Gulf War. "The 'pool' system employed in Desert Shield/Desert Storm was widely detested by reporters in the field, most of whom felt it was a system to control the media," he said.

He also notes that there were only a few unilaterals at that time, among them his friend Chris Hedges of the *New York Times*. "I believe the impulse for control was, at least in part, due to the Saudis who were appalled at the idea of hundreds of Western reporters wandering freely." He also said that some commanders were holding down the corporate fort at the Dahran International Hotel, which was the only place in the theater from which he could feed high-quality audio. He said some commanders—General Walter Boomer, for example—were savvier with the media than others—such as General Barry McCaffrey—which is why the marines got a lot more ink than the Twenty-fourth Infantry Mechanized Division.

"My only personal experience with the pool was a day trip to visit with some A-10 pilots—obviously, the military took us out there because they thought it would be a positive story. The public affairs officers asked us not to report the altitude they were bombing from or the fact that all the aircraft of this type were at one base, both of which seemed reasonable to me," he said. "As the war moved into Kuwait, the pool system broke down completely; as soon as we crossed the border, everybody was a unilateral."

Taking matters into their own hands, Conan said that several journalists who drove together in a convoy seized the cabanas around the pool at the Kuwait International Hotel and reached an informal, voluntary agreement to share information. "We scattered to various places during the day and coalesced beneath the one working lightbulb to write our stories in the evening."

Although Conan said that he "saw the embed system only from afar," he thought it was clearly better than the pool. "Obviously reporters traveling with small units only saw a small part—the 'soda straw' effect—but many saw plenty, and most seemed able to report on what was happening with the soldiers in the front lines."

As far as the effect of being embedded, Conan said, "Sure, there's a natural tendency to identify with the troops you live and travel with, who also happen to be the guys on whom you depend for your security. Some did better than others with this." He didn't think it was as good for the unilaterals because of the danger. "Overall, I think we got extraordinary up-close views; historians will eventually be able to piece together a remarkable mosaic of the view through all of those soda straws.

"Some commanders, as in Desert Storm, made it difficult, but these tended to be much more junior officers this time. It wasn't perfect but much, much better than Desert Storm," he said. He added that his friend Richard Pyle of the Associated Press (based in New York) had an interesting aside. "He covered Desert Storm from the headquarters in Riyadh. He believes the embed system was a vast improvement, but that access at HQ was much, much worse because it was used primarily to provide the party line and spin. So while we got great snapshots, the media were unable to get the broader picture that would have enabled us to better understand what we were seeing."

# Managing the War:
# The Military

# WHAT WILL WE DO WITH SIX HUNDRED JOURNALISTS?

Pinpointing the exact moment when the idea of embedding journalists began to take hold in the Department of Defense (DOD) is as difficult as grabbing quicksilver. Both the media and the military wanted a way for journalists to report from the front lines. Ultimately, the embed program became the means to that end. Although the actual evolution of the embed program is difficult to trace, there is general agreement that Secretary of Defense Donald Rumsfeld had to sign off on it. Chairman of the Joint Chiefs of Staff, General Richard Meyers, also was in the loop. A classified message that outlined the importance of media involvement was sent early in the program to the unified commanders and to some of the other people involved with the war planning. The commanders were told to cooperate and support the media and the public affairs officers in their endeavor to tell the story. Both Rumsfeld and Meyers signed the document. An unclassified version of the message was sent out later.

Some media reports give Victoria Clarke, assistant secretary of defense for public affairs, the credit for either coming up with the idea or at least convincing Rumsfeld that the program had merit. Both Clarke and Bryan Whitman, her assistant during the major military action, minimize her involvement in originating the idea. However, there is little doubt that Clarke championed the program. She also said, at a Brookings Institute seminar that served as a "debriefing" of the program, that she thought the embed concept was likely here to stay. However, after Clarke resigned her post in mid-June 2003, such open support for the program ceased.

# BRYAN WHITMAN
Deputy Assistant Secretary of Defense for Public Affairs,
Department of Defense, Washington, D.C.

Bryan Whitman, deputy assistant secretary for media operations in the Department of Defense, said that the embed program planning began in late summer or early fall of 2002. Although media accounts often give Victoria Clarke the credit for the program's existence, Whitman said that "there is plenty of credit to go around for this." In fact a large number of DOD personnel and media representatives shaped the program. Although he was given the opportunity to manage, develop, and implement the embedding program, Whitman said that none of it would have happened without "the strong support of Secretary of Defense Donald Rumsfeld; Chairman of the Joint Chiefs of Staff, General Richard Meyers; the vision and enthusiasm of people like Victoria (Tori) Clarke; and all of the public affairs officers who really made it happen in the field." He also noted that it wouldn't have happened without all the hard work of the Washington bureau chiefs for the major news organizations. "I worked with them on a daily basis as we started to put this together, developing a construct that would allow them to accomplish their mission without interfering with our mission."

A number of Department of Defense personnel, including Clarke and Whitman, met with a number of representatives from the various Washington media bureaus at least three times between November 2002 and February 2003 to discuss issues of media access and the embedding process.[1] "When I began to fashion the ground rules, I took it right to them [the bureau chiefs]," Whitman said. "Tori and I held a lot of bureau chiefs meetings. We made this as transparent as we could. We recorded the sessions with the bureau chiefs, and we posted the transcripts on the website. We wanted everybody to know and be able to witness our discussions with them, to allow areas of controversy to be discussed, and at the end of the day to come up with a means to let them do what they want to do: cover the war from the front lines and to do it in way in which our commanders in the field were going to feel comfortable that the embeds wouldn't compromise the mission or endanger any of the personnel."

Public affairs officer Major Tim Blair was ultimately placed in charge of matching journalists with the combat units who were deployed to fight the Iraq War. Whitman said that getting six hundred journalists hooked up with combat units was no small task. "Colonel Guy Shields, first in Kuwait and then in Baghdad, was directing the efforts of his staff and placing all these journalists when they would show up in Kuwait having nothing more than 'I'm assigned to the Third ID [Infantry Division] or the First Marine Expeditionary Force . . . how do I get linked up with them?' He actually got them out there, making sure they got their equipment and knew and understood the rules of engagement."

Quoting from a letter sent to him by Tori Clarke, as she was leaving her job at the Pentagon, Whitman said, "As architect and building and general contractor of the embedding program, you ensured that millions and millions of people saw what you and I know: The U.S. military is truly the world's finest.

"I certainly don't like to take more credit than I am due because I certainly had a wonderful opportunity to manage and implement this program. I couldn't have made it successful without people above me and below me," he emphasized.

Although Clarke stated at a Brookings Institute debriefing following the end of the major combat phase of the war that "the embed program is here to stay," Whitman, who succeeded her in the Defense Department, has taken a more cautious approach. "I would like to hope that we have done a tremendous amount to improve the military–media relations here. I think that the military has gained an enormous amount of respect for the media, and the fact that there are large numbers of professional news correspondents who are willing to put their lives on the line accomplished a very important mission. I think the news media also has a newfound respect for the military and what they are willing to do, their dedication, their professionalism, the care they take in executing their very lethal duties," he said.

Whitman also pointed out that a by-product of journalists being in contact with soldiers on a daily basis, especially in a "difficult wartime situation," was their ability to witness the U.S. military's efforts to prevent civilian casualties and collateral damage.

Whitman's caution in declaring the embed program permanent is that every military conflict is different. "Every military situation has to be looked at for its uniqueness and then [I must] determine, from my position as the deputy assistant secretary for media operations in the department, how best to accommodate the media in being able to do what they want to do and for them to accomplish the task of informing the American people. So if there is another conflict tomorrow that is of the same nature as Afghanistan, it would be very difficult to replicate the opportunities that I was able to provide the news media in Operation Iraqi Freedom."

He says that the situation in Liberia offers another example. "Because of the embedding success, there are a lot of news organizations looking at the situation in Liberia and saying, 'If the president decides there's going to be a military mission involving a unit, as you are doing your public affairs planning, we would be very interested in embedding with that unit.' Well, that unit, by any comparison, is going to be very small. The demand from the news media to accompany that type of unit is going to far exceed my ability to embed anybody." In cases like this, Whitman said that he would be "forced" to rely on a pool situation in which a small number of journalists are selected to cover the story for a large number of news organizations. Other factors include the media's being able to get in by themselves—that is, unilaterally—and the general environment surrounding a military conflict.

"You can't just automatically say embedding is what we always do in the future. I would like to hope that we will never have any conflicts, but that's probably unrealistic. What is more realistic is that I hope that this experience has demonstrated that the media and the military can work side by side and that when conditions permit, we can place correspondents with our commanders in the field so they can observe combat and observe our forces," Whitman said. "We are very proud of our forces, and we want people to see how well trained, how well equipped, and how well led the U.S. military is. You can't spend any time with our forces and not walk away with a tremendous amount of respect for their dedication and for their professionalism. And we think [media observation] is good, because it is the American people who pay for this standing military that we have, and they ought to see it; they ought to hold it to a high standard."

Although Whitman concedes that the access and coverage of the Iraq War is very different from that of the 1991 Gulf War, he isn't comfortable making direct comparisons. "I always tell people that it isn't very useful to compare conflicts in some respects, because the situations are so different. And the news media and the news industry changes every time. If you look at the advances that have been made in the news business since 1991, we couldn't have done this [embedding program] in '91. The news media didn't have the capability to be able to file from the field in real time. You had to get back to where there was bigger, more stationary type of equipment to move video. You didn't have computers that were small enough, rugged enough, and durable enough and with the transmission capabilities to be able to send copy." He also sees the military objectives as being different in every conflict. "The military mission also dictates what you're able to do. Not much time passed between the conflict in Afghanistan and the conflict in Iraq, and yet the coverage was somewhat different because the mission was very different. In Afghanistan for weeks all we had were very small numbers of Special Forces on the ground that infiltrated into very arduous conditions and in very small numbers, which was not conducive to being able to put any significant number of reporters on the ground."

However, some journalists were embedded during the military action in Afghanistan. "We had reporters aboard the ships at sea on the first day of the war, when the Tomahawk shooters engaged targets. The media were on those ships in significant numbers," Whitman said. "So there's always going to be a numbers factor that dictates how you are going to best accommodate the media in covering any sort of military conflict. And the mission certainly is going to be one of them. The conditions in which you operate is another, and then just the technology as it continues to improve in the news business is a third."

Several journalists complained about their treatment by the military in Afghanistan, and some, such as CNN's Christiane Amanpour, refused to be embedded because of her experiences with the military. Whitman, however, discounts reporter dissatisfaction as a catalyst for the embed program. "First of all, I do like to think that we are a learning and growing institution and that we will get better at doing this over time. But I don't think that Afghanistan put any pressure on us in that regard. Afghanistan again presented a completely different set of circumstances and is a completely different type of combat, and it was a unique force structure. This is why I don't think it is very useful to make these hard and fast rules: embedding was successful in this conflict, so we should use it forever and always. I just can't say that. I've got to look at everything anew and use my experience of the past and use what has worked and what people feel is a good approach to things, but at the same time I think I have to leave my mind open to other opportunities as well. There may be something that comes along that enables me to modify the embedding program and make it even better. We are going through a comprehensive lessons-learned process that we want to capture those things that worked well, those things we could do better, and then see how they might be applied in future situations.

"We just celebrated the thirtieth anniversary of the all-volunteer force, so we've had an all-volunteer force for some time. It's also been said that across various segments of society, whether it be Congress or the general public, there are fewer and fewer people who have a brother or sister or relative or someone they know personally who is in the military. So to the extent that the American people get an opportunity to have some insight into the military, I think that is good. And there probably is no better way to do that than with independent, objective observers reporting on their activity," Whitman said.

Whitman did not discount the dangers for journalists on the Iraqi battlefield, especially those who were not embedded in a military unit. "The independent, or unilateral, journalists out on the battlefield had everything wrong that could go wrong happen to them. They got killed; they got injured; they got captured; they got lost. Every bad scenario that you could think of happened to them. And that is not to say that it wasn't dangerous for embedded journalists either." In fact, two embedded journalists—Christian Liebig, a reporter for the German weekly magazine *Focus*; and Julio Anguita Parrado, a correspondent for the Spanish daily *El*

*Mundo*—were killed in a rocket attack in the outskirts of Baghdad. They were both foreign journalists who were embedded with the brigade headquartered there. A number of soldiers were killed in that same attack.

Whitman said that there is no doubt that being with U.S. military forces afforded a certain amount of protection that unilaterials did not have. Although all journalists were independent regardless of their embed status, dangers to journalists was a major reason for the development of the embed program. "There is no more dangerous place to be for journalists than being out there running from the sounds of the guns, to be getting intermixed between enemy and friendly forces. It is a recipe for disaster for journalists," Whitman said. "So to the extent that we could provide them an opportunity to get that firsthand account without putting them in excessive danger by making them be out there between our forces, we thought that was good. They will always tell us that we have no responsibility for their safety and security, and that's true, but we still care. We don't like putting anybody in jeopardy."

Whitman thinks that news organizations have weighed, and will continue to weigh in the future, whether putting unilaterals in the field is worth the risk. "They'll probably use this experience as a prism to some extent to determine if what they got from their unilateral journalists was better or different or more unique than the reports they got from their embedded journalists. I can tell you that some weighed it in midstream. There were some news organizations that made the decision that the risk, that the cost-to-benefit [ratio] was just too high. They pulled out all their unilateral journalists, and they asked me for additional embeds. To a large extent, I was able to accommodate them because I had a strong desire not to see journalists in danger," he said.

Matching journalists to units was a subjective process based on objective criteria. "I decided right from the beginning that I wasn't going to play any favorites with journalists. I wasn't going to deal with a single journalist. I was going to deal with news organizations, and I was going to make the bureau chiefs partners in this process for a couple of reasons," Whitman said. "Who knows better than the bureau chiefs and editors out there who they want and who's best qualified to go out on these types of assignments? What I needed to do was to take a look at what was in the best interest of this country in terms of making sure that the right news organizations were in the right positions on the battlefield to be able to give the American people the most comprehensive look."

Whitman wasn't concerned with only the American audience. "I also had to look at the international audience. I heavily weighted toward domestic media because, after all, it was the American people who were paying for this conflict, and they were paying for it not only with their dollars but with their sons and daughters. So I felt an obligation to heavily weight them, and I did."

The split was about 80 percent domestic media to 20 percent international, but in today's world of global media, sorting out which was which was not always easy.

"I considered AFP [Agence France-Presse] a foreign news wire and AP a domestic news wire. They both overlap in the United States. Reuters—the same way—I consider them international, but you will see Reuters's reports in the newspaper every day. So I just had to make some of those judgments," Whitman said. "Then I felt I had a real responsibility to make sure that reach and impact was a factor. I had to look at those news organizations that had the kind of reach and impact that were going to be able to hit the wide audiences out there. So I looked at the major media markets. I looked at the top one hundred newspapers. I tried to look at where there were force multipliers out there with newspaper chains, like Knight Ridder, Scripps Howard, Copley, and all those where one reporter is actually reporting for a number of different newspapers. So I put that all into a mix, and then I just had to start making some assignments and allocating embed opportunities. At the end of the day, while I used a lot of different objective criteria, is it subjective? It certainly is."

The gender of the embed was not a consideration for slots, at least from the military perspective. "I couldn't tell you today exactly how many women reporters were embedded," Whitman said. "We have a list, but not all names are easily identifiable, especially when you get to the foreign correspondents, as to whether that was a male or a female. We were completely gender blind."

It fell to the news organization to decide who would be embedded, so if any gender bias occurred, it was at that level. "We had nothing but positive experiences with the process," Whitman said. "In Afghanistan we embedded women reporters with our Special Forces units. Katherine M. Skiba, Washington correspondent for the *Milwaukee Journal Sentinel*, had a great experience during Operation Iraqi Freedom. Her unit was completely gender blind to her, and that is the way it should be."[2]

Whitman's staff was also responsible for the boot-camp training offered to journalists. "We developed the curriculum. If we were going to put large numbers of reporters out there, I felt that it was important that we give them some basic skills training for a couple of reasons," he said. "First of all, I wanted reporters to have the confidence they needed in themselves to be able to go out and spend extended periods of time with U.S. forces in the field. It was also to give my commanders out there confidence that reporters with their units had basic skills and would not compromise missions or endanger personnel." Among the skills Whitman thought necessary for journalists were putting on a chemical protection suit; reacting to indirect fire; knowing the basic principles of cover, camouflage, and concealment; and knowing basic first aid.

"We don't want the reporter to be a liability out there on the battlefield. So it was a very basic program of instruction. It was designed to be an opportunity for a reporter to do some self-assessment. It wasn't tremendously physical, but there were some physical aspects to the training. We didn't keep grades or say, 'This person is never going to be embedded' or anything like that."

Training didn't guarantee that a journalist would receive an embed slot. "I only trained 238 reporters, and I embedded more than 600. I knew I wasn't going to be able to train everybody. So I couldn't make that a factor for selection. Also, many news organizations, because they had to expand their pool of foreign correspondents, weren't going to send their seasoned, wartime correspondents to my training. They were going to use training for that journalist who might never have been in combat or lived in the field or lacked exposure to the military. I wouldn't want it to be an excluding factor," Whitman said. Although he wonders how many of those who went through training got an embed slot, he has not had the time to do that research.

## NOTES

1. Defense Department participants listed on the Department of Defense website include Victoria Clarke, assistant secretary of defense for public affairs; Bryan G. Whitman, deputy assistant secretary of defense for public affairs; Rear Admiral Stephen Pietropaoli, navy chief of information; Major General Larry Gottardi, army chief of public affairs; Brigadier General Andrew Davis, Marine Corps director of public affairs; Captain "T" McCreary, chairman of the Joint Chiefs of Staff for public affairs; Colonel Jay DeFrank, director of the Department of Defense Press Office; Lieutenant Colonel Catherine Abbott, deputy director of the Department of Defense Press Office.

2. Skiba was embedded with the U.S. Army's 159th Aviation Brigade, a part of the 101st Airborne Division. The brigade is 2,300 strong and features pilots flying Black Hawks and Chinooks into battle.

## MAJOR TIM BLAIR
MEDIA OPERATIONS, DEPARTMENT OF DEFENSE, WASHINGTON, D.C.

April 18, 2003, was the date Major Tim Blair "popped a bottle of champagne" to celebrate a milestone in the embed program. "That was the day that we at the Department of Defense passed the embed program to Central Command [CENT-COM, now headquartered in Florida]. We had maintained the reins of the program and had been the gatekeeper, if you will, for people getting into the program. We never said the program was done, but we did relinquish control."

That was such a memorable date for Blair, manager of the embed program, because for months he had been completely absorbed in figuring out how to match journalists to military units, in monitoring the reporting done from journalists in the field, and in feeling a personal loss when some reporters were killed. Furthermore, Blair had to fend off initial skepticism on behalf of reporters and journalism organizations who thought the promised access to the battlefield was merely a Pentagon ploy. "I remember an interview with the *Columbia Journalism Review* prior to the war. The published article indicated that our media embed program was just a front—that we would never grant the level of access that we said we would give," Blair said.

Blair, a self-proclaimed computer geek, was assigned the task of putting together the embed program in late December 2002. "Some of the initial planning had been done when I came aboard. I assisted in setup of the media boot camps, and I helped with administrative tasks, such as setting up the matrices in an Excel spreadsheet and how to track and do some different things—just basic computer assistance. That was my undoing because when the boss, Colonel Jay DeFrank, director for press operations, recognized I could do that, he came to me and said, 'Hey, I've got a job for you. Do you want to manage the embed program since you know how to use Excel and you're familiar with the media? It would be a natural extension for you to just jump into this job. Do you want to volunteer for it?'"

Blair said that he was warned that the job was "going to suck." He was told, "You are going to spend long hours every day in the office; you are going to deal with some unruly media because everybody wants slots. It's going to be like herding cats." Blair was "convinced" to take the job because "it's going to be a part of history." Never one to back down from a challenge, he asked, "When do I start?" He was told that he had already started and to get busy. The rest of the story truly is history.

"As I went into the embed program, I was the European command liaison, I had the assistant secretary of defense for international security affairs in my portfolio, two deputy assistant secretaries, ninety-plus countries, two-and-one-half continents, and a unified command—those were my responsibilities when I started the embed program. I ended up having to give all of that to one of my coworkers, Lieutenant Colonel Dan Stoneking, who took all of my old accounts because the embed program was literally a seven-day-a-week, twenty-four-hour-a-day job. We did have one day off a week scheduled, but you would still get calls, even on your day off. I had several folks in the office who were die-hard helpers who helped run the program with me," Blair said.

The beginning stages of the embed program were classified because at that point the official decision to go to war had not yet been made. "We were making the plans to go, and getting things staged in-country, but the large units were already in theater—specifically the Third Division and some of the marine units," Blair said. "A lot of the units here, in the United States and elsewhere, were given deployment orders to be prepared to go."

Public affairs guidance (PAG) was developed for each of the commands, which outlined how to handle the embed program. Although PAG is not normally considered part of the public domain documents, Blair said that this PAG became such a hot commodity that it was made available to the public and to the media so that they could see the ground rules and guidelines. "We in the public affairs community develop PAG that we send to our internal community on how to handle any event, or happening or operation. It basically gives you statements that are okay to use. In any operation you do ground rules for handling the media," Blair said. "So when we developed the media embed program, we developed PAG for the embedded media programs, and we sent it to all the commands. Each of the units, as they received this PAG, then tailored specific ground rules that they would use with the media in line with the beginning guidance. The reporters, as they would sign on to their embed, they would sign and agree to a set of ground rules for their reports based on this initial guidance." (See appendix A.)

Blair said that the overall objective of the embed program was to get the widest possible dissemination of information, to counter the propaganda and misinformation for which the Iraqis were famous. "We went into the embed program trying to get the widest dissemination of accurate and true firsthand information from the embeds as we could," Blair said. "The best way to do that was to ask, Who has the broadest reach? Who has the most circulation? Who has the largest viewership?"

The first step in the embed program was to ask the units to develop the number of media representatives they could handle if the United States went to war. Blair said that the actual number of embeds allowed came from the units themselves. "Speaking hypothetically, let's look at the Third Infantry: The initial number they provided us was around seventy news media representatives that they could handle, and that number increased a little over time. They ended up having a little over eighty. That's how we came up with a number of media we were going to be able to embed."

Blair said that the Department of Defense and CENTCOM looked at all the units that were currently in the neighboring countries preparing for war, as well as the units that were identified throughout Europe and the United States and other places who were going to go once the decision was made to go to war.

"We then started compiling a list, and the list was very basic in the beginnings. It would just have a unit: the Third Infantry Division, the First Marine Expeditionary Force, the 101st . . . the large major units that were going to be part of the war. We put down the number of media they said they could handle—sixty, eighty, one hundred, whatever the number may be. We started from there," Blair said. That was the easy work because at this stage they were basically feeding information provided to them into a computer. The next step involved determining how media slots would be allocated:

70 percent national media,

10 percent local media, and

20 percent international media.

The expectation was that the deploying military units would identify and take along local or regional media representatives with whom they had previously established a relationship.

"We then started refining things," Blair said. "If a unit said, 'We have sixty or seventy slots to fill,' we would automatically off the top look at the national and regional news organizations that we were going to target first." He pointed out that integrating the media with the military was not a new thing but that the scale was much larger than anything previously accomplished.

The national television network assignments were relatively easy since there are only five: ABC, CBS, CNN, FOX, and NBC/MSNBC. "Our goal throughout the embed program was to give them representation in all the major units that were going to be in the war and give each of them the same number of slots across the board. If NBC got twenty-five slots, then so would ABC and CNN and so on. The networks were the easy part of the puzzle. We determined they would have a slot everywhere, and to each unit they went to they would have two positions, usually on-air talent and a cameraman. So for the 101st they would have a two-person slot; for the Third Infantry Division, they would have a two-person slot. We expanded on that some as time went along and other slots became available," Blair said.

Blair said that they decided not to try to separate entities such as NBC and MSNBC. Rather, they gave the parent company the maximum number of slots and let news managers select the journalists they wanted to send and which news programs would be represented. For example, CBS decided whether *60 Minutes* and *60 Minutes II* would each get their own embed team. The Department of Defense had no say in specific allocations within a news organization.

The wire services also were easy allocations because of the small number and the differences in reach. Reuters, the Associated Press, and Agence France-Presse were given the largest number of slots, while Knight Ridder and United Press International were given fewer.[1] However, even smaller wire services were given a small number of slots. "We did our best to evenly distribute among the major wire services. We treated them pretty much the same as we did the television networks. We gave them representation in each of the major units—a little bit more because lots of people buy the wire service products, and we knew there would be wider dissemination of a product by getting the wire service reporters and photographers out there," Blair said.

Newspapers provided more of a challenge. Blair and his team began by developing a chart from the top one hundred newspapers. "We were inventing criteria as we went along," Blair says. "Our starting point for newspapers was the top one hundred circulation lists, but we had to find a subjective way to look at how we were going to slot the newspapers."

With the overall objective in mind, they looked at the top one hundred list and decided that the top five newspapers in the country would get the most slots, then papers six through ten would get fewer slots, and so on. The newspapers ranking between fifty and one hundred received only one or two slots. "Because the news business is a competitive business, you wouldn't want to give two slots to the top-rated-circulation paper in the United States and then the twentieth-rated-circulation newspaper gets ten slots. It just wouldn't be equitable based on what their markets are, so we developed a systematic way to look at this. It made for slating these embeds a lot easier. It just took us awhile to develop the thought process to do that," Blair said.

Rather than look at newspaper companies, they looked at markets and then determined which newspapers best served those markets. Consequently, a particular company such as Gannett could end up with more total slots than smaller companies, but that was not a concern if the criteria were based on reach and circulation. "It was probably a thought we had, but we still couldn't be exclusionary just because a particular newspaper was part of a parent organization," Blair said. "We looked at the newspaper itself, its circulation, and the area it circulated in more than we did the actual ownership of the news organization."

Blair said that they looked at national and regional media and then tied the regional paper with the closest unit that was going to be going. "So, if it was Midwest media, we were looking at the units out of Texas or other places like that. If it was East Coast media, some of the naval installation and Fort Bragg, North Carolina, for the army. We tried to affix regional media with their markets so they could give as much of a human face to their region that they could." He did expect bonding to occur between the journalists and the soldiers. "It's human nature, especially in the environment that they are in. You build a kind of bond while you are there, but I would think embeds could still maintain their journalistic integrity to report what they see in an unbiased way." The most difficult aspect of embed slotting was by far the international media. "It wasn't for lack of the international media contacting us, wanting to be embedded, because I had far more contacting me than we were able to embed," Blair said. "It was simply knowing who they were." Blair and his team had little expertise in international markets. They didn't know which publications and broadcast entities provided the largest audiences. "It was very difficult to have an international news organization call me and say, 'I want to be embedded. I'm from X television station in X country.' It was a difficult task."

They called on Colonel Rick Machamer, a Department of Defense liaison in the State Department, and the Foreign Press Center in the State Department.[2] "Colonel Machamer was my sounding board for international media. I would send him a list of my international media to get with his experts in those different countries to determine who they were, what their viewership was, et cetera," Blair said. "The other assistance we received was from the embassies. I would call directly to their public affairs officers and say, 'Can you send me a prioritized list of the media from your country so that when I'm considering embeds, I'm picking the right ones, as far as circulation goes, so that your country gets the widest dissemination of news and information.'" Blair said that they started approaching the embassies late in the game and that if he were ever to do this kind of program again, he would involve them up front.

The Department of Defense was also concerned about the journalistic standards and motives of some international journalists. State-controlled media and media located in countries that were recent allies or who had been former foes were particularly troublesome if they were located in major markets. "Each time we would scrub our list of international media, we would check them off, looking at the globe saying, 'Okay, we've got the Asian market covered with these particular news organizations, we've got Europe covered with these news organizations, we've got South America covered, and so on. We had to break down each section of the world almost a little more micro than a continental basis, and it was a pretty difficult task."

**Number and Percentage of Slots Allocated to Media**

| | | |
|---|---|---|
| Army | 351 slots | 45.29% |
| Marines | 214 | 27.61 |
| Navy | 124 | 16.00 |
| Air Force | 71 | 9.16 |
| Special Operations | 15 | 1.93 |
| Total | 775 | 100.00 |

*Note:* Total percentage reflects sum of percentages before rounding.

There were around 920 official embed slots offered to the media. "What that means is we did the planning based on units that were already in-country and units that were planned to go. We had to plan for units—the First Calvary Division and First Armored Division, for instance—that during the war were not on the ground but we still had to plan embeds for them. A couple of army divisions and other units we planned for actually didn't go." In addition, some slots went unfilled. Blair said that he actually offered about 900 embed slots. When he tabulated the acceptances from the media organizations, the total was 775.

Blair said that the high watermark for embeds was right at 600 at one time. Journalists would come and go at different times, so not all slots were filled at the same time. He said that the 600 figure represents a little more than 250 news organizations, whether magazine, newspaper, radio, television, and so on—both national and international. In other words, that many different outlets were represented in the embed program. The slots were allocated as above, by service component.

Other than the day he handed over the embed program to CENTCOM, the most memorable day for Blair was February 11, 2003. "I almost thought my world was going to end because that was the day I attempted to send invitations to the news organizations. This was the big day for me. All of the planning finally came to a head. I got the nod from the Pentagon to send the invitations to the news organizations. I had everything ready. I had the preform e-mail package set; I had the list of addressees to send it to." The timing was crucial because, publicly, the Bush administration was saying that war could be averted, that no decision had been made to go. "We didn't want to breach the operational security level by giving these invitations, because it was just one more indicator that this was an imminent thing, that it was going to happen and it would seem that we have accepted the fact that we are going to war. But finally on the eleventh, that morning, my boss, Bryan Whitman, came and said, 'Send the messages.'"

After all the careful planning and waiting, sending the messages should have been a great relief and a heady experience for Blair and his staff. It wasn't. They had a couple of hundred e-mails to send, and it was going to take several hours if everything went well. It didn't. "The first e-mail invitation I sent [to a major network] bounced back. I couldn't figure it out at first. And then I realized that because a lot of people were using the network on any given day, you're limited in the size of e-mails you can send. Our cap was ten megs or something close to that, and our storage was one hundred megs. I had never looked at the size of this message. It was a text message in e-mail format with four or five attachments: a PDF [portable document file] on smallpox and anthrax, a 'hold harmless' agreement, and procedures on a few other things. The message itself was ten megs. So, the first message I sent bounced because the network I sent it to would not accept a file that large." It sunk in that the news organizations on the list couldn't accept the important message Blair was trying to send. To further complicate the matter, after he sent ten messages, his own mailbox was at its storage limit, and he couldn't send any more. He wanted a copy of every message he sent for the archive, and that put even more strain on the system. "I was pulling my hair out. All the other folks who were helping me had the same problem. We had a quick huddle, and one of my buddies [Matt Konkler] said, 'Well, why don't we scan all these documents you have as attachments onto the Internet and just put hyperlinks in the message.' It was the greatest idea in this whole program."

Blair said that he was so focused on the situation that he was unable to think outside the box, but his friend solved the problem. "Within ten minutes of this major catastrophe that I thought was going to end my world, we had the solution. We scanned the documents, put them on as hyperlinks and—bada-bing, bada-boom—we're sending messages."

Blair and his three counterparts spent February 11 and 12 sending e-mails out to news organizations that included information on the different inoculations that embeds could voluntarily take and an Excel spreadsheet that had their units of assignment with blanks for filling in the future embeds' names. "All we sent to the news organizations was how many slots you had and which units they were assigned. What they were required to give back to me was the name of the reporter. They had a week to send it back to me," Blair said. Media organizations had until February 19 to send him the names. By Friday, February 21, Blair sent to all the news organizations who had responded a point of contact for the units they were assigned to and, with a touch of humor, added, "Yea, verily, by the power invested in me as the embed manager, you can now contact the units and begin your embeds." February 21 was the official start date for embeds.

Journalists joined their units in several ways depending on their locations. Journalists embedded in the Third Infantry Division, which was already in position, had to find their way into Kuwait to link up with the unit. Several of the news orga-nizations already had reporters placed in Kuwait, so they could make an easy transition. Jounalists assigned to units like the 101st Airborne Division[3] (out of Fort Campbell, Kentucky) and the Fourth Infantry Division (out of Fort Hood, Texas) could join them in the States and perhaps get a week or two of training, thus getting the opportunity to visit with the unit and then fly to the region as part of the unit.

Although the gender of embeds wasn't an issue to the Pentagon, it was to some women's organizations who suspected that female journalists were being denied an opportunity to participate. After reviewing representative slices of news reports coming from the region, such organizations concluded that there was too small a female representation and started complaining to Blair. "Since my name was synonymous with the embed program, I started getting hammered by different prominent women's activist groups asking, 'Why didn't you select more women to fill these slots? Why were you exclusionary toward women in these slots?' One of the ladies who contacted me—even after I explained it to her—still didn't like it. She said, 'Well, you should have asked. You should have known. You should have pressed for more female representation.' I just didn't think that should be my position to do that. Then, after I explained to them that, first of all, the news organizations themselves picked the reporters to fill the slots—that I simply asked for reporters to fill the spots and that I didn't ask gender nor care [about] gender for who was going to fill the slots—that pressure subsided from me and, I think, was refocused on the news organizations."

Although there was no "gender" column in the matrix that Blair used to track the embeds, he said that the women who complained inspired him to take a second look at the names and to estimate the number of women included. Based on the names given, approximately eighty-five were women (about 11 percent). Female representation in the military is around 14 percent.

Because the military was so invested in the embed program, the question became, Was the safety of unilaterals of little concern? "I would never say we had that mentality. All throughout this process, when we had the bureau chief meetings prior to the war, we issued warnings of how dangerous it was going to be. While we would never intentionally target places where we knew media would be, we couldn't guarantee their safety on the battlefield just because of the sheer environment they were going to be in," Blair said. "One of the main reasons we were doing the embed program was to give a kind of protected way for the media to cover the war, fully knowing there would be unilaterals on the battlefield. I would never say we were indifferent to their safety. I would actually say there were times when we probably went out of our way to protect media that were not embedded. I can think of a couple of instances, as a matter of fact, but I can't elaborate on them. We would receive reports—even during Afghanistan I was called at two o'clock in the morning one time—telling me the coordinates of their truck while driving from one point to another point to make sure they didn't get bombed while they were moving and be mistaken for a target. We would get calls from different news organizations that would tell us, 'We are moving on this road or that road. Please don't shoot us' or 'We would have reporters at this place or that place; please be mindful when you are targeting that we are there.' Those things didn't fall on deaf ears. We made every effort with precision targeting that the Defense Department does to account for things like that. So, were we conscious of the unilaterals? Yes. Did we condone them? No."

Blair said that he has wondered, "What if we hadn't embedded, and we went with this war and not included anyone in our coverage and [had] given the unilaterals the run of the battlefield?" He believes the coverage would have been worse and that the number of fatalities within the media community would have been much higher, as clutter on the battlefield increased. "It is also interesting to see the news organizations we offered slots to who turned them down, saying, 'No, we don't want to send anybody.' And then when they saw what was happening and saw the benefits of the program, they came running back and said, 'Hey, we recanted. We want our slots back.' It was very difficult sometimes." Blair said that some of the units who were moving would actually grab unilaterals as they were moving along and just integrated them unofficially, knowing that was probably the safest place for them. "I worried about unilaterals in my job because the majority of unilaterals I knew about on the battlefield were folks [to whom I had] said, 'I can't embed you,'" he said. Molly Bingham, a freelance photographer from Louisville, Kentucky, was one of them. She, *Newsday* reporter Matthew McAllester and photographer Moises Saman, and photographer Johan Rydeng Spanner of the Danish newspaper *Jyllands Posten* were taken from the Palestine Hotel on March 24, 2003, and held prisoner at Abu Ghraib, the most notorious prison in Iraq.

"She was in our office. I actually talked to her. I could not give her an embed slot. So when I saw on the news that she was captured, I felt partially at blame because here was someone I couldn't give a slot to who went on her own and now she's captured. If I'd given her a slot, would she be in the same situation? So the day I was watching the news footage of her crossing the border out of Iraq [and into Jordan], I breathed a sigh of relief because that was one less thing I had to think in the back of my mind that I could have had an effect on."

Blair said that one international journalist who actually had an embed slot to a unit that hadn't deployed to theater yet decided he couldn't wait, so he joined up with another crew and went off unilaterally onto the battlefield only to be captured by the Iraqis and held prisoner. "We were contacted by their news organizations, 'Please help us. They are captured. We don't know for sure where they are.' I even received some diplomatic pressure on this as well from the embassy of the country involved to see what we could do. I'm sure they were contacting the State Department, as well. This lasted a day or a day and a half. In the meantime, I got word back they had escaped because we had bombed a target nearby, and, while we were bombing the target, their captors went to where they were bombing, so they jumped in their vehicles and drove off. But it was pretty much an accidental rescue. We were just attacking a military target nearby and created a diversion for them, and they were actually able to make it out of there."

There were four embedded reporters who died during the first two months of the war. NBC correspondent David Bloom died on April 6, 2003, of a pulmonary embolism while traveling with the U.S. Third Army Infantry Division. Michael Kelly, editor at large of the *Atlantic Monthly* and a columnist with the *Washington*

*Post*, was killed while traveling with the U.S. Army's Third Infantry Division just south of the Baghdad airport, according to a statement from the *Washington Post*. According to press reports, when the Humvee in which Kelly was riding came under Iraqi fire, the soldier driving the vehicle tried to evade the attack, and the jeep ran off the road and rolled into a canal. Both Kelly and the driver drowned. Kelly was the first U.S. journalist killed while covering the war. Christian Liebig, a reporter for the German weekly magazine *Focus*, and Julio Anguita Parrado, a correspondent for the Spanish daily *El Mundo*, died in an Iraqi missile attack on April 7, 2003, while accompanying the U.S. Army's Third Infantry Division south of the capital, Baghdad. Both Liebig and Parrado were embedded with the division, according to Agence France-Presse. According to *Focus* editor in chief Helmut Markwort, the two men had decided not to travel with the unit to Baghdad, believing they would be safer at the base. Two U.S. soldiers were also killed during the attack, and fifteen were injured.

"I actually met with Julio Anguita at the Pentagon," Blair said. "He and another Spanish reporter came in looking for an embed. I got to talk with him in person and meet with him. A large news organization in the Spanish market gave him and another news organization the embed slot. This was kind of a personal one because this was somebody I knew, somebody I had met and talked to. So those are the only four embeds. When I was at the Pentagon, I was actually keeping track of both embedded and unilateral reporters who died in-country. In some cases we helped to bring the remains of reporters who were killed there out-of-country for some of the other news organizations. I know in northern Iraq, we helped countries and different news organizations get bodies out of the country."

A significant issue related to unilaterals was the use of nonmilitary vehicles. "The decision was made to not allow media vehicles in our convoys. If you were going to be embedded, you were going to be in military transportation. The unilaterals spent a lot of money outfitting vehicles. They bought Humvees and painted them the same color as ours, so they outfitted them to look like our vehicles. We made a decision that we weren't going to allow media vehicles. I'm sure there were a lot of reasons for that. First and foremost I would think that reasons would be, as a news media representative, you are a noncombatant. If you are driving a vehicle that looks like one of ours, who is to determine if you are a combatant or noncombatant? The Bloom Mobile was a military vehicle. It was a recovery vehicle that he was just riding on the back of. It was going along the way, providing a venue and a platform for him to conduct his news on this vehicle. NBC didn't buy it. It had to be there. I think it was an M88 heavy recovery vehicle.

"I can tell you from reading some of the reports from commanders on the ground and some of the public affairs officers who were managing the embeds for their units, even though we had guidelines out there that said no media vehicles, I can tell you that the media had vehicles that they took with them regardless of what our guidance from on high was. We definitely didn't condone it—actually strongly didn't condone it—and told the different commands not to have media vehicles."

With the vehicle issue, there was a satellite telephone (sat phone) issue. Nearly all the journalists who covered the war had sat phones that were used to keep in touch with editors and producers and to file stories. The embeds had to tie into military electrical power sources. "We did tests at the Pentagon to show news organizations how to tie into military vehicles and use the power generation system from the twenty-four-volt evo systems and how you could use inverters and converters, and all the different aspects of how we would be able to operate in a field environment. So, it was quite an undertaking," Blair said.

The military banned one brand of satellite phones, Thuraya, because it integrated a global satellite-positioning feature. There was concern that the enemy could zoom in on the transmitting signal and thus target U.S. troops. The CEO of the Saudi company that manufactured the phone system, Mohammad Omran, disputed the U.S. claim, but the military held firm. "If I'm transmitting with this phone from a unit on the front line and my opposition has the ability to zero in on this signal, then they know where to target a round. The messages and guidance that went out from CENTCOM was specifically directed at the Thuraya cell phone because it had the capability of being traced when it was active. That was particularly troublesome because a lot of news organizations relied on the fact that they could use their Thurayas. In some instances they were completely forbidden to use them because of the fear they could be traced. In those cases, other media organizations would help people transmit their product, and even the military would help them transmit if they could not use their Thuraya," Blair said.

Although there has been no official end to the embed program,[4] most embeds voluntarily left their spots when one major goal of the war was achieved. "They reached Baghdad and our numbers just stopped. The [military] units were continuing to move north and west, but the embeds just stayed in Baghdad because that was the goal line," Blair said.

Blair has thought a lot about the benefits of the embed program. He has concluded, "We really educated three different cross sections of American society and, in some instances, the international community. First, the embedded media now have an understanding of military speak, the military way of life, the hardships and the trials that service members go through. So they are educated in that fact. Second, you also have a military that are the obverse of that. They are better educated on the needs, wants, and desires of the media: how they report, how they operate, that they are not the bad guy. But they are there to tell a story, to pass information as they see it firsthand. Third, the American public, or the world at large for that matter, has received a bird's-eye view from the soldier, sailor, airman, and marine on the ground of what they do, with the hard work they do, the trials and tribulations they go through as servicemen on the ground performing their jobs. They have an understanding of how hard, how difficult, and how dangerous their roles in mission are. Those are the three communities I think this really had an impact on."

The media, at least, expect the embed program to continue in some form. "Once the hostilities started to wind down, I would start getting calls from media saying they wanted to get on the next embed list and asking if I could go ahead and take their names," Blair said. "One journalist called me and said, 'I want to sign up for Operation Syrian Freedom, Operation Liberian Freedom. . . .' He listed every country that had any potential for any type of military action and wanted his name placed on a standing list."

## NOTES

1. United Press International was purchased by News World Communications, a newspaper publishing company owned by the Unification Church, which is led by the Reverend Sun Myung Moon. The company publishes the *Washington Times,* the *Middle East Times* (Cairo), and the *Zambezi Times* (Zambia).

2. The United States Department of State has Foreign Press Centers (FPC) in Washington, D.C.; New York; and Los Angeles. The Foreign Press Centers support U.S. policies by helping foreign media cover the United States. Their goal is to promote the depth, accuracy, and balance of foreign reporting from the United States, by providing direct access to authoritative American information sources. FPC briefings are for foreign media only and are on the record unless otherwise stated.

3. The 101st Airborne Division (Air Assault) is formed of three brigades plus Division Artillery, Division Support Command, the 101st Aviation Brigade, 159th Aviation Brigade, 101st Corps Support Group, and several separate commands.

4. Approximately twenty-six journalists remained embedded through September 2003, and some continued to stay with the troops well into 2004.

# Managing the War:
# The Media

## EASON JORDAN
EXECUTIVE VICE PRESIDENT AND CHIEF NEWS EXECUTIVE, CNN, ATLANTA, GEORGIA

As executive vice president and chief news executive of CNN, Eason Jordan was the network's architect for its war coverage. In 1991 CNN found itself with the only news team broadcasting out of Baghdad as American bombs fell on the city. But in 2003, CNN found its reporters expelled from Iraq, and the network was facing a myriad of competition, from American and foreign media, most notably Al Jazeera. In the United States, CNN's competition includes not only the traditional news of ABC, CBS, and NBC but also the other twenty-four-hour news networks, FOX and MSNBC.

Still, CNN was prepared to provide the kind of coverage that put the network on the map more than a decade ago. "CNN stands out from the pack in the sense that we've had a bureau in Baghdad since 1990," Jordan said. "We've been there pretty much nonstop except for a few occasions when we were thrown out of the country. So, we had a pretty good sense of what was going on in Baghdad."

Jordan said that CNN reporters were kicked out whenever the Saddam Hussein regime didn't like the reports they were seeing. "Our one and only ever Baghdad bureau chief, Jane Arraf, was expelled from the country forever, at least as far as Saddam Hussein was concerned, for reporting on human rights violations," he said. "If you are going to get kicked out, that is a great thing to get kicked out for."

Jordan said that in Arraf's case, she wasn't kicked out of the country immediately but that when she left to take some time off, they wouldn't let her come back in. "In other cases we had people kicked out on the same day, and some people were never permitted to go into Iraq in the first place. Aaron Brown and Wolf Blitzer could never get a visa. They were just on the blacklist from the get-go. Other people, like Christiane Amanpour, were let in several times, and the reporting over time was deemed to be too tough, and they generally wouldn't let those people back in," he said. Jordan personally went to Iraq again and again to argue on behalf of these reporters.[1]

He said that it became clear during the summer of 2002 that a big military conflict was likely to play out in Iraq, so CNN started putting a game plan in place. "A number of people here and overseas were involved in that process. Several months out from the war, we starting weekly meetings, when everybody in the company could come, and we would talk about various challenges, progress that had been made and what we needed to do to prepare for war. Those meetings started out with a handful of people, and by the end we had a couple of hundred people in the room at a time, talking about war coverage preparations," Jordan said.

The embed program, from his point of view, had its roots in the problems encountered in media coverage of the 1991 Gulf War. "Nineteen ninety-one was different from a logistical standpoint, from a technical standpoint, and from a competitive standpoint. There is very little in which it was the same. The war in '91 was not in Iraq, at least from a news coverage perspective, aside from a very small reporting presence inside Saddam Hussein–controlled territory," he said.

The military did permit embedding in 1991, but Jordan said that the "process in '91 was a joke. It was a disaster." He said that the reporters who went through it were determined not to get caught up in it again. "There were a lot of journalists who understandably were jaded about the whole process this time around."

Jordan said that he spent a lot of time at the Pentagon before the war and had traveled with then-CEO Walter Isaacson around the region[2]—Kuwait and Qatar and Bahrain. "I'd actually spent a couple of days and nights out on an aircraft carrier in the Persian Gulf in late December 2002 meeting with the ground forces commander and the naval commander before the war to talk about how embedding would work," he said. "One of the things that I was most surprised and impressed with was the fact that it was the field commanders more than anybody who felt that embedding would be a good idea. Not that they felt like it was a slam dunk, because they knew there would be pros and cons in the process. There were a lot of commanders who knew either firsthand or through the grapevine what had happened with the news media in '91, and they felt like there were a lot of great stories in '91 that didn't get told because the news media were kept away. They felt that if they could get up close and personal with journalists and vice versa, that important, compelling stories would emerge; and, in fact, that is what happened."

There was also an embedding track record of sorts in Afghanistan. "There was some embedding in Afghanistan that I think was deemed to be successful by all sides," Jordan said. "Afghanistan was the worst as well as the best of media–military relations. In the early going, it was a train wreck from the news coverage perspective. We got into things like Operation Anaconda, where CNN, for instance, had an embedded team. I think the military saw the embed process could be very successful if executed in the appropriate way. And the media, which in the early going in

Afghanistan had a really hostile relationship with the military, began to see the merits of working together as well.

"A lot of journalists early on got corralled and basically shunted aside and put in little pens in Kandahar and Kabul. Over time that changed. Things ended up going very well as things progressed, but it took months," Jordan said.[3] In the meantime, a number of reporters who were there in the early months, including Christiane Amanpour, refused to be embedded in Iraq. "She just saw how poorly the relationship worked in Afghanistan in the early going, and veterans like Christiane not only had the Afghanistan experience but also [experience] going back to the 1991 Gulf War. Come hell or high water, they were not going to allow themselves to be embedded in a way that they would be constricted or constrained in any way," Jordan said.

Jordan said that he and Isaacson toured the region because "we thought that the closer we got to war the more the Pentagon would lose control, to a degree, of the embedding process." They expected that some journalists would get an embed spot through "wheeling and dealing in the field" rather than through edicts from Washington. "That turned out to be the case," he said

Jordan said that he and Isaacson went to Kuwait and spent two hours at his command post in Camp Doha, Qatar, with Lieutenant General David D. McKiernan (commander of Third U.S. Army), the ground forces commander through the entire war.[4] "We convinced him to let us put a crew with him for most of the war and actually watch from headquarters the war being executed from the command post. That happened only because we made the trip. There was no dictate from Washington. In fact, Washington was never told that sort of side deal was being done," he said.

CNN embedded nineteen journalists. "One of the reasons that we ended up with nineteen embeds, when I don't think anyone else had more than a dozen, was the fact the we went out there and pushed hard, especially given the competitive situation and the fact we felt like CNN made its name in part because of Iraq in '91. Expectations for CNN were very high, so we felt like we needed to put as many players on the chessboard as possible, so to speak," Jordan said.[5]

CNN had forty-five correspondents covering the war (including the nineteen embeds). Jordan said that a number of his colleagues likened covering the war as an embedded correspondent to covering the war through a straw. "We needed to get as many straws out there as we could to get as full a picture as we could of the conflict," he said. "Some of the most compelling reporting comes from that narrow [embed] perspective because you are dealing with people—real people—it's not some view from forty thousand feet, where it's a very impersonal conflict, which is exactly what it was in 1991."

Jordan said that CNN's nineteen embedded correspondents were "an interesting mix of really seasoned veterans and people who pretty much had never been in war. The reason for the eclectic mix, in part, was because some of our most seasoned veterans refused to be embedded because they had become so jaded from the failures with the previous couple of wars and they would not get involved."

Jordan thinks that the embed program was "absolutely" a good thing. "In my mind it wasn't a perfect process; we didn't expect it to be a perfect process. We were realistic about hiccups in the process and bumps that would be in the road along the way. On the whole I think the media won in the process; the military won in the process; and most importantly, the news consumers in the U.S. and around the world won in the process. It was a win, win, win from my perspective. Not to say that it's perfect. Postmortems galore will take place, and hopefully next time things will go even better, but I think it went far better than 99 percent of people on the news team ever anticipated."

Perhaps because of the 1991 war and several military operations since then, a number of high-ranking retired military officers—ones who openly expressed skepticism about the war strategy—served as media military analysts. Vice President Dick Cheney, speaking to the American Society of Newspaper Editors the morning that Baghdad fell, referred to them as "the armchair retired generals who are embedded in television studios."

Jordan said, "I understand why people who are in the present-day regime don't like getting second-guessed by the previous regime. It is a pain in the ass." However, he doesn't believe that the military commanders in charge blamed the outlets but rather felt somewhat betrayed by the second-guessing generals. "In the eyes of present-day military people it is like sacrilegious almost for a military veteran to criticize current military leadership. Government officials criticize the news media damn near every day. But it is rare that you have former senior military officials, generals and so forth, come out and publicly criticize the Pentagon, and that is extremely irritating to them."

He defends CNN's use of retired military people, one of whom was General Wesley Clark, who later launched an unsuccessful presidential campaign. "We went after the best guys we thought we could find out there. General Wesley Clark commanded the last major U.S. war in Yugoslavia, and obviously he was somebody who had experience fighting a war and also had experience in the region because, as the NATO military commander, his command extended into northern Iraq and the Kurdish area, so he was familiar with the region," he said. "The other two guys we had—retired brigadier general David Grange and retired U.S. Air Force major general Don Shepperd—had experience from the 1991 war. We just thought they were the best guys to have."

Jordan characterized General Clark as "really outspoken" and representative of "the old-school army view—strength in numbers." Jordan sees the conflict between the previous and current military commanders as a mirror image of the conflict between the Colin Powell doctrine and the new, Rumsfeld doctrine—respectively, "Have a clear goal, and go in with an overpowering force and kick some ass" and "Go in with a smaller and more elite force, and do it more effi-ciently with a more efficient team."

He said that he thinks the military analyzers added to CNN's overall coverage. "I think it is important to try to decipher the Pentagonese, so to speak, and in hu-man terms to just spell it out for people in layman language as to how and why the war is being executed in such a way. It makes a lot of sense. It's better to have smart, enlightened people doing that than having people who don't know what the hell they are talking about. If you relied exclusively on the government to tell you everything, I think it would be a disservice to consumers everywhere. You've got to try to interpret and analyze the best you can for the benefit of news con-sumers."

## NOTES

1. CNN reopened its Baghdad bureau as soon as Saddam Hussein fled Baghdad, before the war actually ended. Since then, the bureau continues to have a large staff to cover the ongoing struggle to stabilize the situation in the war-torn country. Two CNN employees—producer Duraid Isa Mohammed and his driver, Yasser Khatab—were killed in an ambush on the outskirts of the capital, Baghdad, on January 27, 2004 (see appendix F).

2. Walter Isaacson left his post as CNN chief in April 2003 to become president and chief executive officer of the Aspen Institute.

3. Operation Anaconda was designed to destroy Taliban and al Qaeda strongholds in the Shah-i-Kot mountains of eastern Afghanistan. After the first week of battle, 8 U.S. and 3 allied soldiers were dead, and an estimated 450 enemy personnel were killed.

4. Lieutenant General David D. McKiernan assumed command of Third U.S. Army/U.S. Army Forces Central Command and the Coalition Forces Land Component Command September 4, 2002.

5. Major Tim Blair, who was in charge of the embed program for the Pentagon, acknowledged that some deals were made in the field that were beyond Pentagon control. However, he disputes Jordan's assertion that CNN had more embeds than other television networks.

## BRUCE CONOVER

SENIOR INTERNATIONAL EDITOR, CNN, ATLANTA, GEORGIA

Bruce Conover, senior international editor for CNN, managed the CNN Embed Desk and was the primary liaison between the Atlanta headquarters and the embedded reporters. He was concerned with logistics and staff issues as CNN geared up for, and then covered, the Iraq War.

He said that the embed program "gave relatively unfettered access to soldiers once a level of trust was built up." Once soldiers who are fighting wars and reporters whose lives are in their hands establish a rapport, "political correctness goes out the window," he said. "We actually were surprised by how open communications were once our reporters were embedded."

He was concerned, however, about the tendency for reporters to identify with the soldiers in their units. "There is a danger of losing one's objectivity," he said. CNN editors consistently warned their reporters to use the word *they,* rather than *we,* in reports referring to military activity, especially in live reports, when they were under the most stress.

His main complaint about the program was reporting limitations. "It's a small view down a narrow hallway, and reporters were unable to lag behind advancing U.S. troops in order to establish what actually happened in many situations," he said. "Access to troops, and even civilians on the other side of the front lines, is essentially impossible for an embedded reporter."

CNN had, and continues to have, a relationship with Al Jazeera. He said that the Arab network wielded considerable power during the war because of the access it had to the other side that was not readily available to Western media. Al Jazeera also became the primary conduit for communiqués from al Qaeda and, later, for messages from the Iraqi guerillas opposing U.S. forces in Iraq.

Language barriers also existed. Most Iraqis that the journalists met were well educated and spoke either English or Russian. He said that Saddam Hussein and members of his regime would skew information, and journalists who didn't understand Arabic might not have been aware of that. "We counteracted that by adding reporters and editors who speak and read Arabic, so communication was not a problem as it is in other countries where we don't have the resources to place native speakers of the local languages."

Conover also noted that Afghanistan was originally planned to be the proving ground for the embed program but that the U.S. Department of Defense decided to pass on the embed program during operations there. Access by journalists to U.S. forces during Afghanistan was extremely difficult. U.S. soldiers and Special Operations agents avoided journalists when possible and were extremely reluctant to speak frankly about operations. "In Afghanistan the Special Operations guys were cautious and not happy to see journalists," he said. "But now, after Iraq, there is a greater level of trust, and they are more likely to share information with journalists they trust."

Conover has attended several military–media conferences since the war "ended," where journalists and the military analyzed the embed program during the Iraq War. "I would say that there is a greater willingness on the part of the military to trust journalists—not all, but certain journalists who have 'proved' themselves in a prior embed situation."

Conover says that his conversations with officers, however, lead him to believe that there is still a fundamental misconception on the part of the military about the role of the embedded journalist. "Many of the officers I have spoken with are very enthusiastic about expanding the embed program in the future because they believe that an embedded journalist will function as a kind of public relations officer for the brave men who are fulfilling their duty," he said. "That may have been true of the Iraq War, but there are many hypothetical military scenarios where a journalist's duty to tell the truth is going to come into open conflict with warfighting goals of military strategists.

"As conflicted as the relationship between the media and the military is likely to remain, I still believe on balance that the American public is better served by having reporters embedded with the military than not," Conover said. "But I do see a need to continue to put journalists 'on the other side' wherever and whenever that is possible. However, with the emergence of Islamic militants who perceive journalists simply as a differently equipped version of Western and anti-Islamic 'crusaders,' I suspect that getting the 'view from the other side' is not going to be very easy over the next few years."

# EARL CASEY
SENIOR EDITOR, CNN, ATLANTA, GEORGIA

Senior editor Earl Casey was involved with training and equipment issues for CNN. He said that the embed program worked better than any other approach to war coverage since he's worked at CNN. "In 1991 there was no freedom of access. It wasn't perfect, but Iraq was not conducive for unilaterals because the chance of being shot up by the U.S. was high." He said that because of CNN's fifteen-year history with Iraq, CNN producers and correspondents recognized that the situation was deteriorating. By evaluating the situation in Iraq and by gleaning subtle hints from Pentagon officials—namely, from their references to the weather and to moon phases—CNN decided to prepare to cover a war. CNN started gearing up in July 2002. "By August, we had a clear outline of where we would staff and a rough idea of what personnel and equipment would be needed. But that began to flesh out over the fall months into considerably more detail," Casey said.

Although CNN's most recognizable veterans were largely missing from the embed lineup, most embeds had experience in Afghanistan or in other hot spots. Casey agrees with other media managers that Afghanistan is where the first tentative steps toward a trusting relationship between media and military began.

CNN offered its correspondents survival training for a hostile environment—a weeklong program offered through AKE, a British company with a branch in Washington, D.C. The company's promotional material proclaims:

> In today's uncertain world, the security of businesses and professionals is at a premium. In a high-risk geographical, legal or technological environment, you need to know how to protect your investment, facilities, staff and yourself. Otherwise, the result could be failed projects, reduced efficiency, additional costs, injury, illness and even death, along with high insurance premiums.

Casey said that AKE training, at CNN expense, was required of everyone working in the war zone, including Kuwait, Iraq, Jordan, Israel, and others. He said that initially two hundred staff or freelancers covering the Iraq War received the training. By March 2003, about four hundred CNN employees had taken the basic course, with some taking an additional training in chemical/biological/nuclear weapons. "The main AKE war-zone training course is five days long," Casey said. "The chemical/biological/nuclear weapons training was an additional two days, usually offered at a different time, most of it in theater, nearer the conflict itself. That was the scariest part of the experience because of the suits, respirators, injectors—and the reality."

He added that CNN sent "only a dozen or so" journalists through the Pentagon's weeklong training course. CNN paid for any transportation and out-of-pocket costs for the training with the military, but the military provided the training itself at its own costs. "We sent some field personnel and engineers to a multiday exposure in the field to shake out the equipment compatibility and battery-charging questions," he said.

Casey said that CNN, as part of the embed training, put some experienced photographers and engineers into the field during military exercises so that they could determine what vehicles they would likely be traveling with and what the options were regarding power-battery recharging. "From that, we learned of some simple but necessary adapters we'd need in the field," he said. They used the weeks of waiting in Kuwait to complete training and field-test their new technology, including hardware and software. They practiced with satellite technology, trying to crash systems and then debugging them.

The training and testing paid off. "We had surprisingly few equipment failures in the field. There was a lot of dust, and it held up. We did not lose much equipment—a handful," Casey said.

CNN managers also planned ahead to be sure they had enough bandwidth on satellites available when the military started to need a great deal of satellite resources once the war started. They purchased as much space as they could in advance, well before most of the other American media, and had very few problems during the war. They used Inmarsat ship-to-shore equipment that provided tremendous geographic coverage. They also used Thuraya cell phones from a company based in Dubai, United Arab Emirates. Casey said, "This particular satellite telephone system only works in the broad Mideast region . . . service into Afghanistan and Pakistan on the east . . . probably into northern Africa on the west. It embraces the entire Iraq theater. We also used a separate service, which is global, called Iridium."

He said that Thuraya was CNN's preferred brand because the phones were somewhat smaller. "At one point in the conflict, the military required that Thurayas no longer be used and at one point actually required that the phones be surrendered for the interim. This was a security-and-monitoring issue that we were expecting, due to our conversations with the military in advance of the conflict. However, another satellite system we used to transmit live and video, which we refer to as Inmarsat, was still in the field and in daily use. It is how we moved our video into the network, and thus we had phone connection through that device as well."

# BRUCE DRAKE

Vice President of News and Information,
National Public Radio, Washington, D.C.

As vice president of news and information for National Public Radio, Bruce Drake devised and instituted a plan of action for coordinating war coverage among the stations that form the public radio system. NPR's managing editor and foreign editor handled most of the day-to-day coverage, whereas Drake was looking at the bigger picture. "A big part of the efforts was on behalf of the public radio system. The greatest logistical effort—greater than mobilizing people in the area—was a game plan that worked for the public radio system," he said.

NPR faced a much different set of circumstances than did cable networks. "CNN controls the air. We don't control the air of our stations. They use our programming the way they want to use our programming," Drake said. The public radio system includes 273 principal stations that control more than 700 signals. Drake said that the stations NPR serves have a variety of formats, including those that are all news. "Those are the easiest ones to work with because they are essentially all-news stations. But then there are stations that have mixed news–jazz formats, mixed news–classical formats, and those stations that only take our newscasts. There are stations that have different views about when they want to scrap their normal schedules and take special programming," he said.

Along with the months of planning that went into just how NPR was going to cover the war were months and months of planning and consultations with system stations to devise a game plan that worked for everyone. "We have five levels of coverage, with 5 being the highest and 1 being the lowest. [Level] 5 is coverage like 9/11 or the start of the Iraq War, where we know that at least for a time we are going to go twenty-four hours, or we are going to go much beyond our regular programming. So we had to have a plan that worked for the system as a whole. Otherwise, you are dealing with a lot of conflict," Drake said.

The five-level system was linked to radio "clocks." "It's like a pie that represents the hour, and one sliver represents a five-minute newscast, another sliver represents the size of the news segment, and another sliver is the size of the cutaways for the stations to put local information in," Drake said. "So at level 5 we are using a special coverage clock. All we have to do is say 'level 5,' and they know they are not going into local cutaways, because we are going to be staying on the air. It also signals a dramatic situation where we decide that funding credits are inappropriate, and we drop those. It is a lot easier if you are CNN, but for us that is a very complicated endeavor, and it took a lot of work."

NPR started preparations to cover the war in August 2002. "We were doing it on two tracks. One was the five-level system. The other track was making the advanced lists of who was going to do what on short notice and figuring out who was going to go where," Drake said.

NPR sent correspondents, especially those without much war coverage experience, to train at Quantico Marine Corps Base in Virginia or to Centurion Risk Assessment Services training in England. Then, selecting the reporters who would embed was the next step. "We gave the names of whom we wanted to the Pentagon. I don't remember anything in terms of having to give further information or vouchering them. Is this the right person? I don't remember getting anything qualitative from them other than having to sign whatever waiver it was. The Pentagon did decide in which units they were placed. We were very lucky because the two places we got in with were in the center of the action.

"First of all, we had formed a national security team [Steve Inskeep, before he became the weekend host of *All Things Considered*, Tom Gjelten, and Eric Westervelt]. So it was clear that someone from that team was going to go. Eric was an obvious choice. Then for your other choices you just look around for your most compelling reporters. Anne Garrels had this kind of experience, and John Burnett by any standards ranks high on both those scales. So he was a choice. So that was the first wave. Later on, Steve Inskeep did go in and embed."

NPR prepositioned correspondents in the region months before the war began. "Anne Garrels must have gone in and out of Iraq about six times during the period," Drake said. "Other reporters, like Ivan Watson, went in." Drake said that preparation is what sustained Garrels and raised NPR's confidence level about letting her stay in Baghdad during the early days of the war. "She was able to network and fall back if she had to lay low. She was experienced enough in Iraq that, as much as anybody can in that situation, she constructed safety nets for herself."

Drake said that NPR has a lot of correspondents on the national desk who gained a lot of experience in Kosovo, Bosnia, Afghanistan, Indonesia, and Iraq. "We are lucky to have a pretty savvy, battle-hardened crew who know how to do these things," he said.

NPR had its logistical plans for correspondents in place when the embedding opportunity came up. Drake said that NPR was offered more slots than it took.

"We only took two slots because we wanted to have a mixture of ways to get at the story, including the embedded reporters, reporters like Ivan Watson and Anne Garrels, who were prepositioned in the region, reporters that we would have in Doha for official briefings or in Kuwait, which was another listening post. So we only took two of the slots." Some of the journalists who assisted NPR during the war were doing double duty with other media outlets. John Lawrence, for example, was also reporting for *Esquire* magazine.

"We weren't shy about using other people's embedded reporters to help flesh things out," Drake said. "Rick Atkinson of the *Washington Post* had covered the military for years, and he had a very good berth. He offered his services before he went, and we regularly went to him for reports. The *Los Angeles Times* was also interested in exposure for the fine work their people were doing. I think what it all added up to was that we tried to take advantage of this in two ways. It was not only the benefits of reports from the scene but also using them to paint the bigger mosaic."

NPR's coverage strategy was to first describe the "big picture" and then move to the building blocks of the stories. Drake was understandably proud of the reporting team that earned one of broadcasting's highest honors—a 2003 Columbia duPont Silver Baton for coverage of the war.

Clearly, Anne Garrels "struck a chord" in the public radio system. Drake said that this was in part because of her courage but also due to her ability to get people to talk and open up to her. "She didn't hype the fact that she was the only U.S. broadcast journalist in Baghdad. She reported. At the end she was frustrated almost to tears because she wasn't getting a correct translation [from minders and government translators], and she didn't speak enough Arabic to double-check it," he said. "The thing that Anne was able to do—that may be a little easier in print but very hard to do in broadcast—was she always had a way to talk to people who were scared to talk and to convey the fact that they weren't necessarily thrilled with Saddam Hussein. She was just a master at doing that from a country where, unlike other places, you can capture people vividly on tape."

Eric Westervelt covered the ground combat, the ongoing attacks on U.S. forces, and the struggle to rebuild the country. "Eric was right at the point of the spear, and several of his pieces made it clear that the vehicle he was riding in was fired on and took some hits. There was one piece where you could hear a rocket-propelled grenade go right by him," Drake said.

John Burnett, who is normally based in Austin, Texas, for NPR, was another one of the veteran reporters who had been in Afghanistan and Pakistan. He was well placed with the First Marines Expeditionary Division. Of the two prongs going toward Baghdad, Westervelt was in one, and Burnett was in the other, allowing NPR a chance to cover the main military action.

In Kuwait was Mike Schuster, whom Drake described as one of NPR's most experienced correspondents and an excellent writer. "He is a person who is very good at taking lots of information from lots of sources and constructing them into an overview," Drake said.

Drake has pondered the contributions of the embed program to war coverage. "We were pulling information from many, many sources—briefings, reporters. I'm not sure there was all that great stuff from unilaterals, because even though they weren't restricted, there were places they couldn't get to. If you read some of the stories by unilaterals, they had to survive by trailing the military almost as if they were embedded."

He thinks NPR's coverage benefited from embedded reporters. "Eric Westervelt was going up through Najaf in central Iraq where there was resistance. He provided a counterweight to the rosier reports about the progress of the troops coming out of Doha. I think the fact that we knew they were meeting more resistance in the south than had been anticipated was information that largely came from embedded reporters—at least at one point in time. I look at the embed program as one piece of the puzzle."

Drake said that some news organizations may have overemphasized the bad, but that is a function of writing the first page of history. He also doesn't believe the military used the media to shape the news. "There is no evidence that the embed program was used in any significant way to feed misinformation, deceptive information, or was used to coerce reporters. I don't have any major criticisms of it. I haven't received or heard one account of a reporter in retrospect saying that he or she had been fed misinformation," he said.

However, whether Drake would make the same decision to embed reporters in the future depends on the kind of military action involved. "If there is another situation like this and the military makes that kind of offer again, I'd have to make my own assessment of the situation because every situation is different. If the new situation were anything like what we went through in Iraq, then we would go."

Because of the characteristics of the medium, Drake said NPR's coverage was different from that of television. "We did a lot of live, but we didn't do much that was the equivalent of Walter Rodgers [senior international correspondent for CNN based in London] and others doing a mad dash north. Nothing was really happening, other than you were seeing those pictures of the mad dash with him saying whatever he could say. We didn't do a lot of that. It wouldn't have had much value on radio."

NPR relied more on packages that editors put together. "When the reporters had the time to get out in the field, and they had some downtime in terms of not being on the move, then they would transmit their spoken tracks and actuality and sound, and those would be mixed back here in Washington, D.C."

NPR also paid attention to whether reporters were overidentifying with the soldiers they were covering. "On the 'we' issue, that is something we are very sensitive to. Do some of the reporters naturally form some kind of bond or friendship with the people they are with? I'm sure that camaraderie develops," Drake said. "I listened very carefully to the stories, and—whatever was in Eric's head or John's head—you would not come away with 'I'm part of the boys here,' whether they felt that way as human beings or not. Eric's pieces, mostly combat pieces, were very straightforward. It was very straightforward war reporting. Also, I think our reporters put a higher premium on the frequencies of produced pieces rather than stand-ups. So, if you are doing a produced piece about a firefight that day, it's going to sound different than a breathless CNN reporter like Walter Rodgers in the prow of the tank doing a live satellite video remote piece because it's not the same adrenaline. I think that also gives some of our coverage a different tone."

NPR was just as committed to the new technology as the other news organizations were. "All of our foreign correspondents have sat phones now," Drake said. "Because of the situation in Baghdad with power, Anne Garrels had a car battery wherever she went. Sat phones have now become a lot simpler to use since the early advent of it. We used to send engineers with it to operate it, but that is not true any more. Sat phones enable us to have the highest quality sound for reports. It's expensive. We're easily going to spend triple what we budgeted for sat phones this year."

Satellite access created some problems. "There were some times when that was true, especially after the fall of Baghdad, when so many other press came in. But there were certain periods of the day and night when there was some other problem with getting connections because of atmospheric conditions or something that had nothing to do with traffic volume."

Although Drake declined to be specific about how correspondents who go into harm's way are compensated, he did say that such duty is not considered a routine part of the job. "The people who had the greatest hardship assignment obviously got a reward for it."

Sometimes, though, it's not a monetary reward that is most needed. "When somebody comes back from a dangerous assignment, I or somebody else always calls him or her up and says, 'Listen. You've just been through a grueling thing. There is an employee assistance program at NPR like many other organizations have. Here's a telephone number of someone there, and if you feel you ever need to talk to them, this is part of your company's benefits. Nobody knows if you talk to them. I don't know it. Your manager doesn't know it. It is entirely in confidence.'"

Drake said that giving people time to decompress is a matter of company policy. The foreign editor Warren Jenkins also was in almost daily contact with spouses or other family members of the journalists who were most clearly in harm's way.

Although Drake believes that NPR correspondents such as Neal Conan (host of *Talk of the Nation*), Tom Gjelten (who covers the Pentagon), and Steve Inskeep (who covered the Pentagon before becoming the weekend host of *All Things Considered*) are well respected, he said that it is a fact of life that Washington administration officials are made more available for television appearances than for radio interviews. He finds this attitude frustrating since "even though a lot of times people can go on CNBC or something like that, the audience dwarfs. Look at the number of cable users."

The expectations for NPR have changed since Drake came there to work in 1991. "At that time, during the Gulf War, NPR was not thought of as a source of news. Listeners turn to it for a lot of reasons, but it wasn't a place to turn to because you thought you were going to get everything you got watching CNN or reading the *New York Times*. The decision was made at that point in time that NPR could be that and should be a place where you could come for news. About $1 million was raised from the system to beef up resources," he said. "That became one of the turning points where NPR, while still continuing to do the back-of-the-book kind of programming that we still do—features and things like that—started its move toward being a primary provider. If news happens that's worth reporting, we do it that day and not three days later and call it analysis. It was a big culture change that accelerated in the late nineties, and with 9/11 it got cemented in. The public radio system itself is changing because now there are major markets that have gone to all news/talk, so the need and demand was out there.

"If there is a difference in emphasis, it is that we want to be quick with the news, and our stations expect us to be quick with the news in a way that was not expected in public radio five or six years ago," Drake said. "I feel very strongly, and I communicated very strongly downward, that we are not going to have our decisions driven or distorted by being the first to say that the port of Umm Qasr has fallen or something like that. I'd rather be right and late than first and wrong. So, to the extent that while we see something on CNN, we react and try to go out and find out if it's true, I resist the kind of competitive pressure to show up in Lisa de Moraes's *Washington Post* TV column because I beat NBC by nineteen seconds. I don't think our audience cares about that or expects that of us."

He thinks the audience does expect to be able to "turn to NPR like any other news source and be confident that we are telling them what they need to know. Just being first for first's sake is not a very highly held principle around here."

Drake said that NPR has a personal connection to its audience. "There are a lot of listeners who feel like they are part of the family, and they know the voices of Anne Garrels and Scott Simon [host of *Weekend Edition Saturday*]." However, he said that the public radio system makes it difficult to determine just how much feedback NPR gets from the audience. "It's hard to scientifically count it because e-mails come into so many different places here. Some people write to the shows, some to reporters."

NPR's audience has grown in times of crisis and public anxiety. "With every major story over the last three or four years—the presidential election in 2000, 9/11, and the war in Iraq—times when we did a lot of special coverage, we have hit a record audience," Drake said. "While it is not unusual for newspapers and broadcasters to have a spike when there is big news, the difference between the trend at NPR and the other places is that for the most part when we have spikes, we hold most of those people. They don't go away. We are also blessed to have a very sought-after and ideal audience."

The NPR website experienced a "monumental" jump in the number of hits during the major military action of the Iraq War. "I don't know whether it was as heavy as 9/11, because 9/11 was so heavy we had to change our homepage to a stripped down version," Drake said. "I would say we're in a different position on-line than CNN or MSNBC or some of the networks that have very well-resourced sites. I mean we just don't have the resources. I think we know that NPR listeners do not come to us for headlines the way they go to CNN or MSNBC. They come to us for time shifts—for information or programs that they missed. They come to us for our audio archives to hear pieces."

However, the website did permit NPR to do special coverage that was only available online. "A lot of our correspondents in regions filed reports that they didn't do for radio, some of which were very nice. Some of them had digital cameras and sent back pictures. So, we experienced a traffic jump like a lot of news organizations did. But in terms of whether we served the public [online] like we served them on radio, I don't think we had the resources to do that."

NPR, like other national news organizations, decided to cover the war first and worry about what it was costing later. "That's what we did with 9/11, with Afghanistan, and that's what we did with this. Our company is committed to covering it, so I never got in the position where I had to go upstairs and say, 'Can I spend this money?' We were very quick to try to make projections about what this is going to cost. We expected it would cost a million beyond what we had budgeted. This is roughly a hundred-million-dollar company, so you squeeze elsewhere. The management of this company—both due to our mission and what we heard loud and clear from our stations—was committed to doing whatever we needed to do to resource this story."

## LEONARD APCAR
EDITOR IN CHIEF, NYTIMES.COM, NEW YORK CITY

Leonard Apcar, editor in chief of NYTimes.com, said that the Iraq War demonstrated "quite markedly" that Westerners get their news from a variety of sources—television, newspapers, magazines, and increasingly the web. Apcar spends a lot of his time looking to the future of online news. He believes that the Internet's role is to provide comprehensive information. For example, the *New York Times* produced a package of stories that detailed the events that led up to the Iraq War, what happened during the war, and what continues to happen in both Iraq and Washington. This package can be kept on the website indefinitely.

The *Times* has about ten people working in the *Times* building who write and edit almost exclusively for the website. About thirty-two NYTimes.com editors and producers are off site because of lack of space in the building. They tape-record correspondents and produce links and packages.

The newspaper managed the correspondents during the height of its Iraq War coverage, but the website was right alongside. The *Times* set up a bureau in Kuwait City, with Patrick Tyler as the bureau chief, two to three weeks before the start of the war. Producer Naka Nathaniel, overseas editor for NYTimes.com, coordinated the coverage with the correspondents and Tyler.

Tyler wrote overview stories, whereas Nathaniel put together the *Times*'s war coverage in the region and in Washington. The embedded reporter with the Third Infantry wrote for the newspaper and the website.

Apcar said that early on in the war there was an issue about photographs that the Iraqis released of captured Americans, the troop that included Jessica Lynch. "Reuters had them and circulated them. The *Times* didn't run them because, one, showing captives is against the Geneva Convention; two, we had no idea whether the Pentagon had notified family members about their capture; and three, they didn't know the circumstances under which the photograph was taken: Were they under duress?" The *Times* opted to run military-issued mug shots of Lynch and a group shot of prisoners.

Although the *Times* does not have written policies for photograph content, Apcar said, "We don't show gruesome shots or dead bodies in any conflict. It is generally standard practice for photographers to take what they wanted and then let editors decide if they should be used." Apcar said that the role of the online newspaper is extremely important, especially in a situation such as the Iraqi War. "Iraq is eight hours ahead, so the morning is just beginning when the *New York Times* goes to bed between midnight and 2 AM. The online newspaper can pick up the coverage and update it as it is happening in Iraq. Our website enhances the newspaper's coverage and then picks up where the paper leaves off. It provides information not available on cable television or websites that are not being updated quickly."

## MARIA C. THOMAS

VICE PRESIDENT FOR NPR ONLINE, NATIONAL PUBLIC RADIO, WASHINGTON, D.C.

Marie C. Thomas, vice president for NPR Online, makes it clear that she is a businessperson and an Internet person rather than a journalist or a media person. However, she is responsible for all the content on NPR.org, and that has involved creative ways to "shift time." The term *time shifting* generally refers to listeners being able to access programs and news reports when they want them rather than when they air in real time.

When it came to Iraq War coverage, *time shift* also meant working with at least an eight-hour time difference between the United States and the Middle East. "The first things are practical," she says. "With the time difference between here and Iraq, much of the news was coming out during the workday. The fact that many people are at their desks and on their computers all day long is an opportunity for a workday audience to receive news in a new way."

Another aspect is the advancement of technology since the last war. "The fact that audio and video compression technology make it much easier to receive audio and video over the web in a much more high-quality way—it's just easier to do it. It's becoming more commonplace to click on a news site and expect to find rich media—audio and video in addition to text and pictures. I think societal change in general about the Internet as a medium has changed the expectations about how people consume information," Thomas said.

Technology has increased the expectation for immediacy. "It's basically about technology," she said. "The fact that these people were embedded with digital cameras and satellite phones, making it possible for things to happen quickly, and the fact that things do happen quickly, raises the bar in terms of people's expectations about how quickly they can consume media.

"One thing is very important if you are comparing our websites to other media's websites," she said. "When you compare the NPR.org website to, say, a newspaper's website, or a TV website, a huge difference is that newspapers and TV start with their original, off-line product; their product is a visual product. It's a visual medium. A newspaper is in print. A TV has a screen. Since they started their businesses, they were already in visual businesses. That's really different here. It affects everything we do, war or no war. We are not a visual product in our core business. Our original business is radio. We here at Online work on a visual platform. So it is a place where you can, quote, 'see' NPR. And that is really different than a newspaper or TV. That's starting point number one.

"Concerning how we put audio on the site so quickly, there are several points to be made," she said. "One is that there is an actual process that has to happen in order to make the audio consumable on the web. It doesn't just sort of magically go from the microphone into a digital storage place and then magically appear on the web. There is a process of encoding, which means putting it into a format that can be read by the players on your computer. There is a technical and labor process that it has to go through to make that happen.

"The second point is that we, I believe and have the research to confirm, add value to the process of archiving the audio. To simply archive everything you hear on NPR programming is already valuable because, for you as a consumer, the radio is a linear medium—meaning that if you miss it, it is gone. You don't have twenty-four hours a day to listen to the radio. But you have specific interests, so we make it possible for you to go back to the web and listen to only those things that you are interested in. That's already a valuable service, but I think we add even more value because we tape those programs, such as *Morning Edition* [a two-hour program]. We not only make it possible for you to hear the whole program on the web at your convenience, but we also cut it up to the individual stories and also the music that is played between the stories—that is very important. So the value comes in the form of time shifting. You do it on your time and your convenience. But also, you maybe don't have time to listen to the whole program so you want to hone in on your interest."

NPR uses music to segue between news and information segments. A feature of NPR.org is *All Songs Considered,* an exclusively online multimedia music program. It started after listeners wrote in asking about the music played between news stories on *All Things Considered.* "There is a lot of interest in the music that is played between the segments, and one of the values that you can bring on the web is to inform the listeners—well, what was that music? And we do tell them what it was and make it possible for them to hear it because they are coming to the website because they don't know what the music was. And the only way to know is if you hear it again. It is really a big part of our listeners' enjoyment because the music sets the tone for the stories.

"After September 11, we produced a show that was September 11 music. We had a lot of comments about how important it was for people to express their feelings and grief and sorrow through music. I think it is another phenomenon," Thomas said.

Thomas said that NPR has used Nielsen Net Rating, the leading web metrics provider, to determine the number of hits the website receives. "Since we've been getting reliable numbers, which is a few months before the Iraq War, hits have been steadily increasing month to month," she said. "We definitely had a huge spike during March and early April for the war. And, in fact, Nielsen Net Ratings came out in April with a ranking of the fastest growing news sites as measured from February to March to sort of take a count for the war, and we were number nine on that list," she said. "I think Al Jazeera was number one, because obviously no one looked at Al Jazeera in February, and then everyone looked in March. So, yes, our numbers are increasing. That relates primarily, I think, to the fact that we are cross-promoting on air what's going on the web, because there are a certain number of listeners who are going to come to the web anyway because they are just naturally inclined to do so. But if we tell them on the air, 'Hey, did you know you could actually go and listen at your own convenience?' . . . We have to educate listeners, and we're starting to do that."

Since it is a not-for-profit organization, NPR cannot put traditional advertising on its site, just as it does not run traditional advertising on the air. The challenge for Thomas is to figure out how to financially support the website operation. "I think we have an uncluttered underwriting environment at the moment. I think we have little data about the trade-off between whether people really value that or even recognize it versus our need to subsidize the cost of what we are doing," she said.

"The technology to put the audio on the website costs money. We have never changed anything about the fiscal operations of this company to reflect the fact that we added this whole operation called Internet that costs real money," she added. "So, actually one of my objectives is to find an appropriate balance between offering underwriting online for real money, and yet we will never do some of the things you see on commercial websites, ever. But certainly it's appropriate to try to replicate online the type of underwriting that one hears on air. The hard thing about that gets back to the first thing I said, which is the air is not visual and online is visual so immediately you introduce a new element. And suddenly people think, 'Oh.' And I think we can work that into an opportunity, and we are just starting to think about that."

Thomas is optimistic that online media sites can eventually pay for themselves. "The *New York Times* is making money. The Internet has been around only since 1994, basically. But the actual commercial applications of the Internet really didn't get started until around '95 or '96. We are still in the big picture. It's still not a long time. The idea of the *New York Times* even making a marginal profit is interesting," she said.

Thomas said that any media on the Internet trades off between the subscription model and the advertising model. She thinks in the long run it will be a balance of both. "I think the model is cable. People pay for cable, but there is still advertising-supported 'free' TV. Since its early days, the Internet has evolved as the ultimate democratic medium. People still have the notion that it is free, but I think that is going to change."

Thomas said that adding visual elements to a radio website enhances its value, as it did during the Iraq War. "We were able to send some digital cameras out with folks on the ground and get pictures back from the front line. We are not in the business of professional photography, but I think despite NPR's powerful on-air storytelling that sometimes there is a visual element to a story that is really best captured by a photo. The best example of that actually was not in the Iraq War but rather in Afghanistan in 1992, when we gave Steve Inskeep a camera. I have a little piece here from Poynter: 'Radio doesn't need pictures. That is the old way of thinking. . . .' Then it talks about what Steve Inskeep did."

Inskeep had a breaking news story when he was in Afghanistan. "The photos that went with it really allowed us to talk about it a lot more. His story was on the radio, but it helped us talk about it a lot more, and it helped us get from my perspective—PR—some television coverage. We were able to use a visual with our story, so our story could be told on all different media," Thomas said.

Also, NPR.org coverage included some "web-only" content. "There were stories to be told that reporters on the ground felt they wanted to tell, but they didn't have enough airtime for whatever reason," she said. "We actually had many submissions in the form of essays from people like Sylvia Poggioli, Guy Raz, and Ivan Watson. Even producers who aren't on the air contributed from their perspectives. Charlie Mayer submitted photos and essays. I thought a very interesting one was Guy Raz's story about the last Jews of Baghdad."

Raz visited the only known synagogue left in Baghdad and met some of the thirty-five Iraqi Jews still in the city, descendents of slaves brought to Babylon by Nebuchadnezzar twenty-five hundred years ago to build the famed hanging gardens. "It was on air, but he did more online. And that is a model that will evolve for us. The reporters and correspondents who are inclined to embrace the web will plan their stories. They know the story to be told will take X number of minutes, but the available time on air will be Y number of minutes. They know that X–Y will be on the web. It is a way that we can evolve to have complementary mediums," she said.

"Increasingly, we are offering audio on the web. For instance, when Anne Garrels came back from Baghdad and did an interview with Susan Stamberg—I don't know how many minutes they were on the air, but we had a lot more on the web," Thomas said. "So it's a way to say to the listeners, 'This is really interesting stuff, and we know you want to listen. We only have so much time; go to the web and finish reading it.'"

## GERRY BARKER
EASTERN REGIONAL DIRECTOR OF NEWS AND OPERATIONS,
BELO INTERACTIVE, DALLAS, TEXAS

## CHRIS KELLEY
EDITOR, BELO INTERACTIVE, DALLAS, TEXAS

Chris Kelley said that the Internet "changed everything" in war coverage between the 1991 Gulf War and the Iraq War. "We didn't have online coverage in 1991. It was a major part of our coverage this time," said Kelley, editor of Belo Interactive's Dallas websites, which include DallasNews.com and eleven other sites.

"The war certainly kept us busy," said Gerry Barker, who is eastern regional director of news and operations for Belo Interactive, headquartered in Dallas. In addition to the *Dallas Morning News,* Belo's Dallas broadcast properties include WFAA-TV and the TXCN cable system. All of the company's online resources were available to support war coverage, which Barker and Kelley made as interactive as possible.

During the major combat phase of the war, Belo had a dozen embeds, equally split between print and broadcast journalists. A section called "Dispatches: Exclusive Reports from Our Belo Interactive Correspondents" was quickly added to Belo sites. All of the embeds were given the opportunity to provide firsthand accounts of the war and share their personal experiences.

The broadcast journalists were sending back video that was used on TXCN and WFAA-TV and then streamed onto the websites. War images were edited together in "War without Words," which included video and still photographs.

Kelley said that weblogs, or *blogs,* added another dimension in coverage. Not only were embedded journalists able to blog, but soldiers and family members were also able to provide personal insights. This phenomenon was not limited to Belo's operations. Kelley pointed to Anne Garrels's book *Naked in Baghdad* as another example of how blogging worked. "Garrels's husband was sending e-mails to family and friends, updating them on her daily adventures as a reporter staying in the Palestine Hotel in Baghdad during the military operations. His blogs were included, making the book much more insightful."

Readers were able to e-mail the embeds, giving them feedback and helping them focus on local angles. As part of an ongoing online project, members of the U.S. military can post their photos and add messages for friends and family on DallasNews.com.

Kelley, like many of his counterparts at other online newspapers, wrestled with the decision about whether to display the graphic photos of Saddam Hussein's sons, killed in a shootout with American troops. "We waited until the last minute to decide if we would even post these photos. I wanted to see how distasteful they would be. I discussed [it] with all our news partners [newspaper and television news executives] in advance, and they agreed on the approach we ended up using," Kelley said. He put a teaser on the home-page that linked to a warning about the graphic nature of the photos, which in turn linked to the photos. "Interestingly, of the twenty-four thousand page hits we got on the homepage tease, we received ten thousand hits from folks who actually went on to view the photos. In other words, about half the audience who clicked on 'View the photos' did not choose to go on to view them. The warning worked as I had hoped . . . giving users the choice to view something that we told them in a separate warning would be graphic."

Kelley said that the photos were clearly an exception to their policy of not showing graphic content on the sites. "Frankly, my concern was not so much the graphic content but more about whether we played into the hands of the Pentagon's spin machine. I don't like feeling used by government to spread what was unquestionably a propaganda move, but I felt the news value warranted publication using the guidelines we followed."

"I think this was the perfect application for the web," Barker said. "I wish the *Dallas Morning News* had resisted printing the photos and instead referred readers to the web." Instead, the newspaper published small photos inside the next morning. Kelley said, "To my knowledge, no complaints were received over that decision." The graphic video of the bodies was not streamed on the website.

# Visual Journalists

# CHERYL DIAZ MEYER

PHOTOGRAPHER, *DALLAS MORNING NEWS*, DALLAS, TEXAS

When Cheryl Diaz Meyer asked her supervisors at the *Dallas Morning News* to "put her name in the hat" as they were considering potential candidates for the embed program, she had no idea what she was asking. As she was leaving Kuwait to start her assignment, she had to check in with a military public affairs group that happened to include female officers. "When one of the women called me up and asked which group I was with, I said, 'the Second Tank Battalion.' She turned to me and said, 'Oh? You're in the Second Tank Battalion?' And I said, 'Yes. Isn't that right?' At that point I couldn't even get all the names of the military units straight—battalions and regiments—so I thought I'd made a mistake. But she looked at me and said, 'You know, if you were a woman marine, you'd be making history. There are no women who will be as forward in battle as you will be.'"

Diaz Meyer said that she realized she was going to be on the front line as the Second Tank Battalion moved toward Baghdad. There were a couple of women in the regiment, but not in her group, the Second Tanks that included the Fox 2/5. "I was in the battalion by myself. So that made me stand back and take note of the situation. I had a few questions regarding privacy issues, such as, What do women do when they are out in the field? What's the protocol? And that is when I learned that I was going to have to make it up as I went along because there were no other women." She said that in other circumstances, women would help each other maintain privacy. "Usually there are a few women together, and they cover each other so that one of them holds up a poncho and watches out to make sure nobody is coming while the other woman is doing her business on the other side."

Eventually, a master gunnery sergeant helped her out. He ordered that she be given a poncho, along with a spade and a bucket—military issue affectionately referred to as "a shovel and shitter." "I ended up finding out how I was going to do

it. That poncho never left my side. I just kept thinking, 'If my mother only knew.'"
Showering was also an adventure that required assistance from a male soldier. She
had her first shower in the engine compartment of an assault amphibious vehicle
(AAV). "The compartment was pretty sizable, probably four feet by eight feet wide
and six feet tall, so once I stepped in I could hunker down and tried to keep the
poncho up above my head." The soldier opened the engine compartment, brought
her the water, and got everyone off the top of the AAV.

Her transportation vehicle varied. "Sometimes I was with an AAV, which is a
big metallic vehicle that has two long strips on the top. The top just opens up with
two jacks. At some point, once we had crossed the border into Iraq, for a few days,
maybe a week, I was in a Humvee." She usually slept on the ground in a sleeping
bag or bivy sack, sometimes on her poncho. She had a tent, but it wasn't very useful. "I don't think I set up the tent even once because we were moving at such a
rate that if they said, 'We need to leave,' you have to leave then and there, and just
collecting your things is enough without having to tear down a tent." Some of the
things she had to gather included her gas mask, helmet, and bulletproof vest—
and, of course, her camera gear and backpack. "You know if I had to tear down the
tent, I'd be holding the place up."

Diaz Meyer said that the soldiers she was accompanying were very accommodating. "We took up space, but they made sure that when I wanted access, they
would make room on the AAV so that I could look out and photograph. They
were very supportive." They were also more protective of her than they probably
would have been of a male journalist. "At one point, we had an incident where a
fellow was accidentally shot by a .50 caliber. Two tankers had just parked. We had
just driven some ungodly number of miles that day. Everybody was really exhausted. The .50 cal went off, and we thought we were under fire. It was so incredibly close that had we actually been under fire, I don't know whether any of
us would have escaped. At that point, one of the marines threw me to the ground
and covered me with his body. And when there was a pause, people were sort of,
okay, what is going on? He got up and dragged me to the back of a vehicle, lifted
me up, and threw me into the back of this vehicle." She doesn't believe he would
have done that for a fellow soldier. "I was a woman there, and I think there was a
real sense that they wanted to protect me as they would their own womenfolk.
They didn't want anything to happen to me. But did they make any special provi-
sions for me? It just depended on the situation."

She was dependent on power provided by the military vehicles to send her
photos back to the *Dallas Morning News*. "I had two digital camera bodies with
lenses. You couldn't have photographed with film unless you were with a magazine and could somehow get it out of the country. That's really tricky. Everyone
was using digital cameras. There was no way to cover this war any other way."

She also had a satellite phone and a laptop computer. "I would photograph and
download it to my computer, and then from my computer I would send it via my

sat phone. We had changed one of the cords from my sat phone to my computer, and, for some reason, the connection was very tenuous. Often my computer would shut down the sat phone as soon as I tried to transmit. There were times in the beginning when I was spending four hours of the day just futzing with the sat phone." She says that she needed to finish before dark because she didn't want light shining on her nor did she want to be in a position to be accidentally run over by a military vehicle. "That's how you get friendly-fire incidents," she said. "So, the whole thing was extremely stressful.

"To get power, we used an inverter, which we hooked into the battery of the AAV; or when I was with the Humvee, the guy sitting in the passenger seat ended up giving his seat to me because it took so long to recharge batteries. If anybody was going to be dislodged, it should have been me. Finally, he gave me the seat next to the driver that had the battery under it, and I would just go somewhere else while it was recharging. It was very difficult," she said. "Several times the batteries on the vehicles just died. That was perfectly dangerous. You've got to move in an instant, and you've got a dead battery. You're not going anywhere. Even in the AAV, which is an enormous vehicle, we ended up draining the battery as well. So, it was a big sacrifice for those guys because they had to run the vehicle often every hour [to recharge the battery]. Sometimes I would say, 'Okay twenty minutes, and we are going to start the Humvee again.' I'd have to time it.

"I pretty much photographed what I wanted to photograph. Sometimes, I broke the [embed photography] rules," she said, "We weren't supposed to photograph prisoners of war, and I did." She said that those prisoners provided the only interaction that the soldiers in her group had with Iraqis. "We didn't understand them. They were all Hajji [someone who has been to Mecca]. We had one translator for a while, which enlightened a lot of things for them. But even then I don't think there was a lot of understanding," she said.

Diaz Meyer said that although she knew she risked being pulled from her embed slot, "I told my boss that I didn't want to pre-edit myself. I'm just going to make the pictures and send them. I don't have time to think. If I pre-edit myself, I'm going to stop myself from doing things, and I don't want to do that. You've got the rules as well as I do. I'll send the photographs to you to decide if this is okay or not okay."

Diaz Meyer said that "without a doubt" she would embed again. "There was no way you could have covered the news, the way we covered it, to such an extent, without the embed process. People ask me, 'Can you be objective?' No! I'm not objective—not when you are nearly killed with these people. You know what they are going through. You know exactly how they feel because you feel it. You feel just as filthy; you feel just as scared; you feel the terror, the weakness in your stomach every time a bomb goes off; and you think it might end up landing near you. Is it wrong that you feel that way? You just do."

She has little patience with the policy that some news organizations had requiring their embed to always use *they* rather that *we* when referring to the soldiers that the reporter was accompanying. "People say, 'Don't say *we*.' I'm sorry, but until you do the embed thing, you can't talk about *we* and *not we*. It's generally people who have not been embedded who say, 'You can't say *we*.' They didn't live it."

Still, she insisted, "If I'd had something bad happen while I was embedded, I would have reported it." She also acknowledged how difficult the experience was for her physically and emotionally. Married only a short time before she left for Kuwait and Iraq, she missed her new husband and her family.

Diaz Meyer remained with her unit until they reached Baghdad. "We came from the south and got maybe fifty miles south of Baghdad, and then we headed east. We circled Baghdad and ended up in the north. The tank battalion positioned itself up there. I ended up spinning off from them and joined the infantry division and went into Baghdad for a couple of days with Fox 2/5, and then went back up and met them. At that point things were pretty much over.

"It's really a guessing game about whether journalists were going to get a good embed or not. David Leeson [fellow *Dallas Morning News* photographer] and I happened to get lucky, and we ended up at the tip of the spear so to speak. He ended up seeing a lot of action," she said. "But the work that a tank battalion does is generally outside a city because cityscapes put the tanks at risk and don't use them to advantage. So they didn't actually enter Baghdad. Some tanks did enter, but not this battalion. They ended up, from what I understand, heading south eventually. They positioned themselves in a place where a lot of the bones of torture victims were excavated."

Once she left her embed position, she was transferred to the regimental headquarters and then to another group, who helped her find a hotel in Baghdad. Once she was settled, she hired an interpreter and kept working. "I was really focused on shooting: What was the perspective of the Iraqi people on this whole thing? How do they feel about it? Who were the people who were injured and affected by this war? So, I went to hospitals. I ended up going to cemeteries. People were discovering for the very first time where their brothers, their sons, their fathers were buried, with just a number marking their grave," she said. "They had discovered somewhat afterward that there were thousands and thousands of files of people who had been tortured and killed by the regime. That was twenty-five years under Saddam. They would have the photos in there, like how this person had been killed. It showed the torture method, and it would show a mug shot and then a picture of the person dead. Then the family would have to go to this particular place to find out where the grave was, then go to the cemetery and dig up the body and bring it to their hometown or take it to An Najaf, which is considered a very holy place for people to be buried."

While visiting one of the cemeteries, she photographed an Iraqi man kissing the skull of his brother. "I think that the Iraqi people are psychologically maimed by Saddam Hussein," she said. "Twenty-five years of him has destroyed their initiative and their sense of responsibility. That photograph symbolized facing up to all these bones that were just in mass graves or in numbered graves and was part of reclaiming all of the grief and all of this pain and really coming to grips with how awful he was."

She said that people coming to collect these bones created an incredible scene. "There were just arms flailing, throwing sand in their face, howling, weeping to discover after so many years what they already feared and from an Iraqi perspective what that meant."

She learned a lot about the Iraqis through her translators. "I really, through my translators, fell in love with the Iraqi people because they taught me who they were. At first I hired a female translator and then I hired a male, and I think that was the best of both worlds," she said. "There were some stories that were better done with a woman, and other stories that were just better done with a man, because two women traveling together, even though we had a male driver, the uncle of my translator, there was still a lot of danger.

"I was riding in the back of a car with my [female] translator heading to a mental institution where I was working on a story. A man looked through the window of our vehicle and saw two women riding in the back and made an indication that he'd shoot us. My translator said, 'The people here are so bad that even the thieves joke about how awful they are.' So, he was joking that he would kill us. That's how bad the area was."

Diaz Meyer said that the photograph that people seem to connect her with the most was a photograph of two men helping an Iraqi civilian in the middle of an ambush. "He had raced in, and his truck had been shot up. It was burning. He had been taken out of the vehicle, and then they were trying to treat him. The medic in our vehicle, an ARV [army recovery vehicle], jumped out—we were the closest to the scene—so he started helping the guy, trying to stop the blood flow. I jumped out to photograph the scene—the angst, the tension of the battle, you know . . ." The photograph ran on the front pages of sixty-eight U.S. and international newspapers.

"For the most part, I gained access to both men and women. A lot of male photographers couldn't do the stories that I did, such as a women's mental institution story. They didn't let guys into the women's section; and if so, it was very brief, and it was guided. Someone was standing over their shoulder the entire time. Whereas with me, I could have sat there all day, and they wouldn't have cared. I could have sat in the men's section. Their main concern there would have been for my safety.

"Very quickly after I arrived, there was an organization called the Hosa, the academy of the Shia people. They were beginning to take over a lot of these organizations, such as orphanages, mental institutions . . . things that here would be run by the public government. There was, all of a sudden after the war, no support for them. No money was coming in. The doctors weren't being paid. The facilities were being looted. It was just complete and utter chaos. And so, the Hosa would come in and take over."

To gain access to these places, she had to don traditional Islamic dress. "When I was in Afghanistan, I stayed covered the entire time, but in Iraq it varied. If I were going to a place with religious connections, I would have to wear a scarf, or an abaya if I was wearing pants and needed to cover my entire body."

Ultimately, the most emotional part of being in Iraq was not the danger but witnessing the effects of the war on the Iraqis. "I was at the mental institution, and at one point there was a very old, sick woman who was very frail and very tiny. She wasn't doing well, because the hospital had been looted on a couple of occasions, and even after I worked on the story, it was looted again. They would come in, and they would rape the women. As I was leaving, we knew for sure that one was pregnant. Some never made it back."

Both the hospital's stretcher and ambulance had been stolen, so they had to transport the frail old woman in a blanket. "So here she was, just a bag of bones. They had to move her, and the pain in her eyes . . . this was a moment where I just bawled. I saw this woman. I thought about my mother. And I thought, I would never ever want my mother to experience anything like this. Just to see her in this kind of pain. . . . They took her out in this blanket, and they transferred her up to the back of this truck, and she just laid there in complete agony." A man got some plastic bags of water for the woman from the Red Cross. He poked holes in the bag, but she couldn't drink from it. "He would pour the water into his hand and drip it into her mouth, and like a bird on the ground, she would open her mouth and just make this rasping, gulping sound. . . . When I saw that, I just completely broke down. To see such pain and such suffering, and that wasn't even the gravest of the suffering. For some reason it touched a chord in me that I just personalized it."

Diaz Meyer had to deal with these emotions eventually. "I was doing pretty well when I first got back actually," she said. "But then the longer that I've been home, I think, little by little, it's sinking in, and I feel actually sadder about it. I feel closer to tears more often."

She knows other journalists have had similar feelings that are very close to the surface. The *Dallas Morning News* has counselors available to employees at any time, whether they are on the job or just coming back from being abroad. But Diaz Meyer didn't spend much time feeling sad. When Saddam Hussein was captured, Diaz Meyer returned to Iraq, stood in the now famous hole where he was hiding, and took photographs. She and fellow photographer David Leeson shared a Pulitzer Prize for their war coverage in the "Breaking News" photography category.

# JEROME DELAY
## PHOTOGRAPHER, ASSOCIATED PRESS, BAGHDAD, IRAQ

Jerome Delay, Associated Press Photographer of the Year (2003), covered the Iraq War from a different perspective than that of most other journalists. "I had absolutely nothing to do with the U.S. forces. I was covering the other side. I was pretty free to move around, but I knew what I could and could not do," he said.

Before his stint in Iraq, Delay spent a week aboard a U.S. aircraft carrier in the gulf. "When I was on the aircraft carrier, I only wanted to photograph the flights out. I was not interested in taking photos of soldiers in the kitchen and other parts of the ship. The military didn't quite understand that. I would ask them for things they didn't expect, like being hooked up with a belt on the tarmac so that I could shoot the F18s taking off using a wide-angle lens. There were a lot of 'yes sirs' to those photos."

He left Baghdad in November 2002 to cover the Turkish elections and then again for the Christmas holidays. Upon his return to Iraq, he stayed in Baghdad until a few days after the city fell to U.S. forces. "At first we stayed at the Al Rashid Hotel, a fine place. We moved because it was in the heart of the targeted area, and also we thought there was security in numbers. Everyone moved to the Palestine Hotel, which had a good viewpoint for photographing the bombing." Although the U.S. military was aware that a number of journalists were staying there, the hotel was deliberately shelled on April 8, 2003. The military claimed that Iraqis were firing on them from the hotel, but many of the journalists on the scene dispute this claim. Regardless of the reason, the result was tragic.

"That was a very bad time," Delay said. "I was on the seventeenth floor with a group of photographers taking pictures of fighting on the bridge. We saw them looking at us, but we didn't think much of it. We saw a flash of light, and then the building shook. We thought the shell had hit close by. We didn't see damage from our vantage point, but then we saw people pointing to the building where we were hit. We took the emergency exit down to the fifteenth floor, where most of the others were already evacuating. We went to the room that had been hit. Some of the wounded were being evacuated already. There was mayhem. When I reached the room, I found my friend Taras, lying on his back, his guts open. I opened his jaw and got him breathing again. We put his guts back in and carried him down in the elevator, which took a long time. We put him in a taxi, and I got into the car with him. The driver took us about three blocks away to a medical facility. We got him out of the car and laid him on ground. Nurses were there, but they were throwing up because of the terrible scene. We knew that wasn't the place for him, so we carried him back out and put him in the back of the pickup truck, but I lost him about three minutes before we got to the hospital. I returned to the hotel in shock. I had a friend who just died in my arms. I went back out to take photographs and spent the day at the morgue."[1]

He said that the Iraqis would take photographers and television crews to the hospitals by bus, creating a media circus. "I would always go alone or with another photographer. We worked with people and talked to them to understand what happened. We worked in the hospital building, getting close-up pictures of a man with a scratch on his head."

Delay captured one of the most memorable images of the Iraq war: the toppling of the statue of Saddam Hussein near the Palestine Hotel. That image marked the psychological end of the war for most Americans. It seemed to provide proof that Saddam's regime was gone and that the Americans were in control. Delay said that it was "a perfectly orchestrated media event, a perfect photo opportunity."

Delay describes how he captured that image: "I was with a photographer friend taking pictures of looting and burning buildings. Then we decided to make it back to the hotel. [Soldiers were] stationed all over the place. A little group of Iraqis gathered around the hotel. The Iraqis tried to take Saddam's statue down by breaking down the base. But they weren't able to do it. Then the military came in."

In spite of the play the image received around the world, Delay said, "I don't think it was an important image. It showed the quote-and-unquote 'victory.' Statues of Saddam had been toppled everywhere, but there was no press there for those. Some Iraqis knew we were there, but some didn't. The military unit was not supposed to be there that night. We had some friends who were traveling with them and were in contact with them. We had expressed a concern that there was a power vacuum and that the city was being looted. There were millions of dollars of [media] equipment in the Palestine Hotel." The group was able to contact Gary Knight of *Newsweek*, who said that the unit he was traveling with was near the Palestine Hotel. "He convinced the unit commander to keep going to the Palestine Hotel that day to protect us from potential looters."

Delay said that his personal icon of the war was his photographs of bloody feet that he took at the morgue. The *London Guardian* filled half the front page with these images the morning after he took them, but they got no play in the United States.

Delay left Baghdad four or five days later for Kuwait. He "chilled out" there for a few days and then went back home to Paris. By then the unilaterals and embeds were streaming into Baghdad. "What had been six or seven journalists grew to three hundred or four hundred. My job was over. It was time to pack." But Delay wanted to return. "I wanted to go back to see places and people, if they are still there, from a year ago and look at pictures I took and do them again." He did return to do exactly that a few months later.

Delay has been a photographer for twenty years. He covered wars and conflicts in the Mideast, Africa, Afghanistan, and Bosnia. He knows the toll that the profession can take. "We [photographers] see a lot of things, and everyone reacts differently. You collapse, and people around you understand that. You have to deal with [what you see]. You are with a group of people who represent the current generation of photojournalists. It's a tight group, a family. We help each other a lot. That is how we deal with it."

"People [journalists and photographers] were covering things their own way. You were photographing what you were seeing. The way the photos were used was different. I had to put up a fight to stay in Baghdad because of security. There is a difference between my not wanting to be there and being told, 'You should leave.'" At first AP was encouraging him to leave, and then the Iraqis wanted to kick him out two days before the arrival of the Americans. "It is the same everywhere because photographers are seen as a threat. I worked a lot independently, alone or with another photographer. The last two months I was there, I had a minder who became a friend and who translated for me." Being French was probably an advantage because he was dealing with only the Iraqis.

Delay participated in a risk-awareness course at Centurion in the United Kingdom five years before the Iraq War and then completed a quick refresher in September 2002. He thinks training is a good idea because it makes people aware of their environment.

Delay said that he used digital cameras to do his job. He also had a sat phone and was able to send his images to the AP's New York bureau from his hotel room at night. He often communicated with the office using Instant Messenger on the Internet. "During the bombing, I was doing live reports and taking photos."

Delay said that every war is different. "This war was different from the first Gulf War. It is getting more and more difficult to work because [technology is] different. In Vietnam, it took a week for pictures to be seen. Now, pictures come out an hour later. That makes the job more dangerous. Photographers are in greater danger than writers [reporters]. People want to see for themselves and not rely on what others tell them."

However, Delay said that he had seen what he and his colleagues call "lobby journalists," reporters who rely on what other people tell them rather than get the story firsthand. Delay has little respect for them. "I don't do this job to say I was in Baghdad or Bosnia and so forth," he said.

He concedes that photographers need to get close to the action and that they enjoy it. "It's like a drug, a big rush—but, although I am terrified of being dead, wounded, or maimed, I have a duty to show what is happening. You can't stop things. A lot worse things would be happening in the world if we don't show things. That's a romantic view. It's my job. It is what I was meant to do and what I enjoy doing."

Delay is mystified about why a photographer would deliberately digitally manipulate news photographs. "Why would you want to alter an image?" he asks. "You can do something that you would do in the darkroom. If there is a streak of light that is distracting, you dodge it to lighten it. Photography is painting with light. It is true that using a different f-stop can make the image darker and lighter. Taking two images and combining them does have a place in photography but not in news photography." For Delay, credibility is the issue. "It's hard to be credible, and I don't want to add fuel to that fire. All the people whom I work with understand that." He also pointed out that he is responsible for providing accurate information for captions. "If I make a mistake in a caption, that comes back to me."

Like most photographers, he has a strong sense of ownership where his images are concerned. "When AP editors in New York crop my photos, I get upset. I tell them, 'Get my name off it because it is not my photo,'" he said. "But photographers don't control how their photos are used. People pay large amounts of money to get our pictures."

Delay said that he doesn't think the statue picture is the icon of the war, because he witnessed "the total trashing of a country from outside in and inside out." He said, "You just have to see what happened. I photographed the bombing and the daily life of Iraqis. I tried to show Iraqis were not bloodthirsty baby-killers. The majority of Iraqis are like you and me trying to make a living with the rules they live under. I showed the suffering of the population. I saw people die, and I saw people wounded.

"I'm just one little piece of a bigger picture. It was my reality. Other journalists [photographers] showed their reality. Put them all together and then you be the judge."

Delay had to adhere to what he called "silly Iraqi rules" before and during the war. "I could not shoot pictures of bunkers or old cars." He said that getting access to the military was very difficult. "We begged to go to the front lines, but we had to wait for the front line to come to us. I photographed fleeing Iraqi soldiers and foreign fighters. There were rules—and my rule is that rules are made to be broken."

However, Delay said that he faced more rules when he was on the U.S. aircraft carrier. In fact he said that other countries impose more rules and restrictions on photographers than the Iraqis did. "On the streets in Paris I cannot take a picture without prior consent of the people I'm photographing. I can't take a picture of a person in handcuffs because the person is considered innocent until proven guilty."

Although he was not embedded during the Iraq War, the embed process is nothing new to him. He was with the Kosovo Liberation Army in Bosnia. "You embed," he said. "You live with them and eat with them [soldiers]. But you have to take a step back and say, 'Wait a minute.'

"I spent some time with Serbs, and in any system you have restrictions. Our job is to go around the restrictions and break the box. If you have to sign a paper [such as that of the embeds], some say, 'Don't go'; but if you don't go, you have zero access. If I came to your house, I would not be able to photograph the bathroom, the bedroom, but I might look into the living room. But if I live with you, I might be able to take a picture in the kitchen. You have to take what access is given to you and expand it. That is what we did in Iraq."

Delay has worked for the AP since 1991. He studied communications in France and photojournalism at the University of Missouri's School of Journalism for a couple of years (1981–1983).

"We have a saying that you are only as good as your last picture. You do have a little bit of freedom, but you can't abuse it. Working for the AP gives me the widest audience for my pictures. A whole lot of people see it when you get a front page around the world, and that's worth it. That is the main reason I stay with AP."

That doesn't mean that he's always happy with his bosses. "Trust me. We do have arguments. I have quit twenty times, for an hour. But winning the Photographer of the Year Award [from AP] was nice. I was very happy. I was in Spain when I learned I won, and I was speechless. I don't work for awards, but it's nice to get recognition from peers. But it puts more pressure to produce better photos. My biggest fear is that somehow I don't take a good picture."

His advice to young people who think they might want to be a photographer? Get a real job. "They have to have a passion for people, for life, for what you do. Live at forty miles an hour. Sacrifice everything for your job: your family, your friends. Just go for it. Look at other people's pictures, at art, learn history. But if you don't have that passion, forget it!"

## NOTE

1. Taras Protsyuk, a Ukrainan cameraman for Reuters, and José Couso, a cameraman for the Spanish television station Telecinco, died after a U.S. tank fired a shell at the Palestine Hotel, where most journalists in the city were based during the war. At around 12 noon, a shell hit two hotel balconies where several journalists were monitoring a battle in the vicinity (Committee to Protect Journalists; see appendix F).

## RICH JOHNSON
GRAPHIC ARTIST AND ILLUSTRATOR, *DETROIT FREE PRESS*, DETROIT, MICHIGAN

Rich Johnson is a graphic artist and illustrator for the *Detroit Free Press*, a Knight Ridder newspaper in Detroit, Michigan. Johnson was the only combat artist to cover the war in Iraq for U.S. media. He and staff reporter Jeff Seidel spent three months in the Middle East in early 2003, and together they produced a series of sketches and stories that offer intimate portraits of the war—stories of soldiers and everyday people caught in the war's crossfire. Their work carries on a tradition that dates back to the American Revolution and the battle of Bunker Hill. Combat art does not mirror reality in the way a photograph does; instead, it evokes the emotion of a captured moment. Art forces one to consider a different way of seeing, and Johnson says, "What keeps people looking is that joy in the details."

Knight Ridder approached all of its staffers for unique ways to cover the war. Johnson suggested that the company send a combat artist—him. He had a number of reasons for wanting the assignment. "It was a combination of desperately needing to get out of the office, get away from my boss, and do something with my talent that actually had some meaning, value, and consequence. I feel that art has a unique ability to grab readers who would generally bypass a story, and bring them up short. I felt we could tell simple stories of average people under extraordinary circumstances and make people read them," he said. "By reading them, I hoped we could remind our readers that the military is not a big faceless machine but an army of sons, daughters, fathers and sisters—of people just like them. I hoped we could remind our readers that the people of the Middle East, when considered individually, are remarkably similar to them. And I hoped that if, by one sketch, I could make one person read one story about one individual and make them care about that individual, then it would all be worthwhile."

Knight Ridder senior military correspondent Joe Galloway, author of *We Were Soldiers Once . . . and Young,* threw his full-throated support behind the project. In the preface to *Portraits of War: The People of the Iraq War, One Sketch at a Time,* a compilation of the newspaper series, Galloway writes, "We knew it would give Knight Ridder's war coverage something special, something different, something invaluable. We knew it was the right thing to do."

During the buildup to the invasion, Johnson and Seidel spent two months in Qatar, Bahrain, and Kuwait. They worked through the region. They covered stories on personnel in Central Command in Qatar. They pulled a stint on board the USS *Abraham Lincoln* in the Persian Gulf out of Bahrain. They covered Kuwaiti oil-field workers and military-base personnel in Kuwait. They trained in nuclear–biological–chemical gear with the U.S. Army in Kuwait before eventually embedding with the U.S. Marine Corps Sixth Engineer Combat Marines, a unit based in Peoria, Illinois.

"We staged with the marines on the Kuwaiti border in the days before the invasion. It was a constant abrasion of wits and nerves and equipment. The weather stank; a huge sandstorm made everything difficult. Gas warnings came three to five a day, so we were in full gas gear. We faced incoming artillery on the night the invasion began, but returned fire silenced it. We faced Scud missile attacks during the same period. Dozens of Patriot missiles were also launched from nearby," Johnson said.

On the first day of the war, Johnson and Seidel crossed the Kuwait–Iraq border as part of a security element for a larger convoy. "We were in an armored dump truck along with about twenty marines. We drove parallel to, and about a kilometer east of, the main northbound convoy. The idea being that if attacked, our unit would engage the enemy and protect the convoy's right flank. The convoy stopped at each main roadway we came to and blew a hole in it. The hole would be used later for a gasoline pipeline that would follow," Johnson said.

"We drove through the desert at high speed. The desert was awash in unexploded munitions. At some point during the day, we became stuck in a large minefield. It contained a mixture of large and small mines. One of the marines dug under the mine beside the truck with a plastic spoon, discovering it to be a dud. Eventually, a marine from Explosive Ordnance Demolition on foot, guided the truck out. An hour later, we caught up with the convoy again and found the west-flank security truck stopped. The marines in the truck had spotted two Iraqi tanks ahead. We joined the marines' assault on foot, carrying antitank weapons across the desert. Upon closer inspection, it was confirmed that both of the tanks up ahead had been disabled. We ended that night by setting up camp in the middle of the Iraqi desert around one hundred miles from Kuwait. The camp would become Camp Viper. We later discovered that we were near An Nasiriyah."

Johnson and Seidel spent the next four weeks going wherever the marines went. They dealt with local emergencies. "We lost two marines on patrol as they attempted to swim a canal to secure the other side to defend a water-processing plant. We went on convoys, toured villages, went on security patrols, restarted generators for Iraqis, visited hospitals and mobile army surgical hospital [MASH] units, and swept villages for Iraqi soldiers. We were given no special treatment. Wherever the marines slept, we slept," Johnson said.

The two men eventually ended up in Camp Chesty about forty miles south of Baghdad. Around this time Baghdad fell, and the conflict was deemed over. Johnson and Seidel continued to write stories on Iraqis and their interaction with the marines until the pair left for home in April.

Johnson and Seidel did not participate in a combat-training program, but they did attend a two-hour briefing on land mines in Fort Myer, D.C. Johnson went to life-drawing classes to prepare for the job ahead.

The most difficult part of the work for Johnson, who was thirty-seven years old during the war, was the physical toll it took. "The drain was huge. I dropped about thirty pounds. We worked from dawn to dusk and beyond. Mentally, it was an adrenaline rush that lasted three months," he said. "It lent memories of everything that happened to us a peculiar clarity. Emotionally, the helplessness by being baggage was draining, and the inability to do anything of substance to help was equally daunting."

Johnson did not find the rules under which he had to work particularly troublesome. "The marines limited their communications only in the immediate twenty-four-hour period before the invasion. I think eventually I felt like part of the unit. We were treated as any other marine. We carried our own bags, pitched our own tent, slept in our own ditch, got in our own gas gear, and ran for the bunker when they ran. The marines looked upon us initially as 'those fucking reporters,' but after we had been with them through a variety of scrapes, we were referred to as 'our fucking reporters.' I got the feeling they were happy to have us around. They often told us that a mission might be dangerous and offered us an opportunity to stay home, but we never did. We never at any time handled firearms or live ammo, but we would help lug gear around with everyone else."

Johnson encountered both "none and many" ethical dilemmas. He dealt with them "by drawing without judging and leaving it to my editors back in Detroit to sort out." Johnson took with him sketchpads and pencils. He had a digital camera to take pictures of the sketches and a satellite phone to send the digital pictures back to the newsroom, with Seidel's stories. The equipment would regularly be hampered by the extreme weather conditions. When Johnson could not sketch directly, he would take digital photos and he would work from those images and from his memory of the emotion to capture the essence of the scene. He also worked directly from memory.

Seeing a scene through an artist's eyes gives it human dimension and interpretation. Johnson most often reached for his Prismacolor indigo blue pencil because it seemed to add a touch of life to his subjects. In almost three hundred illustrations that accompanied stories written by Seidel, Johnson produced a range of images from Iraq. The drawings offer a more personal face of the war. There is a scene of Marine Lance Corporal Erica Gonzales and Navy Petty Officer Second Class Alejandro Gonzales, husband and wife, meeting on Camp Solomon Islands, Kuwait. It is a close-up of them holding hands, finding solace in each other. There is a frame of Navy Seaman Rosy Vazquez aboard the USS *Abraham Lincoln.* She is balancing across her shoulders the thick, heavy chains used to tie down planes; and looking at her, you feel the weight of her burden. There is also the ghostlike image of an Iraqi child, his hand raised to greet a convoy, his stare direct.

Johnson found the military chain of command organized in such a way that very little information about what was going on elsewhere came down from the top. Johnson and Seidel became a major source of information to the marines in their unit about what was going on in the rest of Iraq. "Someone in Knight Ridder put together an e-mail brief, which we downloaded during our limited logged-on time daily. We then passed the laptop around, and one of the marines would write down key points to then brief his men," he said.

In Johnson's view, the embed program was a success. "It all worked. It gave unprecedented access to the realities of war in all their convoluted confusion. It allowed journalists to tell it all live—no hearsay. It was a brave and open attempt by the U.S. government to show the honesty and integrity of its intentions. The government knew that reporters would see the unnecessary carnage of innocents that war creates, yet judged that their purpose would remain clear to the public around the world. But the rest of the news media back home were not ready for the unprecedented amount of news they would receive. They ended up covering the conflict in a spastic confusion that I am not sure helped readers understand. It took, I think, a clear vision of the important stories long term to explain what was being seen in a way that did not make it instantly forgettable. I am unsure if any news agency accomplished this."

Johnson would do it again "without hesitation. It was by far the most meaningful and useful project I have worked on during my twelve years in journalism. It gave me an opportunity to continue a dynasty of combat artists dating back to the Civil War. Before I left for the Middle East, I visited Howard Brodie, a veteran combat artist of World War II, Korea, and Vietnam. We spent a day talking about what I would face in the months ahead, and he gave me advice. He told me whenever possible to try not to judge my subjects, instead just to draw their humanity and to look upon everyone with a compassionate eye. I followed this rule throughout my time as a war correspondent in Iraq. I hope it shows in my work." Johnson and Seidel's work is posted on the *Detroit Free Press* website—www.freep.com—and is titled *Portraits of War.*

The experience of covering the war changed Johnson in important ways. "I am more compassionate and slower to anger. I am less fazed by the daily grind. Things that seemed monumentally important before are less so now." Johnson believes that the embedding program may also have changed war coverage. "Journalists discovered that military did not need to mean *militaristic*, and the military discovered that not all journalists were sensationalists."

# Print Journalists

## JOSEPH GIORDONO

REPORTER/PHOTOGRAPHER, *STARS AND STRIPES*, YOKOSUKA, JAPAN

Joseph Giordono is currently the Korea bureau chief for *Stars and Stripes*. He joined the paper one week before the September 11, 2001, terrorist attacks on the United States and worked mainly from a news bureau in Yokosuka, Japan. *Stars and Stripes* is an independent daily newspaper covering the United States military, and Giordono had been on *Stripes* assignments to Uzbekistan, the Philippines, Afghanistan, Singapore, and Thailand to cover various military operations.

"Early in October 2002, *Stripes* set up a rotation to staff bureaus in Kuwait and Bahrain. I volunteered for the Kuwait bureau and arrived in early January 2003. Because I was in place and had a good working relationship with the military, *Stripes* asked me to stay until the embedding happened. It turned out that from January to March 2003, I covered the buildup to war, then embedded in mid-March with the First Battalion, Fifteenth Infantry. I did it, in short, because it was going to be *the* story. As a reporter covering the military, I was always willing and eager to 'deploy' wherever the military deployed." Also embedded with the unit were two print reporters, one from the *Daily Telegraph* (London) and one from the *Voice of America* (Prague).

The First Battalion, Fifteenth Infantry, was a mechanized infantry unit from Fort Benning, Georgia. It included a tank company, two Bradley companies, and a Scout Platoon. Giordono rode with the Scouts in a semi-armored Humvee. The Scouts' job was to go ahead of the main units, find the enemy, and call in air strikes. "In the ten days or so that I was embedded before the war began, I spoke with several of the commanders about the best place to be. Because I was both taking photos and writing, it seemed like the Scouts would be the best place—out front, in a Humvee, but not directly in the fight. Or at least, that was the plan. From the first day of the war, the Scout Platoon wound up being in the middle of every serious engagement the battalion had. The unit moved northwest across the border from Kuwait, moving along Highway 8, though Samawah, Nasiriyah, Najaf, and Karbala, then on to Baghdad.

"Most of the encounters were of the ambush type—anywhere from twenty to one hundred Iraqis, mostly the irregulars, would attack with small arms and RPGs [rocket-propelled grenades]. These encounters usually lasted thirty minutes or so. In a few cases, there were more traditional 'battles' but nothing of the armor-on-armor battling that some had predicted. I was embedded until the first week of April, when a combination of factors led me to leave the embed."

Giordono did not participate in any of the media combat-training programs, whether DOD sponsored or private. "It was decided that, since I'd already been with the military in combat situations [such as in Afghanistan], it was not needed. I believe that *Stripes* did send at least one reporter to a DOD training program in the States, though."

For Giordono, the most difficult part of covering the war was "watching people die, watching people get wounded, and watching people inflict death on others. None of the assignments I'd been on before prepared me for what I'd see this time. I'd seen war and its results before, most notably in Afghanistan. But the pitch and intensity of what I saw in Iraq was terrifying. At the end of the first engagement, when the unit I was with took an airfield at Tallil, one of the Scouts and I were standing by a Humvee talking and having a cigarette. I walked off to take a picture, came back about thirty seconds later, and as I was walking back, gunfire erupted everywhere. The Scout was shot through the abdomen and lay prone on the road. He was eventually medevaced and lived. (Later, when I got home, I got an e-mail from the nurse who treated him at a field hospital and had seen his name in a later article I wrote.) Having that happen, being caught in the open in an ambush on the first day of the war, really colored the rest of my experience."

For Giordono, the physical discomfort he experienced was "much as anticipated—going twenty-one days without a shower, having limited water and food. Most of the time, you weren't really hungry and would just smoke a cigarette instead of popping open another MRE [Meals, Ready-to-Eat]. The dust storms were brutal; it was impossible to keep anything clean, especially equipment like computers and camera gear."[1]

Giordono felt generally comfortable with the ground rules of coverage. "The military handed out a long list of ground rules when the embeds began. Chief among them were not revealing operational plans, exact locations, or the names of casualties before the DOD announced them. There were also rules against making pictures of any identifiable casualties—this was a sticky point for many of the photogs. The commander of the unit I was with trusted the reporters completely. On the eve of the war, he gave us a detailed briefing on what our missions would be, and, on an almost daily basis, he made himself available to us in the field.

There were no restrictions on who I could interview or what I could ask them. Nobody read or vetted anything before I sent it out."

During the war, Giordono felt very much a part of the unit with which he was embedded, particularly the Scout Platoon. "The unspoken rule was that I could do anything I wanted as long as it didn't endanger someone else. Endangering myself was part of the bargain, I guess. Many times, the soldiers deemed it quite incredible that I was not armed. I felt protected, or as protected as anyone can feel in the middle of a war. One problem was that, from the first night of the war, everyone was required to wear chemical suits. The suits were desert camouflage, meaning that I was indistinguishable from the soldiers. I'm not naive enough to think that, in the middle of a firefight, someone would stop and differentiate between a camera-toting reporter and a gun-toting soldier. It was a bit discomfiting at first."

In the field, he encountered two different types of ethical dilemmas. "One was an instance in which *Stars and Stripes* altered a photo to fit with the military ground rules. On the morning of the ambush I described above, I took several photos of the wounded Scout. He was lying prone in the road next to a Humvee, as one of his comrades crouched in front of his body, returning fire with his machine gun. Two medics were rushing in with a stretcher. The photos included part of the windshield of the Humvee. As with other military units, the rank and last name of the driver, commander, and gunner were taped onto the windshield. The editors in D.C. decided to digitally blur the names on the Humvee, in order to comply with the ground rule about not releasing names of casualties before the Pentagon did. I did not know about that until after the war when I saw the photo, which ran on the front page of the paper."

The other ethical dilemma Giordono faced was deciding when to leave the embed. "From the beginning I had been having equipment problems, and finally, just outside Baghdad, my sat phone went dead. The other reporters with the unit had moved to different locations, so I could not use theirs. And, for whatever reason, I'd found myself in the middle of a firefight nearly every day. After several discussions with an editor in Europe, a decision was made that risking my life without the ability to file stories was not a good idea. I pulled out in the first week of April, about one week before the major fighting for this unit was over. I'm still not sure if that was the right decision."

Giordono's news-gathering field equipment included a laptop computer, digital camera gear, and a bulky satellite phone. "Working at night was impossible, as the equipment gave off too much light (any thoughts of sneaking a few stories out ended when another one of the Scouts was shot by a sniper in the middle of the night). The dust and sand wreaked havoc on equipment. For reasons that we could never figure out, my sat phone died a few weeks into the war, leaving me with no way to file stories or photos."

While he was in the field, Giordono was only partially aware of what was happening in other areas of the country and in other parts of the war. "The analogy has been made that each embedded reporter was essentially viewing the war through a straw, seeing only what their own unit was doing. In my case, that was very true, but it worked with the plan *Stripes* had laid out before the war—they wanted the soldiers' stories and would leave the bigger-picture war stories to the wire services. I was aware of what my unit was doing but on a day-to-day basis would often be separated from the unit because of the nature of what the Scouts did. Getting information was difficult—I would get snippets in conversations with my editors, when my sat phone worked. The military guys didn't have much information but would give me whatever they had. One of the other reporters had a shortwave radio, which sometimes could pick up the BBC. But a lot of times you'd hear through rumors about events such as the capture of POWs and the deaths of soldiers or marines. Soldiers were constantly asking me to try to get online and find some news."

Giordono believes that the embedding program worked in many important ways. "I think the military got exactly what they wanted from the embed program—mostly positive, admiring stories about the military. Regardless of what any embedded reporter says, it was impossible not to lose some of your objectivity. These were the men and women who were feeding you, protecting you, and befriending you. It wasn't anything sinister—you were a welcome newcomer to the troops, and my role was to tell their stories. And despite everything that happened, I would do it again."

Giordono's father was a career military officer—the family lived and traveled extensively throughout the world—and Giordono believes that this experience as an embedded reporter in Iraq did change him as a person. "It changed me in ways I'd probably be loath to admit. As I said, I'd covered military operations for the past two years, in some of the most desolate and dangerous places you can imagine. I was shocked at how different this assignment turned out to be. I can't really say how it changed war coverage, as my references with war coverage are all within the past two years."

The Society of Professional Journalists presented Giordono with the 2003 Sigma Delta Chi Award for excellence in journalism, deadline reporting (circulation of less than one hundred thousand), for "The Road to Baghdad: A Casualty of War."

## NOTE

1. According to seabeecook.com, each meal contains approximately twelve hundred calories and includes an entrée or starch; crackers; a cheese, peanut butter, or jelly spread; a dessert or snack; beverages; an accessory packet; a plastic spoon; and a

flameless ration heater (FRH). The FRH is a water-activated exothermic chemical heater designed to heat the entree of an MRE by raising the temperature of the eight-ounce entrée by one hundred degrees Fahrenheit in twelve minutes. MREs, sometimes referred to as "meals rejected by everyone" by complaining soldiers, replaced the C ration in the 1980s.

## JIM LANDERS

FINANCIAL COLUMNIST, *DALLAS MORNING NEWS*, WASHINGTON BUREAU

Jim Landers, financial columnist for the *Dallas Morning News*, seems more like an accountant than a seasoned war correspondent. He very matter-of-factly explains that when the Pentagon suggested the embed program, he thought it sounded like a good opportunity. "I wanted to do it, and I volunteered to do it," he said. His background made him a good choice. He has spent a large part of his career writing about the Middle East and the Gulf region. He also can speak some basic Arabic.

To prepare for his embed spot, he participated in a boot camp that the Pentagon offered to journalists. "They taught us a little bit about what combat was going to be like on the ground. We took fire with people shooting over our heads. It was pretty useful," he said. They also learned how to put on the gas masks and suits that were to protect them in the event of a chemical attack.

Landers and *Dallas Morning News* photographer Cheryl Diaz Meyer were embedded together in the Marine Corps' Second Tank Battalion of the First Marine Division. "We ended up with a group out of North Carolina that was attached to a division out of California. So, there wasn't any Texas piece there, but all of our stuff is on the web and available to a national audience," as was evidenced by the thousands of e-mails he received during the war. "The e-mail I got from these families was the most gratifying of my career. They said they would get up and go to the web first thing in the morning. Some days it would be bad news." He regarded his dispatches as letters home for the soldiers in his unit. "It really made me feel bad that those guys got no mail themselves for three weeks. No mail was delivered at all," he said.

He realized that his reports of attacks, deaths, and injuries were difficult for the families of the soldiers in his unit. "We could have reported injuries or deaths, but we couldn't use names. But everybody reading that story had family in that unit, and they didn't know who it was." He said that the military didn't make it any easier: military representatives make sure that they personally notify only the families of the ones who are killed—that is, they don't tell everybody else—thus, many friends and family members do not know whether their loved one is safe. Landers said that the feedback he got from family members about his coverage, however, was always positive.

Landers said that the quality of the embed experience was dependent on the attitude of the commanding officer for the embed's unit. "If you had a good commanding officer who bought into the idea of embedding and was willing to take you in, then you were probably going to have a really good experience," he said. He said that at one point, the colonel that he was working with got word from the division that some journalists had violated the ground rules, and so all the journalists in the division should be denied access to briefings. But Landers said that he continued to go to the briefings, with no repercussions. "The rule was that you weren't going to talk about future operations and identify where you were," he said.

Although he had anticipated that the military would want to censor his reports, no one ever did so. "Several of us went into this thinking about how we were going to deal with censorship; but nobody was reading over my shoulder; nobody was listening to what I said," he said. Although it was possible, in theory, to leave the unit and look around, Landers said that doing so was difficult. "There were reporters I knew who were upset because they couldn't get transportation to go talk to other people about what was happening. The commanding officers wanted us to let them know where we were, if we left the unit. It just didn't seem that it was worth it to move about."

However, because of his ability to speak basic Arabic, there were times when the unit urged him to make contact with some of the people in villages they were passing. "I could give some assessment of what they were concerned about," he said.

Although he listened to the BBC and Voice of America broadcasts, and although he was in contact with his home office daily, he said that it was difficult to know what role his unit was playing in the war. He likened his experience to that of World War II correspondent Ernie Pyle. "He didn't try to tell the whole war story. All you see of the war is a slice."

Landers said that military operations for his battalion were run from an amphibious troop carrier. "We went into battle, so to speak, five or six tanks back from the front." He said that tanks have benches inside where he and the soldiers would sit as the tanks rumbled toward Baghdad. The roof of the tank opened up, permitting a soldier and himself to look out. He was most concerned for his own safety when his helmeted head was sticking up while the tank was being fired upon from both sides of the street as it passed through a town.

In one of his dispatches to the *Dallas Morning News*, Landers vividly describes what it was like to be in a battle:

"Get down! Get down!" yelled Sgt. Jarrell Isaacson. "Sgt. Hale, we need that M-16 up here!" The shouts and the battle began Friday just as the tracked armored vehicle of the 2nd Tank Battalion, 1st Marine Division, rolled behind a flying column of Marine Corps tanks into Yasin Suud, a town about 25 miles from Baghdad.

Six Marines, accompanied by two journalists, were standing on ration boxes, their heads and shoulders above the roof hatch of the vehicle. . . . A bullet went through the windshield of a Marine Corps ambulance and through both hands of the driver. Iraqi Republican Guard soldiers fired from roadside trenches, and then quickly ducked down. The Marines in the armored vehicle returned fire, and empty clips and shells clattered on the floor.

"Ow! Oh! My rifle!" yelled Cpl. William Wadkins of Buffalo Grove, Ill. Cpl. Wadkins ducked down and saw that the black stock of his M-16 was torn open, hit by an enemy bullet. The stock fell off. The aluminum casing inside the rifle was dented in two places. It too fell off. Sgt. Jeffrey Hale of Warsaw, Ind., dropped down into the body of the transport. "God, it hurts!" he cried. Hospital Corpsman Pietro Christofoli pushed up Sgt. Hale's left sleeve, revealing a bleeding cut. "Doc" Christofoli examined the cut and shouted, "You're OK."

Cpl. Jorge Sanchez, meanwhile, continued firing his automatic weapon until there were no more bullets in the 200-round magazine. Cpl. Wadkins yelped, as a hot shell fell on the back of his neck. Sgt. Isaacson slapped it away. "You're not shot. You're all right," he shouted above the roar of the turbo-charged vehicle.

"Is everybody OK?" Sgt. Isaacson asked. Everyone in the transport, journalists included, gave a thumbs-up.

Landers said that his embed experience was both physically and emotionally difficult. "We wore our chemical suits all the time for three weeks. That was very uncomfortable and very demanding," he said. With the desert heat, and with showers few and far between, three weeks in the bulky suits was torture.

However, the emotional toll was more long lasting. "It was hard when the men you had come to know were killed." He personally knew one marine who was killed and an officer who was badly wounded.

Sometimes the soldiers grumbled; Landers reported it, and commanders took note. "They had chickens along as chemical detectors, and all the chickens died in the first dust storm. So then they gave us pigeons. They had to drag these pigeons around, feed them, and clean their cages. They all thought it was pretty stupid. I wrote some of that. Maybe whoever had this idea took offense."

The marine directive to the soldiers was, "Don't talk about what you don't know. Don't give your opinion." Landers said, "The word from the commander was 'Tell your guys not to talk about what they don't know.' The Pentagon would get on their hind legs about breaking the ground rules."

Landers said that he saw unilaterals, but he didn't have interaction with them. "I had good friends before the war who said that unilaterally was the only way they would cover this thing. But if you have a chance to be in the landing craft with the troops when they hit the beach—are you going to say no to that?" he asked.

He did just that, in a manner of speaking, except that his "beach" was Baghdad. He said that the ultimate goal of the troops was to get there. "We passed up a lot of military targets to get there, and we didn't get to see a whole lot of the city." He saw the cheering crowds that greeted the American troops. One man in the throng even asked him for an autograph. "There was no question in my mind that they were happy we were there."

Landers said that he does not regret his choice to embed, but "I don't want to do another war."

# ED TIMMS

STAFF WRITER, *DALLAS MORNING NEWS*, WASHINGTON BUREAU

Reporter Ed Timms has worked at the *Dallas Morning News* for more than twenty-five years. He was embedded with G Troop, Tenth Cavalry of the U.S. Army's Fourth Infantry Division, based at Fort Hood, Texas. Timms was contacted by senior editors at the paper, primarily because of his experience and performance overseas. He had reported on the 1991 Persian Gulf War from Kuwait and southern Iraq, on famine and civil war in Somalia, on conflict in southern Sudan, on Jean Bertrand Aristide's restoration to power in Haiti, on peacekeeping operations in the Balkans, and on the Israeli–Palestinian conflict.

Timms also had spent some time in Angola, Rwanda, and Central America and had a number of reasons for choosing this assignment. "Armed conflict brings out the best and the worst in humanity and amplifies human emotion like nothing else. It's often a baffling mixture of heroism and banality, sacrifice and selfishness, horrific images of death and destruction tempered by displays of compassion and love. As a reporter, I wanted to witness all of this firsthand and try to make sense of it. I also tried to focus on crises that weren't getting a lot of attention, or, within a well-publicized conflict, victimized groups or individuals who were overlooked."

By the time this most recent conflict with Iraq was unfolding, however, Timms was not overly enthusiastic about heading overseas. "Age had something to do with it—I'm forty-six—and my children, ages thirteen and ten, are now old enough to actually know what's going on and to worry. I've also seen a fair amount of death and suffering over the years and didn't look forward to a fresh set of memories. But the curiosity that first prompted me to seek out overseas assignments hadn't entirely left me. I also rationalized that my previous experience in the region might help me to provide my newspaper's readership with some insight into the situation in Iraq," he said.

Timms's unit was a light reconnaissance unit with the Fourth Infantry Division's First Brigade. The unit deployed to the region on April 1, 2003, and entered Iraq several days later. Several journalists were embedded with other units within the Fourth Infantry Division, but Timms was the only one with G Troop. He stayed with G Troop through the end of May.

"Before President Bush declared major conflict over on May 1, we encountered relatively light resistance. That was in part because of the role of a light reconnaissance unit. G Troop's job was to range far ahead of the main body of troops to find out what kind of threat would be encountered; its soldiers were supposed to see what the enemy was up to without being seen. However, after May 1, while operating in the Tikrit area—Saddam Hussein's hometown—we frequently came under fire as G Troop soldiers conducted 'presence patrols' in Iraqi neighborhoods and remote countryside. Typically this involved hit-and-run ambushes."

Timms did participate in a training program before he went to Iraq. "I went through a three-day training program put together by a private defense contractor that trains federal employees who will be working in unsettled regions of the world. It was staffed by former and current Special Forces soldiers. I'd already learned a lot of what they taught through my own experiences and mistakes over the years, but the course was helpful. I picked up some additional knowledge on first aid and evasion tactics in a vehicle. I would have loved to participate in this course before I first went overseas as a reporter."

Timms found the work difficult for a number of reasons. "Combat often involves extreme sleep deprivation, tense or terrifying moments, days or weeks without showers, and crummy food. In the desert, there are also high temperatures and a pervasive dust. I dealt with all of this, to one degree or another, while I was deployed with G Troop."

He did not find the guidelines of coverage particularly troublesome. "I followed commonsense instructions while the unit was in a hostile area, such as not displaying any light when Iraqis might be nearby. If I was reporting on an ongoing operation, I did not identify our specific location or report any information about future plans that I might have gleaned from intelligence briefings.

"I certainly grew to know the soldiers I was with, and they shared with me some of their most private concerns and fears. We shared the same risks and hardships, and I certainly felt a kinship with them. At the same time, I made it very clear that I was obligated to report on the good and the bad and that I was a noncombatant. I believe I maintained a separate identity as a journalist, but I did have empathy for these soldiers. By the same token, they felt comfortable talking to me about things they'd never reveal to a reporter they didn't know," he said.

In the field he did not really encounter any ethical dilemmas. "The soldiers of G Troop did not try to censor, or even influence the tone of, stories I wrote. They talked candidly about situations that did not necessarily put their superiors or the army in the best light. For example, they were extremely upset at the response of higher-ups when an Iraqi woman who'd provided information on Saddam Hussein loyalists in the Tikrit area was threatened. G Troop wanted to escort the woman and her children to safety, but senior officers indicated that they had no means to accommodate her. She was left behind as G Troop was deployed to another part of Iraq. Some of G Troop's soldiers later returned to her home and found it empty. The woman's neighbors claimed they didn't know her. Some of the soldiers are convinced she was killed."

Timms carried with him a laptop computer, a digital camera, a digital audio recorder, a BGAN satellite transmitter, and an Iridium-brand satellite phone.[1] "I used the Iridium for voice communication with my office, but I also could file stories with it in a pinch. It lacked the bandwidth to file photographs. The BGAN transmitter had broader bandwidth, so I could send both story files and photographs relatively quickly. However, there were some days when its satellite was out of service. The Iridium was the most reliable means of communication. I even wrote and filed a couple of stories while on the move in a Humvee, using a car-top-style magnetic antenna to link up with the Iridium satellite network."

He knew a great deal about what was happening within his own unit but could learn very little about what was happening elsewhere. "The advantage of being embedded with a small unit is that you get to know the soldiers very well. The downside is that you have a very limited window on the world. I had an intimate knowledge of what was happening in my immediate area but frequently only had a vague idea of what was happening elsewhere in Iraq. That wasn't necessarily a bad thing. I was not under any pressure to produce 'big picture' stories by my editors. I think they understood both the limitations and the advantages of the embedding process."

Timms went camping "in the wilderness" of Wyoming with his children for a month in the summer after his return to the States to use up his comp time and decompress. "With all my reservations about going overseas put aside, I might well consider being embedded with a military unit again. Even after covering U.S. military operations overseas for more than a decade, I still learned a great deal because I was embedded. I was able to do a much better job of putting a human face on the soldiers who were quoted in my stories, and they certainly had more dimension."

Timms believes that the embedding process worked fairly well overall. "After the 1991 war, journalists had clamored for better access to frontline units. The Defense Department largely provided that. Certainly there were attempts to manipulate the media, but journalists were able to do a much better job this time reporting on the men and women who were fighting. I am concerned, however, that some media organizations embraced the embedding process in part because it was cheaper than fielding so-called unilateral reporters in the region. Ideally, a good mix of embedded and unilateral journalists would provide the most comprehensive coverage, but that wasn't always the practice. Embedded reporters had little opportunity to include the perspective of Iraqis in their stories. Few of us spoke Arabic, and even the soldiers and marines had few interpreters available to them. This is not the fault of the military but a reality for embedded reporters."

Because Timms had also covered the 1991 Gulf War, he was able to compare the two experiences. "I initially was assigned to a pool during the first Gulf War but was extremely frustrated. After cooling my heels in Dharan after the ground war began, I ended up driving up the highway into Kuwait with other journalists. I thought the military did a terrible job of working with the media during the 1991 war. Ironically, once I was able to reach a frontline marine unit, they were delighted to be interviewed. They were involved in one of the most momentous experiences of their lives, and they wanted folks back home to know what they had done and what they had seen."

He does not believe that he experienced any dramatic personal or professional changes as a result of covering this war in 2003. "My defining experiences and memories are still from Somalia and other parts of Africa, where I saw death and suffering on a scale that Iraq, both in 1991 and 2003, never approached. I do think I came away from the experience more sensitive to the difficulties that soldiers face in combat, as well as the angst that their families endure. I hope that this is the beginning of a better relationship between the military and the media that finally gets us both beyond the ghosts of Vietnam. To some degree, that relationship must always have some distance and at times even become adversarial. But I hope that both soldiers and embedded journalists came away from the conflict with a better understanding of their respective jobs and a greater regard for the important role each has."

## NOTE

1. BGAN is a communications system that can be used to surf the web, send e-mail, and transfer data from anywhere within the satellite footprint.

# Television Journalists

## SARAH DODD

REPORTER, KTVT-TV (CBS), DALLAS–FORT WORTH, TEXAS

Sarah Dodd is a reporter for KTVT-TV, a CBS affiliate in Dallas–Fort Worth, Texas. One of the approximately eighty-five women in the United States to be embedded with American troops, she traveled with the Fourth Infantry Division into Baghdad and Tikrit. In 2002, Dodd had twice traveled to Guantanamo Bay, Cuba, to report on suspected-terrorist detainees and the Texas-based soldiers guarding them. That same year, the United States Army presented her the Iron Horse Award for her "fair and balanced" coverage of Fort Hood's First Cavalry Division. In November 2001, Dodd was the only television news reporter allowed into Kuwait immediately after the September 11 terrorist attacks on the United States, and her exclusive coverage was carried on the *CBS Evening News* and CNN.

"I was chosen for this assignment because I covered Fort Hood troops extensively beginning September 12, 2001. I was the only television journalist allowed into Kuwait in November 2001 to report on the increased number of U.S. soldiers patrolling the Iraqi border. Then I traveled with Fort Hood soldiers as they took on the mission of guarding detainee camps at Guantanamo Bay, Cuba. Through these assignments I established positive working relationships with the commanding general at Fort Hood and then was invited to cover the war in Iraq."

Dodd was twenty-nine years old during her coverage of the war and had a number of reasons for accepting the assignment. "I wanted to be able to witness what would obviously become an important part of history. As a journalist, I also felt a responsibility to make sure things were accurately reported. After more than a year chronicling the significant role these troops were already playing in the war on terror, I felt if I didn't travel with them to Iraq, my reporting would not be complete. For me there was never a question of if I would be willing to go into a war zone. I never had any doubts about accepting the assignment. Being a woman,

I also thought it was important to show that women can handle the same assignments as men, even in dangerous situations."

Dodd was embedded with the Fourth Infantry Division's Apache attack helicopter unit, in Kuwait, Baghdad, Balad, and Tikrit. She was in the Middle East for thirty days, from April 1 until May 1, 2003. She and photographer Robert Hall were the only crew embedded with that unit. "We lived in the Baghdad International Airport for a week. We arrived just a day after U.S. troops had taken over the facility. We were traveling by convoy through Iraq, and although we were never in the middle of a live fire exchange, the convoys were extremely intense. There was always an awareness about the potential of an ambush."

Dodd and her photographer took their war-preparation training at Fort Hood, a sprawling army installation in central Texas. "We went through mine-probing training and chemical-suit training. The chemical-suit training was extremely helpful. The first week we were in Kuwait, there were continuous alarms that went off requiring us to use our suits."

Dodd worked a number of long days. "Surprisingly, there was never a time for me when I thought, 'This is too much, too hard, I can't handle it.' I think the challenge of the living conditions was the most trying. Going multiple days without a shower or a restroom was certainly a unique experience. I was also concerned about the emotional impact my assignment had on my family. I am an only child and very close to my mother and father. I knew they were both extremely worried about me, but they continued to be supportive."

She did not find the rules under which she was required to work particularly difficult. "All embedded media signed the same agreement. The main points included not disclosing troop location if it would compromise the mission. Initially, we agreed to let our lieutenant colonel view our stories before we aired them, but that never became an issue. He was so busy, he rarely had time to look at the video."

Dodd felt very much a part of the unit with which she was embedded. "Everywhere they went, we went. We rode on the seventy-two-hour convoys. We went days without sleep, weeks without showers, and survived only on MREs (Meals, Ready-to-Eat). I thought that was the best part of the experience. I didn't want to be treated any differently. In order to accurately depict the situation, it was crucial to mirror the circumstances of the soldiers."

As was the case with other embedded reporters, Dodd was well informed on everything her specific unit was doing. "I attended every briefing my lieutenant colonel was in, and any information relayed to the troops I also received. [The lack of] awareness of what was going on in other parts of the country was very frustrating. It was like living in a vacuum. In many circumstances we did not have television access, so we often depended on a shortwave radio that picked up the BBC. When television was available, we watched CNN. Some information was also relayed through daily briefings."

She carried a laptop computer, laptop video editor, satellite phone, and a small Sony digital camera. Looking back on the experience, Dodd feels that the embedded program was a definite success. "In the end a lot of positive relationships were established between the military and the media. At the start of my assignment, many soldiers were skeptical. By the end, we proved we were fair, accurate, and sensitive to security issues. I also think that the American people were able to see—with immediacy—what was going on in Iraq. Families of soldiers were also able to keep up with where their loved ones were, and in many ways I think that provided peace of mind for many families."

Dodd would not hesitate to take on such an assignment again. "This was an incredible experience, and I'm thankful I had the opportunity to participate. This was such a significant event in history, and being there to witness it, and share what I saw with so many viewers, was more fulfillment than any other assignment I have ever had. This experience made me appreciate what the military does. I have never before seen any other profession where so much of your life is dedicated to your job. These men and women leave their families, put themselves in the line of fire, and put their lives on the line for a small paycheck, but in many cases for an extreme love of country. I was inspired by many of the soldiers I traveled with. And I think journalism was changed because now Americans will expect the right to have journalists covering wars from the front lines. The bar has been set, and the public will not settle for anything less than full access."

# KEN KALTHOFF

REPORTER/ANCHOR, KXAS-TV (NBC), FORT WORTH, TEXAS

Ken Kalthoff is a reporter and anchor at KXAS-TV, the NBC affiliate in Fort Worth, Texas. He has been reporting television news for twenty-four years. He's received many awards over the years, including a 1983 Emmy for his reporting on U.S. Marines in Beirut, Lebanon. During March and April 2003, Kalthoff was embedded with U.S. Marines in Kuwait and Iraq, reporting for NBC, MSNBC, CNBC, and KXAS-TV.

"I was asked to go, perhaps because I had spent substantial time after 9/11 reporting on military activities. I went to Fort Hood half a dozen times or so to do stories there. I was at the Joint Reserve Base in Fort Worth on at least that many occasions and did other military stories as well. At first, prior to the war, I was not sure if I would be an 'embedded' reporter or simply be reporting for the NBC-owned stations from Kuwait, as several other reporters did. But the embed assignment came through from NBC, so we were off to the war." Kalthoff went with KXAS photographer Mike Heimbuch who is a navy veteran. Kalthoff believed that Heimbuch's prior experience would be helpful in their dealings with military people and protocol.

Kalthoff had several reasons for accepting this assignment. "For any reporter this was certainly a unique experience. It takes a lot of curiosity to keep going as a reporter year after year. The opportunity to be on the front lines with the troops is certainly a new experience. We often go to risky places other people want to leave, like hurricanes, riots, crime scenes, and health-alert areas. I knew there would be dangers but felt my years of experience would keep me from doing anything foolish just to get a story. I also thought the marines would take good care of us to see that their reporters were not harmed. I was also anxious to see Kuwait and Iraq and to see this war firsthand."

Kalthoff and Heimbuch were embedded with Marine Task Force Tarawa, which was formed especially for this war from units stationed at Camp LeJuene, North Carolina. The task force included three battalions of infantry troops, an artillery battalion, and a support and command element. The total strength of the task force was around seven thousand marines.

"Within the task force, we were assigned to First Battalion, Tenth Marine Regiment (the marines call it 'one-ten' [1/10]), the artillery battalion of the task force. The battalion had Howitzers that fire a range of up to eighteen miles to support the infantry troops ahead on the battlefield. The major battle for the task force was during the early days of the war in An Nasiriyah, Iraq. For several days it was nonstop artillery fire. The U.S. Army convoy ambush that took Jessica Lynch hostage occurred right down the road from the marine's position south of the city. We were able to see the remains of the army vehicles the next day. After Nasiriyah, the task force was assigned to secure supply routes for other army and marine units heading north toward Baghdad. We traveled to Ad Diwaniyah, Ash Shumali, and Al Amarah. Al Amarah also posed a substantial possibility for battle, but the enormous Iraqi force that was thought to be positioned there just gave up rather than fight."

A reporter from the *New York Times* was also embedded with the 1/10. Reporters for NBC, CNN, ABC, and several print media were also embedded with the task force. Kalthoff was reporting for the NBC network as well as his local station, KXAS, the NBC affiliate in the Dallas–Fort Worth market. "We provided NBC with regular satellite telephone reports and video when it was possible to feed it out. We did not have a videophone or satellite uplink of our own, so we had to rely on shuttling tape to other NBC elements nearby."

Kalthoff and Heimbuch were overseas for a total of forty-three days, thirty-one with the marines. "We rode across the Iraqi border with them on the first day of the war, Friday, March 21, and stayed with them through the first several weeks. We left our unit on April 10, got back to Kuwait on April 11 and left for the U.S. on April 13. By this time, Baghdad had fallen, and our unit was not expected to see major action. The unit left Iraq several weeks later and returned to the U.S. by ship."

Before the war, Kalthoff and Heimbuch did go through a private training program provided by the firm Pilgrims. "It was run primarily by retired British military personnel. It was an excellent course on what hazards a journalist might encounter in a war zone. It included the same things other 'war reporter' schools offer: hostage taking, first aid, biochemical hazard training, which included gasmask training and exposure to tear gas. It was a full, seven-day course in Virginia. Ironically, the February weather for the course was snow, which did not exactly prepare you for the sand and heat of the Middle East, but it was still extremely useful. I do not think anyone should consider going to a place where biochemical warfare is a serious threat without this kind of training. Gas masks need to be second nature to survive in such a situation."

The physical challenges of the assignment were the toughest for Kalthoff. "I never felt that I was looking death in the eye. We were involved in combat, and the hours were extremely long at times, but I did not see blood and death right before my eyes. Being with artillery, we were down the road from where the effects of the massive firepower were felt. Iraqi forces did try to attack the artillery position, but they were not successful and never really got close. The physical challenges were more difficult for me, including relentless dust, no showers, riding in extremely uncomfortable vehicles through the middle of the desert. I gained a greater respect for the challenges marines choose to accept and train for routinely. I was extremely grateful for the small comforts of home when we got back."

Kalthoff did not find the "rules and restrictions" of the embedment particularly troublesome. "We were given remarkable access to the marines and their commanders. We were free to move around the camp as we chose. We could not leave the camp on our own, which would have been very dangerous on most occasions anyway. We could not report future combat or movement plans, but we were given much of that information in advance. We could not report specific troop strength numbers, but once units had arrived at a destination, we were free to report our location and describe in detail what we saw. I did indeed feel protected and often did feel like part of the unit because the marines treated us that way. But I believe they also understood that my role would require reporting the bad things that happened, too. And we did report things that were not good from the U.S. point of view, like a friendly-fire incident in which marines mistakenly fired on their own troops, and the army convoy ambush. The commanders who provided us with information seemed to provide us with at least some of the negatives as well."

Kalthoff did not encounter any specific ethical problems during the time he was embedded with the 1/10. "If really big problems had come up with my specific unit, it would have been a greater dilemma, but big problems did not come up—1/10 performed their mission extremely well as best I could tell. I was sort of torn about leaving early, feeling guilty about the fact that they could not."

Kalthoff and Heimbuch carried a limited amount of news-gathering equipment with them. "We had only a satellite telephone to send back audio reports. We had to shuttle videotape to other NBC elements when we could. This was possible in Kuwait before we crossed the border and occasionally once we were in Iraq, since another NBC crew was with Marine Task Force Tarawa. But it was a big challenge, and photographer Mike Heimbuch was often very disappointed that his fine pictures could not get out. When we did get video out, it quickly appeared on all the NBC programs and cable channels."

As was the case with other embedded reporters, Kalthoff knew a great deal about what was happening with his own unit but very little about what was happening to other units elsewhere. "Our awareness of what was happening in our area was extremely good. The artillery commander allowed us free access to his command area, and nothing was hidden there as best I could tell. The artillery has communication with all the infantry units on the battlefield since the artillery provides the guys up front with immediate support. So the artillery often knew more about the big picture than the infantry units knew about what the others were doing. When the shooting died down, the artillery guys were very anxious to drive up the road to see what had been going on. So they took us along on 'field trips' that allowed us to see things very quickly after they happened. It was an excellent situation from which to cover a war, comparatively safe, lots of current information, with more flexibility than some of the infantry units might have. We did have access to Iraqi people when it was possible to approach them and cross the language barrier. We did not choose the assignment, but we were very fortunate from a journalistic point of view. Our knowledge of what was happening elsewhere in the war was more limited. It came from BBC shortwave radio broadcasts and what I could gather from NBC while waiting on hold to do my own phone reports. Our contact with other journalists was quite limited as well."

Looking back, Kalthoff thinks that the embed program was better than previous arrangements. "The embed program was better than any prior approach I'm aware of for covering a war. There were a few times the military seemed to overreact to the media. There was a last-minute restriction on private satellite news vehicles traveling with a marine convoy, and these vehicles had been heavily rigged and camouflaged, at great expense, to look military, with total cooperation from the marine commanders in the field. (The field commanders helped find a last-minute way to carry the satellite gear on military vehicles instead.) Another time, the military had a sudden fear about reporters in possession of a certain brand of satellite telephone that included some French technology that might have been available to Iraq and that might have allowed Iraq to track troop movements. (Luckily, my phone was not the suspect brand.) But these odd changes seemed to come from Washington or somewhere far away, not from the commanders I dealt with. It was a matter of rapport, like any other people-to-people arrangement, such as covering the police beat. You have to gain respect and give respect. And yes I would do it again, but it would sure be great if it could be in a place with a lot less sand."

Kalthoff was not in the Middle East for the 1991 Gulf War, but he was in Beirut, Lebanon, in 1983 just after the U.S. Marine compound there was bombed. "I was a unilateral reporter in Beirut, and it was a very risky proposition. We did things we probably should not have done to get the story. We smuggled ourselves into Beirut from Israel because there was no airport open and no government from which to get a visa. We drove past the checkpoints of several different armies in hired taxis driven by people we'd never met before. We were very lucky. So I like the idea of having marines around to look after you in a raging war zone. There are certainly times that you would like to go off on your own and talk to more of the local people, get more of the other side of the story. That was very hard to do in Iraq during the height of battle, but we did have opportunities to do this. The marines wanted to see what local people had to say, too. It clearly happened more as time went on, after we left, even as the danger of occasional shooting continued. It was possible to break out of the embed if the time came to do so, and many crews that stayed behind longer did just that. We were asked by our management to return home when the war was basically settled. The access this arrangement provided will undoubtedly change the expectations of viewers and readers for war coverage in the future. And it will be the challenge for journalists to safely and professionally live up to rising expectations the next time."

# RICHARD RAY

ANCHOR/REPORTER, KDFW-TV (FOX), DALLAS, TEXAS

Richard Ray is both a news anchor and a reporter at KDFW-TV, the FOX affiliate in Dallas, Texas. He and photographer Cody Marcom were originally embedded with the Fourth Infantry Division at Fort Hood, Texas, the first week in March 2003. They were fitted for gas masks and chemical suits; given shots; and trained with, and were briefed by, the Fourth ID over a two-week period. The Fourth ID was meant to go in through Turkey and open up the northern front in Iraq. When Turkey disallowed them from doing so, and when it looked as if the Fourth ID were not going at all, Ray and Marcom flew over on a commercial flight and operated as unilateral journalists for the first eight or nine days of the war.

"Our unit did not go into Iraq to stay until after the major fighting ended and we'd gone home. We spent the first days of the war as unilaterals—we'd left our embedded unit at Fort Hood when it appeared they would not deploy—and got into Iraq on three occasions with marine escorts at the beginning of the war. We re-embedded with our unit and made two day-trips into Iraq after the Fourth ID from Fort Hood arrived, but we spent the majority of our time at a camp in northern Kuwait."

Ray has worked for KDFW for twenty years and had originally proposed going to the Middle East to do stories about his son Nicholas, who is in the navy, in aviation warfare. "He's a search-and-rescue swimmer—called 'SAR swimmer' in the navy lingo—and flies in the back of Seahawk helicopters doing some top-secret job he's not supposed to talk about. When I found out about the embedding program, I told my news director. She asked me if I would be willing to become embedded, and I said yes. I guess you would conclude that I volunteered."

Ray said that after the September 11 attacks he, like a lot of Americans, felt compelled to do something more for his country. "I was motivated by the hope that as a journalist I could be of some little service, at least. I'm also certain that my son being over there was part of the motivation, though I never was able to hook up with him. I communicated by e-mail and at one point had worked out a deal with the navy to do some coverage on them. But other things happened, and I had to cancel it."

From Friday, March 21, until around April 1, Ray and his photographer lived in the Hilton Hotel outside Kuwait City, where the military headquartered its public information officers (PIOs). The lead elements of the Fourth ID arrived on March 29. Ray and Marcom began doing stories with them the next day but didn't fully re-embed until April 2. "We spent the first night at Camp Wood, then four or five nights sleeping on the floor of a tent at the port south of Kuwait City, where the Fourth ID was unloading its equipment, and the rest of the time at Camp Udairi on the Iraq–Kuwait border. We got into Iraq three times as unilaterals with marine-escorted convoys—twice to Umm Qasr and the port between Umm Qasr and Basra, and once to the oil well fires in Ramailah—and then twice more after embedding with the Fourth ID—these were day trips on helicopter flights, one to Baghdad and another on a short rescue mission to Nasiriyah. We did not see anything approaching combat. We were in areas where the marines and soldiers were nervous about snipers but never encountered any. We went through dozens of air-raid drills while in Kuwait City, but the only missile that got through hit a shopping center in downtown Kuwait City many miles away from our location." Ray estimates there were thirty to forty journalists embedded at Fort Hood with the Fourth ID, but he and Marcom were the only embedded journalists in their regiment. At Camp Udairi they would occasionally run into other embedded journalists but not on a regular basis.

Ray and his photographer's embedment was with the 2/4 Aviation (Fourth Brigade), a regiment of Black Hawk helicopters. The unit had medevac choppers attached to it but mainly flew supplies, personnel, and equipment in support roles. Ray and Marcom left their unit and flew home on April 21, when it became apparent that the major fighting had ended and the Fourth ID would be involved in peacekeeping. Ray remembers, "Some elements of the Fourth ID had left for Iraq, but the main body was still in Kuwait and did not plan to leave for another five to seven days. My bosses decided, and I agreed, that it was time to come home."

In addition to the training Ray and Marcom received at Fort Hood, KDFW-TV sent them to a one-day crash-course school with former Navy Seals in Virginia. "We got training in the gas masks, chem suits, first aid, how not to be an easy target for terrorists, and that sort of thing. I thought it was all very useful. It certainly made you think about all the different ways you could get killed."

Ray is the father of two sons and one daughter. His wife is a supervising producer at the FOX affiliate where Ray anchors and reports. Looking back, Ray finds the physical challenges of war reporting demanding but not debilitating. "The heat and the dust in the desert of Kuwait were almost indescribable. But, I must say, I thrived physically. My allergies cleared up—no ragweed or pollen there—while other people around me were having all sorts of problems with dust-caused allergies. I'm in very good shape for my age [fifty-two] and really did not have much problem with the physical demands. Others, I'm sure, did. Emotionally, I can only say that I desperately missed my wife and family. We were there more than four weeks, and my wife was not happy with my decision to go. Unlike the soldiers, however, I was able to speak with her on the phone frequently and assure her that I was not in danger, and that helped."

Ray does not believe that the rules of embedded reporting were excessive. "There were not a lot of rules. We were asked never to give out locations. Other than that, they trusted us to know what we should report and what we should not. I made it clear to my commanding officer that if I had a question about anything controversial, I would discuss it with him first. They gave us access to everything, including classified briefings. They trusted us, and I think we were trustworthy. After all, if we reported anything that could harm the troops, we were reporting something that could harm us as well."

Ray did feel very much a part of the unit in which he was embedded, the 2/4 Aviation. He says it would have been difficult not to feel that way under the circumstances. "They looked out for us and were protective in every way they could be. We tried to earn their trust, and I think we did. I felt much safer as an embedded journalist."

Early on, Ray realized that he might encounter ethically difficult situations in his reporting. "Shortly after we re-embedded, there was a minor accident at the port with a Black Hawk on a test flight. No one was hurt but there was a near miss. I sat down with my commander [Lieutenant Colonel Jack Frost], and we discussed how things would go if something truly newsworthy and bad would happen. We asked everyone to realize that just because we photographed something did not mean it would actually end up on television. I assured them that if it was controversial at all, I would have a long discussion with Colonel Frost before we aired anything. I told them we might not agree 100 percent on the wording and the story but that I would certainly hear them out on all important issues. Fortunately, nothing of the sort arose."

Ray and Marcom took small digital cameras; laptop computer with digital video editing software; and, when they went to Camp Udairi, a videophone. They were able to feed most of their stories over satellite from the FOX bureau in Kuwait City, and they did many live shots from there as well. "We often had to use couriers to get our tape back to Kuwait City. We did feed via videophone and do some videophone live shots from Camp Udairi, but the quality of the feeds is not very good so, when possible, we got our tape to the FOX satellite location."

Ray had access to television and the Internet while he was at the Hilton Hotel outside Kuwait City. At Camp Udairi he had Internet access (without e-mail) but relied a lot on telephone calls to Dallas and KDFW. "There was a real information vacuum for many of the soldiers. I was also doing phone work for three radio stations in Dallas—KLIF and the Kidd Kraddick show primarily—and they were helping keep me informed."

While Ray and Marcom were with the soldiers, they ate what the soldiers ate. "While we were at the port in Kuwait we ate a lot of MREs (Meals, Ready-to-Eat), and when we were in camp, we ate at the mess hall. The MREs are actually not bad, although very caloric. They're designed to give a foot soldier enough fuel to go all day. They come with a little chemical packet that you just add water to and heat it up that way. There was a lot of variety in the main courses, and a lot of trading around between soldiers. It was kind of a grab-bag deal. The MRE would say on the outside what its main course was, but there was variety in the desserts and other side dishes. Soldiers had their favorites and would trade with each other. But, bottom line, we ate what they ate. Soldiers stood in line for hours every day to get into the mess hall, often in swirling dust and tremendous heat. Camp Udairi had thousands of soldiers, and they just didn't have a big enough mess hall to feed everyone at once. It was a real assembly line. While we were there, they were constantly expanding the building, trying to catch up."

Looking back, Ray believes that the embed program worked. "The Pentagon wanted its story told accurately and fairly, and by giving journalists access, that occurred. You can't expect to have your story told if you shut people out. You will always need unilateral reporters as well. Embedded journalists only see the small portion of the war that is directly in front of them. But the combination of a lot of embedded journalists and hundreds of unilaterals gives the clearest picture we can hope to get, I believe."

Ray is glad he did this but says, "I would have to evaluate a lot of things before I did it again. I was embedded as a network journalist under the umbrella of the FOX network, and we got a great unit. If it had gone in through Turkey, we would have been very near the action. We were able to fly in the back of the Black Hawks, and that's a great platform for getting video. The medevac helicopters added another element that would have been very interesting if our unit had gotten into combat. But I did not have the technology or the crew, just myself and a photographer, to compete with other network journalists in live coverage. If I had the manpower and equal technological firepower, if my wife, Catherine, would agree—she says now she would not—I would certainly entertain the idea of doing it again. I don't think this kind of war will happen anytime in the near future, however."

During the 1991 Gulf War, Ray did not go to the Middle East, but he did cover it from military bases in Texas. He says there is no comparison between the two. "Journalists were given virtually no access to the war in '91. We had almost unlimited access this time."

Ray is unsure if covering this war changed him in any significant way, but he thinks it has changed war coverage. "I think if we do see another war anytime soon, the Pentagon will once again embed journalists. I'm sure of it; though, again, I don't foresee this type of war again anytime soon."

While Ray was covering the war as a unilateral, he was able to e-mail his son Nicholas. "I told him about accompanying the marines and the first humanitarian relief convoy into the port at Umm Qasr. He e-mailed back that he was flying some interesting missions that he was anxious to tell me about when he got home. Of course, he couldn't be specific over e-mail. A week after I got home, he was able to call me from Qatar. It turns out that while I was reporting from the port at Umm Qasr, he and his crew were flying overhead looking for mines and Iraqi patrol boats."

Ray's personal situation was unique because his wife was a producer at the station for which he was reporting. "I talked about missing my wife. Marcom and I shared everything with the soldiers, all the frustrations over the heat and the dust and everything else. But I had one thing the soldiers craved the most, and that was contact with my loved ones. Many soldiers hadn't spoken on the phone to their family for weeks. I was able to talk to my wife almost daily. At one point, when we first got the videophone up and running, she happened to be in the control room in Dallas. I could see her, and she could see me for the first time in about two weeks. It was a grainy, digitally challenged picture, but we waved and blew kisses and both had tears in our eyes."

## BYRON HARRIS
Senior Reporter, WFAA-TV (ABC), Dallas, Texas

Byron Harris is a senior reporter at WFAA-TV, the ABC affiliate in Dallas, Texas. Harris and photographer Doug Burgess were embedded with the First Marine Division, Command Service Support Group 11, which supplied fighting troops at the front lines. The First Marine Division (called "MarDiv") is primarily based at Camp Pendleton, California. Harris says, "I wanted to do this because it was, and is, a big story. I was selected because of my experience in covering stories like these, my desire to go, and presumably my skill. We were able to obtain an ABC embedded 'slot' because of our long-standing positive relationship in providing and serving the network."

Harris was in Kuwait a week waiting for his assignment to the First Marine Division. Then he was with them for about a week before the beginning of the war. "After the war started, we were with them for about three weeks, until we got to Baghdad, at which point we came home. Total time in Kuwait and Iraq: March 2 through April 12, 2003. We were on the front lines. We were shot at approximately three times. The journalists with our group varied, from a high of eleven total, to a low of six."

Harris and his photographer were trained by both their company, A. H. Belo Corporation, and by the marines. According to Harris, Belo gave all of its reporters classes on surviving in a terrorist/dangerous environment. This training consisted of a three-day course taught by Special Forces veterans in Georgia. "We covered first aid, mines, escape driving, conventional weapons, chemical weapons, and bomb-detection techniques. The marines trained us in donning chemical gear and preparing for attack. The training was useful, but thankfully we didn't need it."

In the field, Harris wore a flak jacket, helmet, and combat boots. He carried a gas mask, goggles, and a water canteen and found the assignment both physically and emotionally stressful. "It was hot during the day and often freezing at night. There were no bathing facilities; we didn't bathe for three weeks. There were sandstorms. Emotional stress arose from the physical danger, which, since we were on the front lines, was ubiquitous. Focus on the work allowed us in essence to put that out of our minds. But it would creep back in idle moments."

Harris interviewed marines in the unit who came from towns in Texas: Austin, Coppell, Seguin, and Dallas. His reports showed viewers how war "gets done"— what it looks like and sounds like. From his position he could show one piece of the larger picture.

He says he did not experience any ethical dilemmas. Other than being prohibited from revealing his location or his unit's troop strength, he had no restrictions imposed on him. "Our unit did not tell us where we were. We were able to glean this information in conversation with unit members. But the only way we knew what was going on elsewhere was by listening to BBC shortwave broadcasts. Our shortwave radio failed after a bad sandstorm, however; and we had virtually no outside contact except what we could get from Dallas when we fed our stories. We slept, ate, and traveled with the unit, so in that sense we were part of it. We depended on them for our mobility. But stories were not suggested to us, and if we were 'managed,' it was not overt."

Harris and Burgess used Sony digital-video (DV) cams for news gathering, edited their stories on a laptop computer, and fed them over satellite-phone uplinks. All of their equipment failed regularly and was difficult to repair.

In evaluating the experience, Harris found both good and bad. "The good side of embedding was unfettered access to the troops, who were free in discussing their opinions with us, and unrestrained access to the battlefield as it unfolded in front of us. The embedding process was necessary from a military standpoint because without it, reporters would have become hindrances to the battle. Most reporters have little or no knowledge of the military and would have been most likely killed by friendly fire. I appreciate the military's practical necessity of managing this problem."

He said the bad side is that the restrictions of the embedding process obviously gave the military a tremendous opportunity to manage the news. "We were tethered to them for transportation. We couldn't break away. If our unit was moving, we had to move with them and could only rarely stop to talk to Iraqis."

Harris, who has worked in news for A. H. Belo Corporation for almost thirty years, says, yes, he would do it again. "As long as the unique situation of the journalists was kept in perspective [that being their captivity by the military], the reports were valuable. This requires some savvy on the part of the audience, and restraint on the part of the reporters, in not purporting to know more than they really do. Reporters really only knew what they saw in front of them. It was up to editors and the audience to synthesize it. The experience reinforced the pain of war and accentuated the frivolity with which our society approaches conflict. It reinforced my appreciation of all human life and improved my mental and physical tenacity."

Once Harris and his photographer were back in the United States, they wrote and produced a special report titled *War Stories*, which was aired in late June 2003 on WFAA-TV in Dallas. In one interview Harris recalled, "It was on balance the most bizarre six weeks I've ever spent at one time. Brilliant, starlit nights punctuated by sandstorms where you couldn't see anything, couldn't move. No showers for weeks. It was a life-changing experience. It led you to reevaluate everything that came before and everything that would come after. There were many times when we were out in the middle of the desert when Doug and I looked at each other and said, 'I can't believe we're here, and I can't believe we're seeing this.' It was stressful psychologically and physically. Many times, no sleep at all or very little sleep, for days on end. You found yourself in the middle of the day awake finding that you'd just been asleep for a few minutes and didn't even realize it. There are many things you don't realize how great they are until you don't have them and then have them again. And what a miracle our lives are compared to so many other people. That's one thing that hit both of us, I think, in Iraq. And when somebody pulls out in front of me in traffic now and I want to get really mad at 'em, it has a new relativism that it didn't have before."

His photographer remembered, "There was always something to do, or somewhere to go, or work that had to be done. When you did have a few minutes, that's when you had time to think about things, and then it became hard emotionally. Or when you had a chance to talk to people back home, then it became hard emotionally. It was almost easier to be working constantly and not think about it . . . until we got back to the hotel in Kuwait City and I took my clothes off and went and showered for however long and came out and I could actually smell my clothes and my belongings. And it was enough to turn my own stomach once I was clean and then you had the perspective of what you smelled like."

Harris does not believe the embedding process changed war coverage per se. "Every war is different. World War II was not Korea, which was not Vietnam, not Lebanon, not Grenada, not Nicaragua. The press has little institutional memory. Journalists have to fight for, and be wary of, access in every conflict."

# BYRON PITTS
CORRESPONDENT, CBS NEWS, NEW YORK CITY

CBS News correspondent Byron Pitts is driven to cover every major story on his watch. He was at Ground Zero on September 11. He was in Afghanistan and covered the military buildup in Kuwait. So, of course, he was going to cover the Iraq War. He was in Kuwait and then Iraq from January to April 2003. He was first embedded with the U.S. Marine Corps HMLA169 (attack helicopter squadron from Camp Pendleton in California)[1] and then with ground troops from the Marine Air Ground Task Force Training Command, TwentyNine Palms, California. He returned to the States a few days after Baghdad fell and then returned to Iraq in July 2003 to cover the aftermath of the fall of Saddam Hussein's regime. Pitts, cameraman Mark Lagaga, and engineer Chuck Rainey went into Baghdad with the ground troops. He and Lagaga had worked together in Afghanistan before the Iraq War. Pitts, forty-two years old during the 2003 Iraq campaign, has been with CBS News since 1998.

To prepare for the rigors of the war, Pitts (and most CBS embeds) underwent military training with Centurion, a British company run by former British Royal Marine commandos, for a week and also went to the Pentagon program for chemical and biological weapons training to learn how to wear protective gear. CBS embeds also learned the military culture and the physical demands of covering the war. "It was clear how physically demanding it would be. One journalist broke her ankle, another injured his knee, and one's clothes caught on fire. It is physical, demanding and dangerous work," Pitts said.

Pilgrims, a British risk-management company, provided security for them in Kuwait. "Most networks have a similar service. They help us assess the risk, and most of the people who were in Iraq for CBS are people who are based in our London office. They most often do this kind of work. So those of us who are stateside depend on their level of experience. We all have some experience. We are a good team," he said.

When they first got to Kuwait, the team stayed at what was supposed to be a secret base for the U.S. Marine Corps HMLA169. "But every pizza delivery boy knew who we were. Once the embed process started, we went there to file reports."

Pitts said the team knew the war had started when there was an air raid on the airbase and Patriot missiles responded. The team then joined ground troops and continued into Iraq with them. They lived inside continually moving armored vehicles. At first, the crew used military equipment to transmit their stories. "Eventually we bought an old pickup truck with a covered bed and turned that into our satellite truck. The only thing we depended upon the military for was protection."

Pitts characterized the embed program as "a good experience for the military, the media, and the nation. Journalism is at its best when it is accurate and when it is personal. By and large the average marine that I dealt with was a good and honorable professional. Most journalists were good, decent professionals doing the best they could."

Concerning the Pentagon rules and regulations for reporters, Pitts said that many were common sense, such as not allowing reports on a mission in progress or on one about to begin. "Do I really want to give up the position with the marines I'm with that would not only put them in danger but me as well?" he asked. "Actually there was no restriction on where we could go. They gave us risk assessment, and we managed to come out okay. It consumed enough of my day to report about the marines I was with that I didn't need to leave the unit."

Pitts said that this experience was quite different from that of the Vietnam era. He pointed out that "for the military the old guard has died or retired. The new generation of military leaders wanted to have a better relationship with the media."

He said that Afghanistan was also quite different. "The U.S. military didn't have an official presence when I was there. They wouldn't even confirm that they were Americans. It was more like the wild, wild West. So many journalists died because they lacked protection."

Pitts said that the military was aware that they were fighting not just a military war in Iraq but also a media-and-information war. "They had to not just defeat the Iraqi army but had to win the war for information. They felt they had a better chance of being treated fairly by Western media than by Al Jazeera or other Arab media. This was part of the military's motivation. We had access to the same basic information as Al Jazeera reporters, but their stories were totally different than the ones we would tell. They have a different perspective."

Pitts said that his team's only ethical dilemma while embedded was whether to let soldiers use their sat phone. They decided to do so to create a relationship that wouldn't otherwise exist, even though that meant not videotaping the soldiers' private conversations. Pitts said that many of these phone calls were the most compelling stories of the war, although they never aired. "There was so little private space for anyone that when marines used our sat phone, we wouldn't videotape them." He vividly remembers some of the slices of life that he witnessed as marines called home. There was a man who heard his newborn child cry. His wife was crying, and he was crying. A young soldier had married a thirty-year-old stripper just before shipping out. The soldier learned in a phone call to his mother that the stripper had cleaned out his bank account and disappeared. Another marine found out his grandmother—who had raised him—had died. "He's sitting framed against the sky in the back of our Ryder truck, with an M-16 on his shoulder. He was quivering because she died and was buried and he wasn't there."

He said that although military rules prohibited showing the face of an injured soldier, marine, airman, or sailor, the reality was that this issue never came up. "We were videotaping injured soldiers with a high level of respect."

Pitts said that his faith got him through his time covering the war. "I was raised to believe God is good. I believed it when I came here, and I will believe it when I leave. As American journalists, we have access to information, and we see the promise of democracy."

Pitts was back in Baghdad when Secretary of Defense Donald Rumsfeld decided to release the pictures of Saddam Hussein's dead sons. He said that a small group of journalists were selected to view the bodies and that he was not among them. "The month before Al Jazeera showed dead Americans. Now the U.S. was parading the dead bodies of Saddam's sons. There is a bridge between U.S. and Iraq, and we both stumbled on it. I was surprised after we released the still photographs that Iraqis were still skeptical. They welcomed the U.S., but they were still skeptical. There is a difference in perspective. We try to believe our leaders, but the Iraqis have been conditioned not to believe their leaders. When the U.S. released videotape, it went from shock to almost humor about how the U.S. military had to give them what they wanted. I think the U.S. government gained something but lost some credibility."

Pitts said that there was personal value in going to Afghanistan and then to Iraq. "I felt all of us [journalists] had some responsibility in what happened on September 11. American journalists had a role to try to help the nation understand how people could hate so much that they would fly planes into the towers. Covering Afghanistan and Iraq would be my contribution. If America had done a better job, pushed harder to cover international stories, and had done a better job of explaining, there might have been a person who would have done something [to prevent the attacks on America]. Prior to September 11, hijacking still meant a free ride to Havana or somewhere. I have five kids, and I have no desire to get hurt or die. But it's important to understand what happened and to help CBS viewers understand. Everyone sacrifices because we think it is important. If you ever hope to have that measure of credibility, then you have to cover every story on your watch. The thing that distinguishes CBS [from other networks] is the context we bring to our stories. I have to cover every major story on my watch.

"CBS did a good job of giving us the big picture. It was my responsibility, my task in the war to cover the story of the marines I was with—period. It was the responsibility of the embedded reporter to provide the slice, while it was the responsibility of CBS in New York to provide the pie."

The embed program gave reporters the kind of access they would not have had otherwise, because of the relationships journalists could establish with military commanders. For example, Pitts doubts that the story about the American soldier who killed two soldiers in his own unit would have been covered—at least so quickly—had Mark Lagaga not built up a trust with the military command. Pitts said that after the major hostilities had ceased and most journalists had left their embed spots, the embeds were "only allowed to have a conversation after something bad has happened—an adversarial relationship. If you are with someone for six days and you see each other in your workplace, you respond differently on day seven when something bad happens."

Pitts saw a shift in military–media relations once he returned to Iraq. "Some of the hostility between the military and media has resurfaced. I never had a cross word with anyone while I was embedded. But the first day back in Iraq, I had words with soldiers. All the good will during the embed process was a honeymoon period. It speaks to the military motive for doing the embed program. There was great criticism of the embed program and the journalists—as being too patriotic. It was all pretty one-sided. It was easy for the media to coexist with the military because it was mostly favorable coverage. Now the news isn't quite as favorable, and the military [has] retreated to old habits. Animosity is being exposed now. The intimacy you got from the embed process no longer exists, because most embeds have gone back home.

"I think the advance of technology allowed the embed program to work to the extent that it did work. There were journalists who had equipment you could fit in a suitcase. Who knows how far it will advance in another war?" he said. " Overall the embed program was good. Gone are the days of Vietnam. Technology will allow journalists to tell stories from the front of the battle. The public will demand coverage. The only concern I have is that at the end of the day, journalism is about words and about information. My only fear is that as we go so far down the road with technology and the U.S. military's ability to kill so cleanly, that journalism will fail to tell people a story and say what it means. We might lose our ability to show and tell people how violent and ugly war really is. Everything looks clean and neat. The U.S. has weapons that can kill one hundred miles away. We will lose sight of the wives who lost husbands and parents who lost children. We will forget how evil war really is."

## NOTE

1. Home of the world-famous Vipers, who provide combat-assault helicopter support, attack-helicopter fire support, and fire-support coordination for aerial and ground forces during amphibious operations and subsequent operations ashore.

# JIM AXELROD
CORRESPONDENT, CBS NEWS, NEW YORK CITY

CBS News correspondent Jim Axelrod began his journey into war at 5 AM on February 15, 2003. "I'm leaving for at least two months, possibly three. My wife is five months pregnant. My two kids are bewildered. We are about to start renovations on our house. Since I don't exactly come from a long line of brave people, I had more than a few questions about just exactly what I'm getting into. I was managing to hold it together until I started down my front steps. All I can hear as I walk to the car is my seven-year-old daughter, Emma, sobbing. 'Daddy! Daddy! Daddy! Why couldn't you be a librarian?'"

That was a question Axelrod would ask himself several times in the course of the next few weeks during his stint as an embedded reporter with the U.S. Army Third Infantry Division. The following day he landed in Kuwait City and went to the Sheraton Hotel where CBS was headquartered. "I was a bit apprehensive—an American in the Middle East, a Jew in an Arab land—but when the clerk handed me the key to Room 666, I thought to myself, this is not the omen I'm looking for. I asked for another room."

For the next three-and-half weeks the Sheraton was home. "Its luxury hardly prepared me for what lay ahead," he said. "But what my time in Kuwait did give me was an invaluable opportunity to learn about the military. I hadn't had a chance to learn much about the military growing up—not a lot of friends joining up after high school, not a lot of fathers and mothers serving in the reserves, not the time or place where you pick up the basics of military life. So in Kuwait I had time to head out to the camps where the Third Infantry was posted to begin learning about the military."

Axelrod was impressed with what he saw. "What I found was an officer corps composed of an impressive group of men and women—diligent, skilled, well ed-

ucated, committed, and extremely hard working. They all could have been making two or three times their current salary in the private sector. But they chose to
stay in the army out of a sense of duty and patriotism. I developed a real respect
for their approach to their training. But that was nothing compared to watching
them after the shooting actually started." He said that it was also a gender-neutral
culture. "I never for a second thought there was any kind of division between men
and women in terms of the military culture. It was as gender neutral while they
were doing their jobs as any workplace I have seen."

The army had all the embed reporters head out to the desert on March 11. Axelrod said that the expectation was that the war would start in a week or two. "This
would help us get acclimated. Acclimated to what? To living and working without
showers or without toilets; to eating military food; to sleeping military hours on
a military cot; to having three pairs of underwear, three T-shirts, and four pairs of
socks total for the next five weeks in triple-digit heat that made you sweat so much
you wanted to change every twenty minutes. Talk about 'shock and awe,'" he said.

Axelrod was with five thousand soldiers of the Third Infantry Division's First
Brigade Combat Unit. "What they did, I did. What they saw, I saw. They were the
first over the border in northern Kuwait to southern Iraq, first over the Euphrates
River, first into the Baghdad airport. So I saw a lot. I slept under rocket-and-
missile fire. I saw burnt Toyota pickup trucks just after being hit by U.S. tank fire,
burnt bodies still strapped in the seats. I saw one of Saddam's palaces, in pristine
condition, abandoned just hours before we got there. But I didn't see everything.
Not even close. My slice of the war was a narrow slice, a very narrow slice. It was
a wild, violent, shocking, and awesome slice but a slice nonetheless." He was riding in the back of a Bradley fighting vehicle, an armored transport vehicle.[1] In the
back of a Bradley, there are slits for soldiers to look through, about six inches by
three inches. "You've got action going on all around you, but all you are looking
at in the back of a Bradley is whatever you can see in the six-inch by three-inch
slit. I don't have the big picture, I have a narrow view."

Despite his narrow slice, Axelrod said that he did not operate in a vacuum.
"One of the advantages of the sat phone is that I could call the CBS war desk and
talk to people like David Martin, who is terrific at pulling together the big picture.
I could find out how the war was going, who had been killed, and so on. But I was
only responsible for my slice."

Axelrod pointed out that satellite communication has changed everything. "My
first inkling was watching the soldiers using our sat phones. We gave them five
minutes each. Most soldiers go weeks, if not months, without talking to their
spouses, to their parents, to their kids. We'd be sitting in our tents, eating some
military delicacy, dreaming of five minutes under a hot shower, when the silence
would be broken by a yell and applause. A soldier outside our tent on our satellite
phone had talked to his expectant wife for the first time since January and found
out that he was a father."

After weeks of acclimation, it was time to go. "On Wednesday, March 18, we moved to another position, still in Kuwait, and the First Brigade began to form its vehicles, its tanks, its Bradleys, its Humvees, its personnel carriers, and its supply trucks into a convoy. The next morning at dawn we were awakened with the news that the U.S. had sent missiles into Baghdad. The Iraqis had fired back. The army told us that the U.S. would invade in a few hours, and that the Third Infantry would be the first over the border."

From Thursday, March 19, until Friday, April 4, when the First Brigade would take Saddam International Airport, the First Brigade was pushing to Baghdad as the tip of the spear. "At the outset we made record time moving the greatest distance in military history, ten thousand vehicles, 150 miles into Iraq in thirty hours. It was swift and steady movement—an army recruiter's dream," he said.

Axelrod, his cameraman, and a satellite technician were traveling in a privately purchased Humvee with a satellite dish mounted on the top. "We could pull out of the convoy into the middle of the Iraqi desert and be up on the CBS television network in New York and talking to millions of people about what was happening in *seven minutes*. It takes longer to boil a hot dog than to tell Americans what was going on," he said. "Satellite technology is not new, but the miniaturization of the components, the quality of the picture, the ease of communicating with technicians in London and New York allowed an unprecedented degree of reliability and ease. With this reliability came responsibility. We needed an acute awareness and sensitivity to the consequences that real-time broadcasting from the front was delivering."

There were not many rules, but Axelrod said that the few there were had to be almost religiously adhered to: never talk about a battle plan, never give away a troop location, and never identify or show dead American soldiers in an identifiable way before the next of kin has been notified. "But by the time the first thirty hours was over, we had had enough experience with these rules to realize they were not going to impede our reporting in any way. I think all we could do was report what we saw as honestly and as objectively as possible."

It looked as if nothing could stop the Third Infantry Division in its initial push up the west side of Iraq. But Axelrod said that two things did appear as potential threats, and neither was the Iraqi military. "We spent the next eight days in a desert camp outside of Karbala. The first two days we endured the worst sandstorm to hit the region in ten years. It was like a hurricane, only instead of water, it was sand. Razor sand, like the wind had teeth. Essentially, I sat in a pickup truck for the better part of forty-eight hours, dozing, filing radio reports by satellite phone, reading, and dreaming about home and the people I missed most. When you go outside, you put on these plastic goggles—airtight we were told. You get out of the truck for two minutes; you get back in and spend the next half hour picking sand out of your eyes. I still don't know how the sand got in there."

As nasty as the sandstorm was, it provided incredible images. "The position of the sun and the light-refracting sand combined to create the most gorgeous rose hue I'd ever seen nature produce. It was breathtaking," he said. "Such incongruous juxtaposition, such beauty created on the battlefield. His cameraman, who had covered sixteen wars and conflicts in twenty-seven years with CBS, told him this was by far the roughest living he had ever experienced. "I think our minds take care of us, because all I remember now from my time in the desert was the exquisite sunsets," he said.

The sandstorm was only partly the cause of the delay. "The convoy had gone so smoothly [and] the Third ID had moved so quickly that they needed to post up while secure supply lines were established and strategies were retooled.

"It was the nature of this war that even though the infantry wasn't moving, the army was fighting effectively, efficiently, and systematically during the sandstorm—during the delay. Most of the fighting I saw was done by captains and majors and laptops in command-and-control tests. It's not hand-to-hand combat. They got the army to the gates of Baghdad inside of three weeks." He said that was possible because of the vast technical superiority of the United States—the howitzers, the multiple-launch rocket systems, the radar that would lock onto Iraqi artillery positions four and five miles away. "Within eleven seconds of the Iraqis' firing, automatically the computer adjusts the targeting mechanisms of the U.S. guns and sends a return volley right down the tubes of the Iraqi guns within two minutes. This essentially rendered Iraqi artillery relatively useless. At any given point in this war they literally had one shot, and then they would be destroyed."

Axelrod said that this meant most of the killing was done long range and out of the view of the cameras. "I did not see hundreds of thousands of bodies piled up on a daily basis. That was not how most of the killing was done in my narrow slice of the war. But each night, as I was sleeping on the desert floor and would be awakened by a whoosh overhead and see a series of white glowing streaks heading off across the sky, I would think that each one of those rockets was targeted so precisely that at that exact moment, there was an Iraqi soldier, sitting next to an Iraqi artillery piece, entirely unaware that he was moments away from his death. And somewhere there was a wife, a mother, and children about to lose their husband, son, and father. That's all I could think about when I would see a burned-out pickup truck on the side of the road with an AK-97 mounted on the back of it or even the charred remains of a machine gun mounted on a bicycle, or when I'd see a pile of captured Iraqi weapons that included flint-lock rifles. They never had any idea what hit them."

The eight days at the standstill combined hours of boredom with moments of terror. "Even if overmatched, the Iraqis were able to kill. A sniper took one soldier one day. A suicide bomber would take four another. This created a certain sort of emotional pressure that I didn't realize the soldiers were facing until one Sunday morning after six days of being posted up and not moving, after six days of this sandstorm, the nonstop firing of artillery, the chemical weapons scares, the daily skirmishes in nearby villages, the loss of several soldiers, the reality started to emerge that this could take awhile—that we'd be living under these conditions and under this pressure for awhile.

"Two days later we were on the move—the final push to Baghdad, around Karbala, across the Euphrates and on to the airport. After eight days in the expanse of barren desert, just moving felt wonderful, though it was going to expose us anew to more intense fighting. In fact as we approached the Euphrates River valley, it felt like stepping onto the set of *Apocalypse Now.* Physically and geographically, everything changed. Endless miles of sand gave way to lush groves of green and thick patches of swaying palm trees."

At the river the First Brigade encountered the most heavily fortified Iraqi positions of its push. "As our Humvee pulled up, Apache helicopters were sliding in and out of the palm trees, popping up to fire at Iraqi positions across the river. There were sporadic bursts of bullets, punctuated by artillery and mortar blasts; tank after tank rattled by, plumes of smoke rising. Our team was in so close that the Iraqi mortars were flying over our heads. This was not good. We were in too close," he said. "You're that close and still able to broadcast. Our satellite operator climbed on the top of the Humvee and got the dish up. So we called up the CBS News *Morning Show* at 8:30 and yelled, 'The battle is raging! We're here! Our dish is up!'"

The first producer he spoke to said, "Well, you know we are in the middle of our nutrition segment. Can you wait a few minutes?" After a few four-letter reviews of this decision, Axelrod demanded to speak to a more senior producer, who said, "Hey, let's do it!" "Viewers got an intimate look at the battlefield," Axelrod said. "It was a different kind of battlefield at that point than anything we'd seen. After a half hour of broadcasting, we put down our dish because we were told it was our turn to cross the Euphrates."

They drove to the base of the bridge, where they lined up and were given instructions. "Now, the bridge is under serious fire. The sergeant is at the bottom of the bridge. He instructs, 'Look, hit the gas and keep moving. They can't hit a moving target. Keep moving! Move! Move! Move! Everything will be fine.'" So, they did as instructed. "We put the pedal to the metal, and mixed with the tension produced by driving under fire was this touch of euphoria as we headed across the bridge. We're crossing the Euphrates! Next stop, Baghdad!"

But then—only halfway across the bridge—their Humvee dies. "Not a sound from the engine," he remembers. "Nothing but a sickening silence." He is thinking that the Iraqis may not be able to hit a moving target, but a sitting duck is another matter. "After a minute or two of immobility, we could hear the AK-47 bullets starting to fly a little closer overhead. And from the sound of things, the soldiers firing mortars and artillery were zeroing in as well. I remember having just enough time to think, 'This is the end,' and repositioned my body to face my helmet toward the direction of fire."

Just then—*BOOM!* He felt a jolt in the back of the Humvee. "It was Ted Koppel's ABC news truck. They had seen the whole thing develop, and they knew that popping the hood and trying to jump out was just too dangerous. So, they did the only thing they could. They locked onto our rear bumper and pushed us across."

Two days later Axelrod and his crew would be the first reporters broadcasting on the runway of Baghdad International Airport. "We would watch more battles and take more gunfire. But I would never feel quite the same kind of fear as I did during those few minutes on that bridge," he said. "I joke now that we were the first American crew to cross the Euphrates—our competition right on our tail."

The question that lingers for Axelrod is, Was it worth the risk? "You know, the families of David Bloom and Michael Kelly will certainly tell you that it wasn't worth it. Here's what it boils down to: this was the purest, most authentic experience of my career—a month in the enchanted forest. It was the kind of month a career in television news does not often, if ever, provide. I'd read about serious, relevant public service performed by reporters in wars past: Murrow, Safer, Rather. But if you grow up in TV news at the time I did, you wonder, Will I ever get a chance at that myself? For a month, I could call CBS News world headquarters and tell them I had news. I had to get on. Put Dan in the chair," he said. "It was relevant news; it was important news; it was news people were watching for and wanted to know about. For a month, I got to watch—not from the front row, but from center stage—what happens when the most powerful country in the history of the world decides to flex its full force of muscle."

For a month Axelrod could watch what the relentless pressure of waging war does to five thousand men and women. He could find out what their limits were. He could find out what his own limits were. "At the end of the day, after almost dying on a bridge, I'll be honest. I'm still trying to find the answers to that question, Was it worth it? For now, I'm going to concentrate on nuzzling my baby girl. And I hope I get an answer to that question before anyone asks me to do it again."

## NOTE

1. The Bradley fighting vehicle provides mobile armored transport of infantry to critical points on the battlefield. The Bradley also provides fire support with a twenty-five millimeter chain gun capable of interchangeably firing armor-piercing and high-explosive ammunition.

## BILL OWENS
PRODUCER, *60 MINUTES II*, CBS NEWS, NEW YORK CITY

When CBS made the decision to send a *60 Minutes II* crew to Iraq, producer Bill Owens became responsible for maneuvering an eight-man unilateral crew through southern Iraq. In a way, this team "came late" to the war because, as a prime-time news program, *60 Minutes II* was in the middle of its season when war became apparent. "We were still in our season and working on stories in progress. So, when we decided that we were going to go over to cover the war, we started working with the Pentagon to find out if there were going to be any surprise embeds at the end—Special Forces or what have you that we may be able to link up with. Short of that we were prepared to go unilaterally," Owens said. Nothing became available that was attractive to them, although the military did offer a number of opportunities. "They were not the kind of things that were really going to help us cover the story in a meaningful way. So, we went unilateral."

Because the Pentagon had been hinting about the timing of the war for a couple of months, by suggesting dates about when the weather would be appropriate, CBS News had been preparing for some time. "You get the sense that it is going to happen. The Bush administration wasn't afraid to show its cards right from the beginning. 'Regime change' was their mantra. I suppose for CBS to prepare to cover the war was a small gamble, but a bigger gamble would have been not to be prepared," he said. So, about two weeks before the war began, his team went to Kuwait, where they obtained credentials and purchased vehicles to transport the camera crew and a flyaway satellite operation.

As a producer for *60 Minutes II*, Owens works with correspondent Scott Pelley. "We do any number of stories together. He has a number of producers doing stories for him. When big news happens, for instance 9/11, it's all-hands-on-deck at CBS News. So for 9/11 we did the *Morning News*, we did the *Evening News*, we did any program all day long. So, the war was going to be like that," he said. "We were fully aware that going over there we were going to be filing our reports for every broadcast, including radio, our overnight programs, and just the special events unit that would handle the beginning of the war while we were on TV for twenty-four, thirty-six, forty-eight hours or something like that. We ceased to become a primarily prime-time team, and we were going to cover the war for CBS News."

Owens had covered the White House for six years and had traveled with President Clinton to Sarajevo and Kosovo when it was relatively safe; but this was his first war. To prepare, he took two training courses, one stateside and one in Kuwait. "In Kuwait City we had our own security—Pilgrims, a British company staffed with former Special Air Service guys. CBS had hired them, so we wanted to go through the drills with them." Owens took advantage of the chemical and biological weapons training to learn how, among other things, to wear a chemical weapons protection suit.

CBS News had established a big bureau in Kuwait months in advance of the war. Veteran producer Larry Doyle (out of CBS's Miami bureau) was in charge. "Our bureau was particularly well supplied in terms of contacts with the military and local contacts. We were in very good shape, so when we got in there very close to the date of the war, we were able to sit down and talk to Larry and offer our services," Owens said. "It turned out that he had struck a deal with a local Kuwaiti businessman/landowner who had a large farm up in what was really the demilitarized zone [DMZ] that the UN used to control the border between Kuwait and Iraq."

Owens, Pelley, two camera crews, and a satellite operator headed to the farm the day before the war began. "We were forward of all known troops, including the British military. We were forward of all of the camps where the military was stationed, such as Camp New York. We were actually in the DMZ," he said. "We got there through cunning and guile. We were able to get through a couple of checkpoints. Part of our team went up really early before the checkpoints were really established. Scott and myself were last and were able to figure out a way through the checkpoints. We got there twenty-four hours before the air campaign began."

Their first inkling that the war was on came when a number of U.S. helicopters began bombing targets on the border between Kuwait and Iraq. "We were able to go on TV to report the ground war had started, because a group of helicopters came up less than a quarter mile away from us and began to just light up the border. They thought they were going to walk right over the border. They clearly were firing on targets that were right on the line," he said. "We found out a couple of days later when we crossed the border and caught up with a marine group that was the first group over the line that everybody was really surprised at the resistance of the border. I'm not talking about the south in general; I'm talking about literally the first night of the ground offensive. They had no idea they were going to meet such heavy resistance. We were right there for that."

Owens believes that they were the first crew to go on the air with coverage of that strike. Pelley was reporting from the roof of this farmhouse, and the camera crew captured video of helicopters lighting up the border and taking out posts that were heavily armed. "Then we watched as columns came up on both sides of us, both British and American, and poured across," Owens said. "I'd say we reported for about twelve hours. We watched a lot of incoming cruise missiles—Hellfires from helicopters—the real start of the ground war, softening up everywhere from Umm Qasr to Basra through the night."

The next morning the crew headed for the border. "We tried for hours and hours to get past the border; but all the checkpoints were sealed up pretty well, and we were unable to talk our way across," he said. "The next morning at first light, we met up with a group of print journalists from the *Los Angeles Times*, *Washington Post*, *U.S. News*, and others." They had seen a British caravan of Fusiliers, the military unit in charge of laying land bridges across bunkers and other structures that could impede the troops' progress. "We had passed them on the road, and one of the print reporters said they might let us through. So we got into this convoy of about a half-dozen cars, and sure enough it was the Brits who let us through. We came across the border, and we saw a number of people giving us peace signs and thumbs-up, and white flags were up on their trucks. We thought, just as the Pentagon expected, people in the south were happy to see Americans come in."

About an hour later the crew ran across a marine checkpoint. "They were very jittery, and we were the first Americans they had seen. They wanted to know who we were and how we got there. They were all on their toes, really looking out at the horizon, and we were just across the border, one half kilometer," Owens said. As the soldiers were asking them for information, there was "a big rip of machine-gun fire" that brought an immediate response from the marines. "They returned fire to what looked like open desert, but there were a couple of small huts there. So we dove behind cars," Owens said. "This was the very big beginning of what became a huge story and a big problem for those first days: the Fedayeen Saddam and this guerrilla war that was going on down there."[1]

Owens said they were expecting to see Iraqi soldiers, but instead they were seeing people driving by in pickup trucks giving them a thumbs-up one moment, and then later a machine gun in the same pickup was shooting at American soldiers. "This was when we got our first taste of 'maybe this isn't going to be what everybody thought it would be,'" he said. The marines told them that they weren't going to let them pass because of the battle that was now going on in Umm Qasr. They were told to go back one or two clicks [kilometers] to the east, to Safwan, a town that they had already passed through. They were told the town was stable. "So, we headed back that way, and came to a big highway intersection where the Brits had set up a small command post and a checkpoint. They had taken about fifty regular army Iraqi prisoners," he said. "It was clear that these guys hadn't been fed in a couple of weeks; they had guns that were being held together by tape, with little ammunition; and they looked pretty happy to be held by the British."

The British were giving them food, water, cigarettes, and blankets. "These guys were all smiling, all being held in a huge semicircle with barbed wire around them. So, these were the first soldiers we saw, and we got a sense of what the regular army looked like, which was what everyone suspected—that the regular army was going to be used as fodder and wouldn't put up resistance." However, Owens said that the soldiers they talked to who participated in that first salvo were surprised that they were getting fired on with all sorts of things.

As they moved into Safwan, they came across ripped-down pictures of a smiling Saddam giving the thumbs-up. "There were people running all over the place, and they were curious to see us. We stopped and took pictures of this. A lot of Iraqis spoke English. They were all thirty-, forty-, fifty-year-old men, all frightened, bordering on agitated, asking, 'Why did the soldiers leave, and when were they coming back?' because it was anarchy in the town," Owens said. "We were standing in front of what had been the Baath Party headquarters. They had broken down the gates and ransacked the place. They were in such a bad way that they were eating the fruit off the trees in the gardens of the headquarters there."

The village men wanted to bring the crew to the hospital to show what bad shape they were in, and how they really needed some order in the town. "They were begging us for order. They needed everything. They needed food and water, but what they needed quickly was order," Owens said. "So, they brought us to the hospital, and they showed us an Iraqi who had died waiting for medical attention. They were showing us an Iraqi who had been killed by American military helicopters. They weren't angry about that. They understood this was part of war."

The irony in the situation was that Safwan had a brand-new large-caliber anti-aircraft gun—a .50 caliber—sitting in front of Baath Party headquarters. But they had only one box of ammunition for the gun. "This was another metaphor for how poorly equipped the Iraqi Army was," Owens said. "So, they weren't angry that this guy had been killed. But they were angry that the doctors and nurses were gone and that electricity and supplies at the hospital were cut off. They went on to explain that Saddam's Baath Party had pulled out all the infrastructure of the town on purpose as part of his war plan. They were going to take the cops; they were going to take the doctors; and they would take all the professionals out of the town hostage and leave the people to try to survive as the Americans came through." Pregnant women, injured people, and elderly and dying people who needed daily care were left without doctors and nurses. "Telling us the stories, they were getting angrier and angrier and angrier," Owens said. "It was a catharsis gone bad." He saw the crowd starting to feed off itself, and he determined that it was time to move on. "We were able to get out of there by telling them [we] were going to try to get some answers, and certainly the next time we came across the U.S. military we would tell them that this town could use some help. But it was time to get out of there. We had seen everything we needed to see in that town. We wanted to get back up to where things were happening." They did keep their promise to tell the military that riots were possible if the town did not receive some basic aid.

The crew headed back toward the American marine checkpoint that had turned them away before. "We got up there, and they were even more on a war footing. They were all on the ground in prone position or in their armored vehicles. There was a tank there, and they made us stop hundreds of yards from them," Owens said. "They sent one marine up to us, running the entire way, to ask who we were and what we were doing there. We told them we were unilaterals not attached to anybody. We were interested in going to Umm Qasr on our own." The marine ran all the way back, had a series of conversations with his commanding officer, and then ran all the way back to the crew. "He hauled me back to the tank, encouraging me to move my ass as we ran because they were clearly still looking out into that field where gunfire had originated before," Owens said. "We went to an armored personnel carrier where the sergeant grilled me. He was clearly in contact with someone above him. Finally, he said, 'Keep your vehicles in single file and one of our APCs [armored personnel carriers] will escort you.' The APC was bigger than a Humvee, equipped with a large-caliber machine gun, but it was not a tank." They rode down the highway to Umm Qasr and into a firefight.

Umm Qasr was the first big objective of the war and the first place where the U.S. military ran into serious resistance. Owens described it as a place that is "broken up" into a working port and an "old town" section that is more of a primitive village. He estimated the population to be about one hundred thousand. Most of those living there work at the port.

"We were watching this hellacious helicopter firefight from above. Our first marine escort dropped us off at a bend in the road. A unit of marines was there getting geared up," he said. "The CO [commanding officer] came up and asked them what we were up to and what we wanted to do. He said, 'We are going into the port, which we now hold more or less. I guess that's where you guys want to go?' We said, 'You bet!'"

So the crew was escorted to the front entrance of the port, which was surrounded by a huge cement wall. "We decided it was a good place to set up camp. We had to go through about three checkpoints there. They searched our vehicles; they searched us." At that point they met Captain Rick Crevier, commander of Fox Company of the Second Battalion, First U.S. Marine Regiment. "The captain comes over and asks, 'Who in the hell are you guys?' We tell him we are CBS, and we're not embeds. And he said, 'Well, we've got our own embeds.'" Owens said that as soon as the captain came over, the embedded reporters came over, too. "They were *not* happy to see us at all. 'How in the hell did you get here?' they asked.

"The captain said, 'Well, this is a pretty dangerous place right now; good to have you here. What are you looking for?' We said, 'Well, sir, we don't want to get in your way, but we are covering the war unilaterally, and we've got all of our own food, water, vehicles. We have our own satellite dish. You tell us where we can and cannot go and what we can and cannot do. We'll abide by the rules. If there is anything you are doing . . . some reconnoitering or whatever you are doing in the next few hours, we'd like to come along. He said, 'Well, we're about to go clear part of the town. There's a lot of sniper fire coming from there. Would you like to come?' I said, 'Sure.'"

At that moment there was a call—"Gas, gas, gas"—which is the universal signal for incoming artillery that had the possibility of including chemical or biological agents. As they struggled into their chemical protection suits, Owens and his crew were able to find out whether their training was paying off. "A marine told me that the reason they took this one very seriously was because the radar set up around the compound had detected an incoming shell, the size and shape of which usually does carry a chemical or biological agent," Owens said. But the shell landed outside the compound. Within an hour, the marines had checked it out and determined that it had no chemical or biological weapons. "So, we stood down. But that was the first real time for a put-on-your-suit-and-see-how-it-works kind of drill."

At that point, it was time to find out what it was really like to work as a unilateral team inside a military structure. "We had a generator that ran our satellite. We wanted to be able to feed in what pictures we had up to that point. The captain came over and said, 'You are going to sleep in that warehouse over there. Move all of your vehicles over there.'" He told them that no "white lights" were allowed. "That's a thing you hear often when you are in the field with the military because that is something that shows up on infrared. So, you've got to use either red or yellow lights," Owens said. "He was giving us the rundown on how he ran his shop, his part of the war. He was a very squared-away guy, very personable, good looking, right out of central casting. I told him that we were much obliged to him for letting us be here. He said, 'Well, I don't know how long you'll be able to stay, because we have all these embeds. If my bosses say you can stay, we are happy to have you. If not you'll have to go.'"

The generator made a lot of noise, and Captain Crevier asked Owens how long the crew would need to keep it running. "I said, 'Well, sir, if it is okay, we need about thirty minutes to be able to do everything we need to do.'" That included setting up the satellite, which required a fair amount of time, and then feeding the pictures up. The captain told them they had thirty minutes and walked away. "We were trying to get the satellite dish up and trying to get the pictures out, when one of Captain Crevier's lieutenants comes over and asked how we were doing. 'You know about no white lights and everything?' he asked. I said, 'Yeah, and I've got to turn off this generator in about five minutes because the captain said thirty minutes. We're still trying to feed out these pictures and have a little more to go.'" The lieutenant told him not to worry about it because a bunch of half-ton trucks were rumbling around, making an enormous amount of noise. "We're not worried about noise; we're worried about lights," the lieutenant said.

Owens believed him and continued to run the generator for an additional twenty minutes. At that point, about fifty minutes into the uploading, Captain Crevier returned and said, "Didn't you tell me thirty minutes for that generator?" Not understanding the situation, Owens joked back, "Yeah, this is the longest thirty minutes in history!" This was not the time to joke. The captain growled, "Unless you play by my fucking rules, you are going to be out of here!"

"He dressed me down, and good for him," Owens said. "He was 100 percent correct on all counts. He had every right to expect his orders to be obeyed." Owens understood the situation from then on. "After you hear rifle fire and machine-gun fire and see helicopters firing missiles and all that, you'd certainly know you were in a war zone. But when someone gets up in your face and explains to you the real meaning of this—people live or die—that makes a different impression." Owens said that another unit had lost someone to sniper fire that morning and that he now understands how anything that can give away position, such as white lights and extra noise, can costs lives. "The sorts of rules that [Captain Crevier] laid out just an hour ago to me prevented things he didn't need to have happen. He had enough problems. From that moment on, we had a really good relationship. I listened carefully to everything that he said." Owens said that he wouldn't even let his crewmembers smoke for the first twenty-four hours after that because of the red ash on the end of their cigarettes. Then the captain told him smoking was allowed.

Owens said that this incident was a perfect example of life as a unilateral. "We hadn't come through their training. We hadn't been with them for weeks and weeks and weeks to know what their rules were. Anywhere else in the world on any other story, having the generator on when one of his lieutenants told me don't worry about it was fine. But there is a chain of command in the military. The captain had told me what to do, and the lieutenant's order didn't mean anything. I fully realized and understand what I'd done. Not with any maliciousness, certainly, but it really was a good thing to happen on the first day after crossing the border, because it changed the way I looked at things and did things in terms of working with the military from then on."

The incident also pointed out one of the problems of covering the war. The embeds, who had been with the units for training and who were by this time familiar with the rules and the COs, resented the unilateral interlopers. It also forced military commanders to think more about whether they had a responsibility to protect journalists even if they were unilaterals. "One BBC reporter objected and asked for us to be kicked out," Owens said. "In the end, Fox Company moved from Umm Qasr up the road, and the public affairs officer [PAO] came up to us and said we wouldn't be able to go. We had been having a conversation with him an hour before, and I think the Pentagon had seen the first report we did. *60 Minutes*

*II* is a prime-time program, and Scott Pelley is one of CBS's more senior, highly visible personalities, one of our best reporters. So, suddenly they were on prime time, and that was a good thing. But there was definitely an official complaint lodged by the embeds that the Pentagon heard."

Owens said that the PAO made the excuse that they would be a "soft target." "There is no doubt about it that it was really dangerous in those moments," Owens said. The crew had been with Terry Lloyd, an ITN (a British news organization) unilateral reporter, as they all tried to cross the border. Lloyd was killed in what was later determined to be a friendly-fire incident. Iraqis were chasing the vehicle in which Lloyd and other journalists were riding, possibly trying to surrender to them. Either the U.S. or British military fired on the Iraqis, thinking they wanted to seize the journalists' vehicle for a suicide bombing, and hit Lloyd's vehicle in the process.

"We knew that it was very dangerous, that we were 'soft targets.' We weren't in any armored carriers. We were in Nissan Pathfinders and a flat-bed truck carrying our equipment," Owens said. "So, that was what the marines told us—that we couldn't move with them any further. But as we continued to talk to them, we were told that their embeds weren't happy about us being there, especially the television embed who was a BBC reporter."

What they did from then on was "surf the convoys." "There was so much military presence that when we moved from company to company, we'd get in a convoy as much as possible. It might make you a military target, but you are protected." It wasn't just Iraqi soldiers that worried them. Owens said he'd been warned about Ali Baba–type thieves. They had two brand new Nissan Pathfinders, expensive satellite equipment, and cash to make deals for gas and food, if necessary. They didn't want to stray too far alone. Owens said that most of the military personnel they met were extremely helpful. "Most of the grunts wanted to know what we knew. They had no idea how the war was going. They had no way of getting news. We took pictures of people and sent them back to wives and mothers via e-mails."

Before they left the compound in Umm Qasr, they covered a really large firefight. "It was basically on the wall surrounding the compound. The Fedayeen tried to make a move into the compound, and the marines all took off up onto this wall and so did we," Owens said. "Scott Pelley was shooting all of this and doing some on-camera work, trying to explain where he was and what was going on. I told him to get those things done right off the bat and then let the cameraman shoot what was going on. I picked up the sat phone and called CBS News, New York, and got on the radio and stayed on the radio for an hour and a half. We were live hourly at the top of the news doing debriefs and roundtables. They didn't want to let me off the phone because for a number of days that was really where the story was—in Umm Qasr.

"Scott and I talked to some of the marines who were up on the wall and involved in shooting the Javelin missile, a new piece of artillery that hadn't been used a lot. In getting them to recount that firefight, we had found out that they were actually the group that had passed us when we were on the farm back in Kuwait. They were able to tell us really early on—from the guys who were doing the fighting—that they were absolutely surprised by the amount of resistance they met coming right across the border. They couldn't believe it. So we sat down and we interviewed all these guys and talked about what that was like."

Once Owens and his crew left Umm Qasr, they moved around looking for good stories. "We were able to do a piece on the very first drop of humanitarian aid. This was serendipity," Owens said. "After we left the marines, we made friends with the Brits at their compound not far outside of Umm Qasr to find out what they were going to be doing and if we could hopscotch ahead. I saw an American major at the compound going in for a discussion. I thought, 'Okay. I'll talk to this guy.' It turned out that he was a civilian-affairs type of person, and he was just about to begin lit-erally the very first humanitarian effort—delivering water to Iraq. It was an amaz-ing scene. Nobody else was there. If the military had been smart, they would have taken some of the embeds there. But this was one of those things that happens on the fly, especially during war, that you can't script. We watched hundreds and hun-dreds and hundreds of people—an unbelievable picture—running out of these lit-tle shantytowns toward this huge tanker truck with water. Saddam or the Baath Party had turned off the taps in Basra about a week beforehand. They hadn't had clean water in over a week. It was just unbelievable." Owens said that in instances like this, instincts take over. "You've just got to keep walking, keep walking, keep walking, and talk to people," he said.

They did abide by the Pentagon's ban on photographing prisoners of war. "We could shoot around that and still say that this group of Royal Marines had taken fifty prisoners. They brought us their weapons, and we could show those." As was the case with many journalists covering this war, Ernie Pyle's ability to tell the sto-ries of the ordinary soldier fighting in World War II was an inspiration to Owens, even if the rules get bent a little. In An Nasiriyah, the team visited a combat sup-port hospital (CSH) that was basically a field surgical hospital.

"A soldier was brought in who had been shot in the leg. He and his buddies had been on patrol in An Nasiriyah, and they saw an ambulance. So, they stood down, and a bunch of Iraqis had jumped out of it and opened fire. So, we interviewed him. The hospital personnel were pleased that we were there while this guy was there because he was being flown out to Kuwait for major reconstruction surgery on his legs. That was the kind of story we had seen in the south—this sort of guer-rilla warfare where there were no white flags because they were using ambulances and things like that."

Owens asked if there was anything they could do for this soldier. Could they let him use their sat phones to let him call home? "There was a question about the military rules about first notification when someone is killed or injured. The army has to get in touch with the family first. They said, 'Well, if you want to let him use your phone, it's up to you.' Well, the phone didn't work within the hospital, but he was eager for his family to know that he was okay. He hadn't talked to them in four months. So, I made a phone call and just said, as we do with characters in our stories, 'Hey you might want to know that your son is going to be in a piece that we are doing. And by the way, I'm at the surgical hospital in An Nasiriyah. He's doing just great. He'll be flown to Kuwait soon. He got shot in the leg, but he's fine. Everything's great.' His mother was over the moon. She was very happy to hear that. I was able to relay a message back from the mom to the kid. He was pretty emotional himself and happy that I had been able to do that. It seemed like a small thing to do. I think that the military personnel who were there were happy to turn around while that happened."

In regard to the question about whether embedded journalists could remain objective, Owens said, "Questions about objectivity were asked in World War II—the whole Ernie Pyle approach. Vietnam was a whole different dynamic. You had soldiers telling the media things that helped to push the coverage a certain way. The things that Walter Cronkite and Dan Rather and Morley Safer found out in Vietnam were the things that people weren't hearing back at the Pentagon. And I think we, at the beginning, did hear some of those things. We had kids on camera saying, 'It certainly wasn't in our freakin' intelligence book that we were going to be getting heavy rounds and RPG-7s fired at us as we were coming across the border. We didn't think that was going to happen for another hundred clicks up the road. It would have been nice to have known that.' For us, it felt real. I didn't have some PAO leading me over to come talk to Private First Class Smith. I went and found Private First Class Smith."[2]

As a producer, Owens was responsible for making many of the decisions about where they would travel and what stories they would do. "First of all you've got to react to what was going on around you. You have to make decisions. I wasn't making unilateral decisions without talking to everyone, but I was suggesting what our course of action should be. You know, 'Let's head back to Umm Qasr. Is everyone comfortable with that? Okay, then let's go to Umm Qasr.' At some point, I'm responsible for the camera crew, and there was another producer with us, there was a satellite technician. We had two 'fixers' [translators]; one was an Iraqi and one was an Egyptian. So I was ultimately responsible for them. I'm also ultimately responsible for the product of what is going to get on TV and where we are in being in a position to offer something to a CBS program. Getting to Umm Qasr, where there was clearly a serious firefight going on, and hooking up with one of the most forward-leading units down there in the south, the Marine Fox Company, was a decision that we all made, but I wanted to park ourselves there and be able to stay with them and find out what the story was."

Although he said that producers and correspondents work together in many different ways, he and Pelley generally sat down and talked about the script and how the piece was going to go. Because Pelley is an excellent writer, Owens functioned more as an editor when they worked together. Although there was a satellite technician along, Owens had to make sure that the satellite was operating at a time that would not interfere with military operations and that would respect the eight-hour time difference, whereas someone in New York would be available to catch their pictures and narrations. He was doing everything from telling people where they were going to sleep to making sure the pictures got to New York. He made sure the editor in New York who was going to put their pieces together knew what they were talking about, line by line. "We didn't have an editor with us. We weren't able to edit our own material. I don't think any of the embeds were really able to do that, either. But we did have the luxury of having a satellite dish, so we could feed whenever we wanted and not [just] when the military said we could. Except on the days when there were still open firefights going on in this compound, we weren't able to feed whenever we wanted, but we had a lot more flexibility than the embeds did, that's for sure."

Owens said that they never had a problem with the satellite. "It was unbelievable. We were in the middle of nowhere and feeding out our stuff with zero problems." He said that they had no problem getting access to satellites either. He credits his satellite technician with keeping all their equipment operating for as long as possible.

It is difficult for him to compare the experiences of unilaterals and embeds. "Honestly, one of the things about being over there is that we really felt at a disadvantage in that we couldn't see anything [on television], obviously. We didn't know how coverage was going. It was sort of fits and starts it seemed for the embeds. We'd hear, 'Boy oh boy, this embed and that embed—they've got nothing' or "Boy oh boy this embed really had something today.'"

After five weeks, Owens and his crew made the decision to return to Kuwait City. "We were up north of An Nasiriyah when we ran into a familiar problem with doing any story out of doors, and certainly in a desert. Our equipment was beginning to die. Since the first night of the war we had lost two cameras, and we were down to our last camera. We lost one tape deck and our second tape deck, which was the only way to get the pictures out, was on its last leg. So, we knew we needed to go and replenish our equipment. There was no way to do that other than to leave the country. So, we went back to Kuwait City."

When he got back to Kuwait, he learned that his mother's health had deteriorated and that he needed to come back to the States. He returned on the day Saddam Hussein's statue came down in Baghdad. Owens, who was thirty-six years old when the war began, had a six-month-old baby, a pregnant wife, and a terminally ill mother at home. "There were a lot of reasons for me to not want to go do this assignment. But this is what we do, and I don't ever not want to be a part of covering an important story. Since I've been at CBS, I've been involved in almost all of them. I didn't want this one to go by without me being involved. I said to my wife at one point, 'There is a community of journalists, and it's really easy for you to think one of the other ones is going to go do it. But this is really what we all do, and it's important that we do it, because if we aren't there to tell the story, who is?' That sounds cornbally, but that is actually a conversation that we had."

Was the danger and personal inconvenience worth spending five weeks covering the war? "Absolutely. Look, the first night of the war we were where we wanted to be. I don't know that the Pentagon wanted us to be there at all. But we were on TV before anyone else was, saying that there is now fighting on the border, and showing pictures of it happening. We were then able to cross the border by ourselves and be in position. Sometimes you're lucky, and we were a lot of times. We were in Umm Qasr when the first major battle happened. We weren't restricted in what we said or did by anything or anyone. That was great," he said. "Is it dangerous? Yes, of course it is; there is no doubt about that. The freedom to do your job without the military telling you what you can do and where you can go doesn't outweigh the safety issues, but it allows you to do your job better. It allowed us to, anyway."

## NOTES

1. The Fedayeen Saddam, or Saddam's Men of Sacrifice, was a thirty-thousand-to forty-thousand-member Iraqi paramilitary group that appeared to be leading guerrilla-style attacks on coalition forces in southern Iraq.

2. RPG-7 is a reloadable, shoulder-fired, muzzle-loaded, recoilless antitank and antipersonnel grenade launcher.

# Radio Journalists

# IVAN WATSON

FOREIGN CORRESPONDENT, NATIONAL PUBLIC RADIO, NORTHERN IRAQ

Ivan Watson, NPR foreign correspondent, is a member of the new generation of journalists who has gotten a lot of on-the-job training covering war. At the age of twenty-eight, he had already covered U.S. military action in Afghanistan and Iraq for NPR and before that was a producer in CNN's Moscow bureau.

Working in Afghanistan proved to be good preparation for covering the war in northern Iraq. Watson said that, in some ways, conditions were worse in Afghanistan. He purchased a generator and car battery that never left his side in Afghanistan, but electrical power supply in northern Iraq was reliable. He arrived in Afghanistan in October 2002 and stayed for about a month before taking a two-week break. He then returned for a couple of weeks.

Special Operations forces were involved in the fighting in both Afghanistan and northern Iraq, which provided a very different working environment than most embedded reporters encounter. "Up until the fall of Kabul, I think I had only three or four sightings of Americans, unlike Iraq, where you would see Special Forces driving on the road every day or so, especially when the fighting started. In northern Afghanistan they were much more discreet until Kabul fell," Watson said.

He also had some unpleasant experiences in Afghanistan. "Some of the most dangerous time for me in Afghanistan was when I tried to approach the Americans, when I'd figure out where they were and tried to go there," he said. "They would have illiterate teenage guards who could be threatening and downright dangerous. I insisted that my driver move us up to where I thought an American aircraft had landed. They struck my driver in the back with the butts of their Kalashnikov rifles, and these kids seemed only a step away from shooting us. They were so agitated and high on adrenaline."

He said that up until the battle of Tora Bora, most of the American military activity occurred at night, and American troops tried to remain hidden as much as possible. "I never chatted informally, much less on the record, with any of these Special Forces soldiers." But later on, when a larger number of soldiers landed and established a military base, Watson was able to approach some of the American troops and have conversations and get interviews from time to time.

Access evolved quite dramatically over a series of three or four months, he said, possibly because the number of Americans on the ground increased. "It's one thing when you've got a couple of teams of Special Forces moving around, and it's another thing when you have a thousand airborne army soldiers conducting an operation such as Operation Anaconda with helicopters. That was a very dramatic change," he said. "The bulk of the fighting that we saw up until the fall of Kabul involved the Afghan Northern Alliance fighters and then American aircraft that would fly miles above the ground. That was about it." But by March 2002, with the launch of Operation Anaconda, there were helicopters racing around, in addition to planes. "You could see far more American soldiers. You just can't hide those people as well."

The two wars have changed things, Watson believes. "Afghanistan really caught a lot of journalists off guard in how difficult, primitive, and backward the whole thing was. People brought that experience to Iraq and were able to use that some. The two wars, happening so close together, have allowed a younger generation of journalists, such as myself, to get a lot of experiences very quickly. I know I learned a lot from that. I now know more of the questions you have to ask when there is an incident or in the lead-up to something. It's been an opportunity to get on-the-job training."

Although he is normally based in Turkey, Watson entered northern Iraq from Iran on February 10. "Almost all of us in the north, about two hundred correspondents in Kurdish-held territory, were unilaterals. A few, maybe four or five, journalists showed up later with the American troops who parachuted in and were embedded with them," he said.

Watson said that after Afghanistan, being in northern Iraq seemed like a vacation, although a dangerous one. "There is no question that compared to what was going on in the south that our experiences were vastly different. Fighting was incomparable to the massive battles that were going on in the south. And we were far more comfortable. We were really living in hotels—not five-star hotels—but it wasn't often camping out; that began after the front was moving forward.

"Compared to Afghanistan this was far more comfortable, and infrastructure was better. The roads were paved; there was a decent supply of electricity and running water; and there were telephone communications and Internet cafés. There also were hospitals and doctors, so that was a bit better. But it was isolated geographically. Because of the politics of the region, it was very difficult to get in and out of northern Iraq through Iran," he said. "It was virtually impossible through

Turkey, except for one brief window when they let a lot of people in. And Syria was also quite difficult. Of course, we couldn't go south into Baghdad-controlled Iraq."

He said there were a number of threats. "There was this al Qaeda–type group, Ansar al-Islam, in the mountains on the Iranian border, and they had been very successful with high-level assassinations of secular Kurdish leadership. There were concerns about the hotels that journalists were staying in—that they could be attacked or something like that. Iraqi artillery was surprisingly good and would come out of nowhere. Not too often fortunately, but it scared the pants off you. It was really terrifying," he said. "I'm one of the believers that journalists overseas are a kind of fraternity—men and women. Once we're in a crazy country, we don't have a lot of resources. We don't have weapons. The U.S. embassies in many countries are not going to do an awfully lot to help me out if I get in trouble. The first people that I'll turn to in any of these countries are other journalists. In many cases you can feel, especially in a war zone, that you can go up to complete strangers and completely change their day by asking them to help you, if you are stranded or in trouble. In northern Iraq, coping methods were what you talked about. When there were fatalities and terrible things happened, you'd sit around and talk about strategies or different approaches to doing things."

A number of journalists were killed in northern Iraq. "There was a BBC team that hit a land mine. They had one fatality and one serious injury. There was an Australian cameraman who was hit in a suicide car bombing around that little Ansar al-Islam group along the Iranian border. There was another BBC crew that was hit in probably the worst friendly-fire incident of the war. Eighteen Kurds were killed in that, including the BBC crew's translator. So there definitely were fatalities up there. It was dangerous, but as is often the case in war or any kind of conflict, it was difficult to tell where the danger might come from," he said.

Watson said that he formed bonds with other journalists covering the war and that they often shared information using Thuraya sat phones, which were banned only in southern Iraq. "I cooperated [with fellow journalists]. One of the fascinating things about this conflict is that the majority of us had these Thuraya handheld satellite phones. With these phones, you can just point out the window of your car or the window of your hotel and make a phone call. They are great," he said. "One function they had was instant messaging as well. So there was a fair amount of chatter going back and forth, especially when the fighting started, using the instant messaging. People let each other know where there was fighting or shelling going on at any one point, how dangerous it was, and would ask, 'Hey, what is going on at your end?'"

Typical messages would be, "I'm at this little border town Chumchumal. The Iraqis withdrew 15 kilometers and then fired rockets. The Kurds have started looting the front lines where the Iraqis were. What are you doing for dinner tonight?"

"It was a really effective way of trying to keep a handle on what was going on all along this front line in an area where it would be several hours' drive from one point to another," Watson said. "There was a great deal of cooperation, and it was interesting how some of it took place. You could compose one little message and send it out to ten or fifteen people, giving them an update of where you are and hear what was going on fifty miles away.

"There was a time where things weren't really moving along the northern front and there had been just one too many of these tragedies, and there was a group of us who operated a lot together, and we knew that one friend, who is technically my competition but who I cooperated quite closely with, had escorted the body of Kaveh Golestan to the border, and we knew we needed a bit of a breather," he said. "We had been there more than a month. We had been sleeping with gas masks beside our bed all the time. There was fear, there was uncertainty, and there was dread because nobody knew what was going to happen. We said, 'Let's just do this,' and we went up to this lake and fished and took an hour-long ride in a leaky motorboat. It helped. We didn't spend an awful lot of time talking about loss and death, and things like that. It was just taking a little breather. As it turned out the following morning, while folks were having breakfast and planning where to go the next day, I got a phone call about the BBC crew who got hit by an American air strike, and I had to rush out to go cover that. But I was glad I'd had that one night, and I think the others were glad as well."

He prefers to deal with his stress and emotions with his colleagues. "NPR offers therapy or group sessions back in Washington, but we're pretty far away from that. Calling home to your friends and family is good, but it is a bit of a stretch for them to understand some of this stuff. Sometimes you talk to them about it, but it can be too much for them. They are worried, too; and they don't understand— I mean some of the everyday stuff can be really terrifying for them. When things happened, I never wanted to lay it on them too much. I want my mother to be able to sleep at night. So, I think some of that really comes out with the other journalists," he said.

He watched the war in southern Iraq on television "just like everybody else." Northern Iraq, under the Kurds, was allowed to have satellite dishes. "This was not the kind of information vacuum we had in Afghanistan, where you pretty much got information from your shortwave radio and satellite Internet connection," he said.

Nearly all the journalists in the north had to compete for translators and drivers. "The typical team up north was a correspondent with a driver and a translator. You should have seen the prices go up as the journalistic population went up," he said.

He had his own fiasco in that regard. "My translator had worked with me for a month, and I'd given him a raise. He was a young guy who was pretty charismatic. He engineered to leave me to go work with Australian ABC television. I was pretty upset about it. He had given me no advance warning. I thought we were better friends! So, he left, and I had to find a translator because I was left in the lurch, and I had to hunt around. Then two or three days later the U.S. launched cruise missiles at the Halabja area where the Australian TV crew was hit in the suicide car bombing. My former translator was burned in the back of the head. He always wore this black leather jacket that he was really proud of, and it may have protected him during the explosion. He told my driver and some of the other translators that he was fed up with journalists, and he was never going to work with them again."

Watson developed ways of determining whom he could trust. "Especially when hiring drivers and translators, you are always careful. Maybe you make little tests, or you make it a point not to exhibit the money you are carrying. Periodically, you do get let down by people you are hiring and rely on, whether it's like little petty theft or suddenly not showing up for work or running to another journalist who is paying more money," he said. "I'd been in northern Iraq a year prior—in Kurdistan, if I can call it that—I had worked with a young university graduate, an aspiring journalist, for several weeks. I trusted her, and she was a good contact for getting in touch with people. I kind of knew Kurds themselves might try to control some information and certainly spin us or bar me from some information. But ultimately we could trust them with our lives. There was no question about that. The Kurds were not out to get us. They were really excited to see us—the factions that ruled the place. I felt really safe with the people, also. Despite a kind of spotty history with the U.S.—a couple of instances when the Kurds said the U.S. out-and-out betrayed the Kurds—Americans were very popular, and the Kurds were very eager to get their stories told, being as isolated as they were."

His work before the war mostly involved figuring out whose troops were where. "I made a number of trips going out to look at Turkish soldiers who had been stationed in what was Iraqi Kurdistan in northern Iraq for six years. About a year ago, after one of the Kurdish factions had denied that there were any Turkish troops on their territory and told me not to go looking for them, I went and found thirty to forty Turkish tanks sitting in an abandoned old airstrip in a part of northern Iraq," he said. "On this trip, one of the first things I did was go to see if Turks were still there and if their numbers had gone up or down. So, when the tensions heated up and a big controversy erupted with Turkey, I monitored it very closely. The Kurds came out very loudly warning of resistance against the Turks. Within a matter of days they had turned from facing south against Saddam, and at least one of the main factions was now facing northwest toward Turkey. So, I spent a fair amount of time covering this. There were lots of rumors of more Turkish troops entering than had already been there. I went on a few wild-goose chases trying to find them."

When the war began, it was much different in the north than in the south. "Unlike the south, the north did not have massive battles involving hundreds of tanks and movements of tens of thousands of troops. There were skirmishes along the front line, with the Iraqi army fighting against a few dozen U.S. Special Forces and dozens of Kurdish peshmerga fighters, and a few American war planes," he said. "That was the battle you had on the northern front—which was not to say that it wasn't dramatic, but the danger there was basically a matter of how close you came to those skirmishes."

The American Special Forces in the area weren't eager to be spotted. "In the month or so before the war started, everybody knew the Americans were there— the Kurds knew it, we knew it. But it was kept out of the public eye. The Americans were hidden off in little mountain retreats and things like that, that belonged to the Kurdish leadership. The Kurds were not allowed to talk about it, clearly, by the Americans, but sometimes hinted at it," Watson said. "Over the course of the following weeks, you started seeing these guys. The Americans would drive around in civilian trucks, escorted often by Kurdish fighters. They were definitely there, and when they saw a journalist, they would jump into their cars and leave. In one case, a photographer photographed one of this group of either CIA or Special Forces or some intelligence group, and the Kurds actually took the photographer's camera and took out the film. They were definitely avoiding us and did not want us to contact the Americans who were based in the area at that time."

Sometimes the encounters took on an almost comical aspect. "There was a really ridiculous moment in one front-line town. While waiting outside a commander's office, several colleagues and I spotted two or three pickup trucks go past that clearly had Special Forces in them, and we jumped in our cars and started following them. We followed them around this little town in circles and up and down a couple of roads. It was a convoy of about six or seven vehicles at this point," he said. "And they went down a road and came to the end of a dirt road that turned to mud, and they got stuck. I stepped out of my truck and went to their truck to say, 'Hey, this is silly. I know you can't really talk to us.' I didn't have a microphone out; I didn't have a camera. I just wanted to make contact. The troops just rolled up their windows, looked straight ahead, and slowly made a three-point turn in the mud and drove away. Their Kurdish guards were friendly—shook hands and everything like that. That was what it was like at that point."

But it was a different story when the bombing started. "The American military put on this great big show by parachuting into an airstrip that the Kurds had been preparing for them for months. Suddenly there were airborne soldiers just standing there; there was no denying it. That was a political message not only in Iraq but also certainly for neighboring Turkey that Americans were officially in northern Iraq."

After that, Watson said journalists had better access. "We could go in and talk to these guys. In some cases in this series of skirmishes along the northern front, Special Forces that were fighting would allow you to sit and watch and would give long interviews and sit and chat for a long time. This was not with any public affairs/press-type person," he said. "You could listen as they called in air strikes, and things like that. Some journalists opted to stay with them overnight to see what they were doing. And when they would get frustrated by the number of journalists who were watching, or if people were rude or taking too many pictures and the situation was tense, sometimes they would just send the journalists away. But you could work and have some access to those Special Forces along those northern front skirmishes and battles."

Watson acknowledges that journalists had a difficult time being objective because of their affinity for the Kurds. "We were definitely with the Kurds; we were alongside these people and were probably influenced by that to some degree, even when you are trying to be very objective. They hated Saddam, and we heard about this. It had become part of their ideology, and we were probably influenced by some of that. We didn't have to sacrifice or make a lot of conditions to work with Kurds. We were pretty free to operate unless they prevented us from going to a place, and often you could sneak around their checkpoints. They would try to bar access to front lines presumably because Americans were operating there, and it became a bit of a game to get around there.

"In the south, if you are working with any group of people and you are side by side with them and if you risk your life with them, there's a bond that is very deep. I said goodbye to my translator who had been with me for the bulk of the fighting. He wasn't an especially talented guy, and we didn't have a whole lot in common; but we'd had to drive in cars with bullets whizzing overhead and drive away screaming. And when we said goodbye, there were a few tears because there was a kind of bond there. I certainly had it with the Kurds as well. When they are celebrating, when they are excited, you can't ignore that," he said. "But part of the job is to be able to report as objectively as you can. The first day I came into Kirkuk, the front lines fell, and I drove across the front line. The Kurds were pouring into this city—this was their so-called Jerusalem, and there were big celebrations going on, and they were doing their own version of pulling down Saddam's statue and cheering and dancing—just a lot of excitement. I was reporting live from right next to that statue, and in the middle of that an Iraqi came up to me speaking in English and said, 'Help! Help! Some Kurd just stole my car.' Now, it's an exciting moment, and there is a sense of victory and a deep bond with the Kurds, but the Kurds were doing this same thing as in the south—they began looting. They were guilty of excesses, and I began reporting on them the same day. You can't blind yourself to that."

Watson also has reported on the political aims of the Kurds. "The Kurdish leadership is on the governing counsel in Baghdad. They've been there since day one. Though the Kurds do want a federal system, they do want to continue to have some degree of autonomy, but they insist they want to remain part of Iraq," he said. "People have been living in northern Iraq in this Kurdish statelet for more than a decade," he said. "The younger generation doesn't speak Arabic too well, which is a big problem. I need to get different sets of translators when I'm working in Baghdad and southern Arabic Iraq; and when I go back up to Kurdistan, I have to switch translators. Someone from Baghdad cannot function in the streets of northern Iraq, even to get a taxi. I know more Kurdish than many of them do."

Watson has seen the frustration with the American occupation. "The frustration with the American occupation is huge, and the disappointment is huge. There is some truth to it because it was pretty remarkable how disorganized the Americans seemed when it came to what to do next. As an American and a patriot, despite journalistic objectivity, I wanted things to improve and get better," he said. "I knew that Saddam Hussein was one of the most evil things ever, and I knew that only a war could get rid of him, as did most Kurds. They were in favor of this; they were the most pro-war people in the world, I think. It was disappointing to see how disorganized and unprepared the Americans seemed to be. In fact, a couple of months later, I don't think any of my Iraqi acquaintances would say their life is better than it was before the war. The universities have been looted. The kids are sitting on the floor only two hours a day. There is a lot of skepticism about the American occupation—why is it happening, what's it for, what do they really want to do, how could they mess up that? To the military's credit, they really spared the infrastructure of the country. And then, everything has been wrecked afterward. That's the ultimate irony of the whole thing."

Although he thought the embed program worked, he had no desire to participate in the program. "First, I'd been in northern Iraq before, and I wanted to cover Kurds. Second, the U.S. military has a publicity machine—it is one. It gets frustrating very quickly to see soldiers looking to their public affairs officers whether they can talk about this or that when you are talking to them. There have been enough times in Afghanistan when the military will say one thing, and then you'd go on the ground to a place and you'd see something completely different. You certainly can't trust everything the military says. I don't think I was very interested in doing the embed program at all. For the next big thing, maybe things will change, but in this one, this is the only way I wanted to do this."

Watson was still reporting from Iraq when Saddam's sons were killed and when Saddam himself was captured. "I arrived in Mosul the night of the battle with Saddam's sons and spent the night on a rooftop fifty yards from the smoking leftovers of the building in which they'd held their last stand," he said. "I was in Baghdad when Saddam was captured, and traveled to Tikrit the following morning for reactions from Saddam's clan."

Although he occasionally takes breaks in Turkey, he has spent much of the year following the major military action and reporting on the aftermath—perhaps putting himself in more danger than he was in during the war. "It's chaotic and crazy. And it's gotten worse. It's inevitable at some stage that the people who are attacking soldiers every day will start turning to other foreigners. This seems to be a logical progression."

### "Journalists and War," An Online Report from Ivan Watson in Northern Iraq

*This essay was filed for npr.org by NPR correspondent Ivan Watson, who has been reporting from northern Iraq and traveling with Kurdish fighters and U.S. Special Forces.*

April 6, 2003—I took a break from the war this weekend, by spending last night at a mountain lake resort called Dukan. This decision came after I realized that too many of the people I eat dinner with have recently been killed or injured covering this conflict.

Since the war began, three of my colleagues have died here in northern Iraq—most recently, an award-winning Iranian camera-man for BBC named Kaveh Golestan.

I can still picture Kaveh's face from when I met him at breakfast in Suleymaniye about a week-and-a-half ago. He was a small, grizzled guy whose face was covered with white stubble. Old enough to be my father, Kaveh had been a journalist covering conflicts around the world while I was still in diapers. And yet he exhibited no bitterness or cynicism. Instead, I was struck by the way he softly enunciated his words, by the way he patiently answered my questions about the Iran-Iraq War in the 1980s, by the way he'd give this funny, sweet smile in between puffs on his cigarette.

At one point, he described how several of his Iranian colleagues recently passed away of mysterious health complications. This happened some 15 years after they had all covered the aftermath of the Iraqi army's chemical weapons bombardment of the Kurdish town of Halabja in 1988. It was the most deadly use of airborne poisons against a civilian population in modern history.

Kaveh photographed the carnage just three days after it happened. He suspected his friends came in contact with the chemicals while trying to help transport some of the wounded civilians. They remained healthy and strong for more than a decade—and then abruptly died from cancer and respiratory illnesses.

Last Wednesday, Kaveh's television crew struck land mines after traveling to the front-line Kurdish town of Kifre, which was under bombardment from Iraqi artillery. Kaveh was killed instantly. His producer Stuart Hughes, a young British guy I'd had dinner with several nights in a row last month, suffered severe injuries.

Stu was just medevacked out of the country. I hear he may lose his foot. Meanwhile, my friend Quill was one of a group of people who escorted Kaveh's body to the Iranian border.

The land mine incident occurred after a veteran ITN correspondent I'd also met at dinner fell to his death mysteriously off the roof of his hotel. This tragedy followed a suicide car bombing in the Halabja Valley that killed Paul Moran, an Australian Broadcasting Company cameraman.

Now Paul's photo hangs in the lobby of the Suleymaniye Palace Hotel. The Kurds are calling him a martyr. At least five Kurds were also killed in the explosion, and dozens suffered burns and shrapnel wounds. One of the injured men was Handren, a chubby, chuckling Kurd who had just finished a month-long stint as my translator.

Over the last week, I've had to dive on the ground three times to escape incoming Iraqi machine gun fire and artillery. The last time came at the end of a day-long battle between Kurds and U.S. Special Forces against Iraqi troops, fighting for control of a bridge leading to Mosul. After burying my face in the dirt of an abandoned Iraqi fox hole during a gun battle, I opted to drive several miles away from the scene of the battle. I stopped at a hilltop where CNN had been camping out for the past three weeks.

A group of us sat there at sunset, watching fighter jets circle overhead, dropping bomb after bomb on Iraqi targets in the distance, when we heard the sudden woosh and subsequent thud of an artillery shell landing several dozen yards away. I was amazed at how quickly the entire group immediately dove on the ground. Then dusting ourselves off, we started nervously walking towards our vehicles. Suddenly another round flew in, landing even closer than the first. All of us fled. The CNN crew didn't even stop to gather their satellite dish and equipment.

Fortunately, no one was injured. Later investigation of at least three nearby blast-sites showed the Iraqis appeared to have been targeting the CNN position from a battery miles away. Saddam Hussein's soldiers are far more skilled with their artillery than I ever imagined.

I am writing this journal entry from the balcony of my hotel room, overlooking Lake Dukan. A storm front is whipping wind across the water.

My "break" is evidently over. I've just received a phone call from a colleague informing me that another BBC television crew has just been hit, this time by friendly fire. The team was driving with American Special Forces and Kurdish guerilla fighters when a U.S. jet mistakenly bombed them. Among the more than 50 people who were accidentally killed and wounded was BBC's translator, Kamaran Abdurazaq Muhamed. Fred Scott, a BBC cameraman I had beers with just a few nights ago, videotaped the aftermath of the explosion. He was bleeding on his own camera.

Unlike the millions of Iraqi civilians who are facing similar threats and dangers, all of the journalists here chose to come to this country. Our motivations vary: glory, duty, curiosity. First and foremost, though, we came to cover the news. We all knew the risks. And yet, I can't help but fear it's just a matter of time before one of us again becomes a casualty of this conflict.

# ANNE GARRELS

SENIOR FOREIGN CORRESPONDENT, NATIONAL PUBLIC RADIO, BAGHDAD, IRAQ

Anne Garrels, senior foreign correspondent for National Public Radio, initially went to Baghdad in October 2002. "It was clear there was going to be a war," she said. "I went there to be NPR's eyes and ears on the ground. Luckily, in some ways, NPR fell beneath their radar and, even given restrictions, I was able to report in a straightforward manner about all aspects of the issues."

Garrels said that the Iraqis didn't pay attention to radio per se. "They were much more concerned about the people they were seeing in real time, like the BBC or CNN. I was far less noticeable. As frustrating as it was, it did seem worthwhile, so I kept going back, and then each time it was enormously difficult to get visas. CNN has admitted, along with other broadcast organizations, that they were under far more constraints because of visas. The Iraqis doled out visas very gingerly and rescinded them similarly. I decided to stay for the war."

She said the decision to stay was a tough call, done in consultation with NPR. "After Bush spoke and set a deadline, it got very crazy. Some journalists just lost it in the tension. Others wanted to stay, but their bosses determined that they would not, or could not, stay. NPR wrestled with it day and night. We took it a day at a time."

Garrels said that she was determined to stay. "I felt committed to being there, but none of us knew for sure if we would be okay. I felt I had a good chance [of being safe], given an extraordinary Iraqi who was working with me. Although there was no guarantee of safety, I had some escape routes if it came to that. Frankly, there were an awfully lot of unknowns. But you work on gut instincts. I have turned down other assignments because they were too bloody dangerous and with no chance of results. But in this case, I gambled and—thank God—it was okay."

Garrels said that her arrangements with her Iraqi driver (who was not a government-assigned minder) evolved slowly over time. "As the war approached, we talked about his ability and desire to continue to work with me despite the danger. He just grew [in importance] with each passing day. It was a relationship and trust that had evolved over many months." Her driver spoke English and Arabic, whereas Garrels could communicate in English and Russian. She said that many Iraqis had trained in either the former Soviet Union or post-Soviet Russia. She had spent time in the Soviet Union as a foreign correspondent, so between her English and Russian and her driver's Arabic, they were able to function quite well.

Garrels said that getting access to officials was more of a barrier than the language problem. "Trying to get to people—given the Information Ministry system, the classic Soviet system was difficult. I needed my Iraqi driver because of the dangers that have become all too clear in the aftermath. People were afraid to be seen around any of us. The Baath Party blanketed the city in the weeks and days leading up to the war and after the war. The Information Ministry system was the classic Soviet system of people squealing on each other—not to mention the fact that every neighborhood was blanketed with security." Given the difficulties involved, Garrels said that her driver became her eyes and ears. "I would give him tasks, and he would go out and do them and come back with a tape. He could move around less noticeably than I, but I also was out every day and still seeing people. I was trying to get a pulse of the various communities, especially during the war."

When she was moving about the city, Garrels said that she didn't have to worry much about conforming her dress to Muslim standards because before the war there was a wide spectrum of attire in Iraq. "Lots of Iraqi women did not wear a veil. More and more were wearing head scarves; and, on occasion, I would wear a silk scarf on my head, but I did not wear the classic Shiite, long black garments. Clothing was not an issue, but it's now becoming one, I think." She usually wore trousers and a long-sleeved shirt while she was working.

She did occasionally have to make some accommodations to Islamic tradition when she was working in Afghanistan. "On one occasion I wore a burqa, and that was at the insistence of the mullah whom I was interviewing."

Garrels, fifty-two years old during the Iraq invasion, uses both her age and gender to advantage in the Muslim world. "I have a lot more leeway than I did as a younger woman. At one level, working as a woman, people just deal with us as sexless Westerners who are journalists. I never had any trouble in Afghanistan—really anywhere—dealing with officials. Even dealing with Islamics in Pakistan, I was able to interview officials. There were a couple of occasions when I was told specifically that they wouldn't see me because I was a woman. But then it was made clear to them that I was over fifty. At that point there was a safety zone. Mullahs who said they would not speak to me did because I was older." Garrels has a sense of humor about dealing with the "younger" mullahs, especially the one who had harbored John Walker Lindh in Pakistan. "When I arrived to interview him,

the people in the village said, 'But you don't look fifty!' and then there was a huddle about how they were going to cope with me." She solved the problem by donning a burqa to placate the thirty-six-year-old mullah.

She said that she was accepted as "Western and weird and sexless," a decided
advantage on more than one occasion. "I've been able to work both sides of the
street more effectively than male journalists because I can go in and see the
women while men really can't, and men don't really think of me as a woman. So,
it actually works much to my benefit. Curiously, in a way, the more segregated the
society, the more access I have."

During the early days of the war, Garrels and the other foreign journalists who
were still in Baghdad lived and worked in the Palestine Hotel, which was inun-
dated with Information Ministry people who were then replaced by security officials. "We didn't know who they were, but we could guess. The [hotel] staff
undoubtedly was debriefed as to what we were doing and what was in our rooms.
The big issue was our means of communication—the satellite phone. I was only
supposed to use it at the Information Ministry. But when the war started, there
was no suitable space to work there, and it was a [military] target. So I removed
myself from there with my phone. That was constantly an issue because I had to
hide it the entire time and was working in the shadows."

While still in power, the Iraqi officials made life difficult one minute and then
sought media coverage the next. "You could get out into the city—it was difficult—
but you could. We bribed an Iraqi official who became our minder—who wasn't
really a minder. So, we had a certain amount of freedom, but it ebbed and flowed
in terms of how strict they were. They would clamp down one day, but then there
would be a bombing or explosion of unclear origin, and they were so keen to as-
cribe it to the U.S. they would say, 'Okay, you can go on your own.' But the next day
you were told you could only go on the [supplied] buses." Garrels said that journalists were permitted to go out for a meal or to buy food, and she would use those
occasions to go see people to try to get interviews.

Some journalists were monitored much more closely than others. She said
John Burns, the *New York Times* correspondent, was watched closely. Garrels's
driver told her that the Iraqis were focusing on her more and more because they
thought she was a spy. "He had to dissuade them from this by saying, 'She's an old
lady who doesn't know what she's doing. Don't worry about it!'" Garrels said that
they never seemed to pull her transcripts; furthermore, because of her driver's
clever response and the timing in general, she had a lot more freedom than she
might have had.

Garrels said that 150 journalists were in Baghdad when the war broke out
(among them, only 16 Americans), compared with upwards of 500 before the war
began. There was no Western television during the war other than the BBC—no
CNN or American networks. The remaining journalists had to decide whom
among their colleagues they could trust. Garrels said that although she did have

some old friends among the journalists remaining, she didn't trust everyone in the press corps. She was not impressed with a young female journalist who told her she would do anything to stay in Baghdad because she wanted to be a star in her native Greece. "You are dealing with a bunch of journalists, many of whom were doing things to stay on and get visas. I know of one young European journalist who was talking far too freely to the Iraqis—sucking up in order to continue to get visas. It wasn't just a question of Arab/non-Arab. You don't know these journalists; you don't know what they've done. I had some old and dear friends from all parts of the world whom I had known for many years and trusted." However, Garrels said that she did not tell the journalists she didn't know how she was getting information or what equipment she had.

She said that the remaining Americans didn't work as a group but that they did look after each other. "We were all friends who crossed national borders. But because we were such a small group, there was a certain amount of making sure we were okay. We talked, compared notes, but did not work as a large amoeba-like group. I didn't know what people were reporting. I was on a different schedule than the others because they were mostly newspapers and photographers."

Peter Arnett, who was part of the CNN team who covered the bombing of Baghdad during the 1991 Gulf War, was fired from NBC and the Discovery Channel because he talked too freely with officials on Iraqi television. Garrels said that some journalists had signed a petition of support for him. "The issue is complicated," she said. "It was not smart of Peter to have done what he did, but it was sad to see the focus become more about Peter Arnett than about the real issues of the war."

She also thinks that the bombing of Al Jazeera's headquarters was not in the same category as the bombing of the Palestine Hotel that occurred later the same day. Al Jazeera television had had its own headquarters, so its correspondents were not working out of the Palestine Hotel. "Al Jazeera was allowed to be free, in the general sense that it had its own building and exclusive camera position. Everyone except Al Jazeera and Abu Dhabi Television had to work out of the Palestine Hotel. Al Jazeera's building was right in the middle of the firestorm. They said they had given coordinates to the Americans, but this was the ground war, and they were right in the middle of it. Nobody in their right minds would have stayed where they were. Initially, after the correspondent was killed in the bombing, the Al Jazeera bureau chief said they were in the middle of a residential district. That simply was not true. They were right next to the Republican palace in the midst of the Information Ministry, just where all the fighting was going on. That was clear and had been for days. The death of the correspondent was a tragedy that could have been avoided. They put themselves in an indefensible position."

Garrels does not think the same could be said for the journalists who were staying in the Palestine Hotel when the Americans rolled in and shelled the building. (Garrels referred to the report issued by the Committee to Protect Journalists, which she said issued an excellent report on the incident.) "The Palestine was the only place in town where all of us journalists were, and it has distinctive architecture. The military has told so many stories, and the initial explanation was not credible." Although the military claimed that they had been fired on from a sniper in the lobby or perhaps the roof of the hotel, Garrels said that that was physically impossible. "We were all on our balconies, facing where the troops were looking. There was no outgoing fire. The distance was also impossible. We were a kilometer from where the troops were. A sniper with a gun couldn't possibly have hit them. None of it added up." Garrels remained at the hotel after the bombing because she thought it would be safer. "There was a day when all Iraqi information and security people just disappeared into the woodwork. That day, we could see the troops and see the tanks but—other than the shelling—had had no immediate contact with them. By the end of the day they took up positions around the Palestine. Because the looting had begun, everyone was quite relieved when the troops got to the hotel, in as much as we all had huge amounts of cash and equipment. Our minders and security people had ripped off many journalists just before they departed. We were concerned we would be a target for looters or assassins."

Garrels stood on a bridge and watched the American tanks roll into Baghdad. "I saw these kids in their tanks, and I could literally touch one of the kids as his tank rolled underneath me. You hadn't met them, but you *knew* them. I thought, 'I bet you're from Illinois'—he looked so young and somehow familiar. I found myself weeping—weeping with relief. Two of my colleagues had been killed the day before. The bombing had been so accurate that it was scary in a curious way, but people were frazzled and frayed. The looting and burning had started, and you wondered where was this going to go. There was relief that they got there without the hideous battle that we thought was going to happen. But when the statue came down, I didn't feel relief."

Garrels was present when the statue of Saddam Hussein was pulled from its pedestal outside the Palestine Hotel. Although the incident was carried live by U.S. television networks and was pictured prominently on the front pages of most American and international newspapers the following day, Garrels thinks the incident was overplayed. "I have seen statues come down in many countries—including in the Soviet Union. Pulling down statutes does nothing to resolve issues of how you got to where you are and how you are going forward. The press didn't encourage them intentionally, and the marines didn't start it. The Iraqis were thrilled that Saddam had disappeared, and it looked like the regime was over. The group at the statue was very small, and they felt protected next to the hotel and with marines in the vicinity. They couldn't have done it in other parts of the city because they couldn't be sure they wouldn't be shot by someone." She said that the Iraqis initially threw the soles of their shoes at the statue, a sign of great disrespect. Perhaps all too symbolic of the relationship between the United States and the Iraqi people since 1991, the Iraqis couldn't pull Saddam down on their own; the marines rolled up with a tank and a boom to help. One of the marines draped an American flag over the face of Saddam and then, remembering orders against displaying American flags, he replaced it with an Iraqi flag.

Garrels said that many Iraqis standing around were saying that pulling down the statue didn't mean anything. "It was too simplistic," she said. NPR asked Garrels to do an update after her initial report. "I've seen these statues come and go. They make great television pictures, but I thought the incident should be kept in perspective, given the events in the rest of the city. NPR wanted me to go much more on the glorious end, and I said, 'Bullshit!'"

Garrels said that her refusal to give the incident bigger play and to avoid the "herd mentality" is one her proudest moments. "I'd been in the hotel eating lunch with my driver when the troops arrived and the statue came down. I ran down to cover the event and spoke to lots of Iraqis who were there and then went back to eat the remnants of my lunch. My driver, whom I know well and who hated Saddam and his regime, was crying, and not with happiness. It was enormously conflicting emotions seeing the marines. Outside the hotel, the attitude of many who were down on the street was, 'Why couldn't we do this ourselves? Why are the Americans here?' I reported that that night while everyone else was going nuts about the statue coming down."

Soon, Garrels had to decide whether to stay in Iraq or return to the United States. "Initially I said I would stay on for another few weeks, but when all the press corps flowed in from Jordan—I saw Christiane Amanpour and Dan Rather walking down my hallway—I knew I was exhausted. I knew the war was going on for a long time. I figured I would leave and let them deal with whatever was going on and then go back."

Garrels had another important reason for taking a break. "I needed to see my husband. I got a sense of just how hard it had been on him. He'd just been so supportive during everything."

Her initial reaction to her boss was, "Oh, I'll stay on for a few more weeks and see this part through, and then I finally realized after about ten days that I was fried and had to get out." Most of the journalists who had been in Baghdad during the bombing left at about that point.

Garrels made good on her promise to return because of "unfinished business." "I have some perspective, and we're incredibly short-staffed. NPR doesn't have a deep bench," she said. "We've had people there all along; and had we not, I would have gone earlier. It's my turn to go back."

Garrels believes that both Afghanistan and Iraq will continue to be major stories for a long time. "Afghanistan is just as important, and NPR continues to be there. We've stayed consistent. As long as American soldiers are dying, it will be a big story. It may well have been scaled back dramatically, had it just been an administrative issue."

Garrels said that although she wasn't in a position to see a lot of the coverage, her impression of the embed program was that it was "enormously successful." "I was in a cocoon and did not have access to a lot of satellite TV, but I know from talking to our reporters how successful it was. I was very skeptical beforehand and did not want to be an embed, given how unsuccessfully the administration had dealt with pool reporters who had been embedded with the military in Afghanistan," she said. "It was quite different in Afghanistan. The Americans kept us very much at arm's length and were not helpful. Those who went in on pools in eastern Afghanistan were unable to report. Our efforts to deal with the military in Kabul were not altogether successful. It's been quite different in Iraq. That was one of the reasons I was extremely skeptical initially of the whole process and what it meant. But it turned out to be a far more fruitful experience for journalists than I could have imagined," she said.

However, Garrels said that the embed experience in Iraq depended upon which colonel and which unit the journalists accompanied. "Everyone saw a small window—whether you were an embed or in Baghdad. Everybody only saw a tiny window of the war." However, Garrels was also somewhat critical of the constant coverage television provided. "The embed experience was demeaned inadvertently by television companies who were running endless coverage. They didn't have anyone in Baghdad, so they were locked out of that story. But they had an embed. Maybe the embed was where there was action and a story to tell, or maybe he was with a unit who was not doing anything. Regardless of that, the embed was put on the air, unedited, for hours showing scenes of the desert. In a sense that demeaned the overall experience. The reporting that came out when it was justified—when reporters had something to say or were with units that were doing things—was overwhelmed by the endless blathering by people who had nothing to say.

"I think a lot of journalists thought this was going to be a cakewalk—that they were just going to drive from Kuwait City to Baghdad. There are now a lot of young men and women out there who know better."

Garrels was totally surprised by the loyalty of the NPR audience who had listened to her reports about the bombing of Baghdad, the reactions of the officials in Saddam Hussein's crumbling regime, the pulling down of the statue, the looting and burning, and the triumphant entry of the American troops into Baghdad. Many of them had sent her letters of support and prayers for her safety. "I did not fully appreciate it," she said. "I had no idea [of the audience's reaction] because I knew what I was seeing was a window. Of course, I'm pleased at one level and proud that I'd done it to the best of my ability. I was so tired and didn't have time to digest everything."

She finds the thousands of letters she received very touching. "NPR had protected me [from growing notoriety] while I was gone. I contributed reports to [NPR shows] *Morning Edition, Talk of the Nation,* and *All Things Considered.* I was working from five in the morning until one the next morning. Then, when I tried to sleep, it was kind of noisy," she says, referring to the bombing of the city. Rather than focus on the political and military side of war, Garrels prefers to focus on war's effects on ordinary people. Her audience clearly is drawn to her attention to humanity.

When she returned to the United States, she experienced culture shock when she found she had become "the taste of the week." She was constantly asked to speak to groups and give interviews. "It was odd for me. That's why I wrote the book *Naked in Baghdad*. I could just disappear for awhile." Garrels said that the book's title has double meaning. On the one hand it refers to her lack of protection during her days in Baghdad; on the other, she would pretend she needed to dress so that she could buy time to hide her sat phone when the Iraqi security people were checking her hotel room.

Garrels said that she did not personally encounter any ethical dilemmas, because her previous experiences gave her a sense of how to do her job. "I just reported what I saw. When you work in a police state, you can't tell the listeners completely how you are getting information because then the people who are getting it for you or helping you get it will be killed. I feel I successfully protected my sources. It's a different dilemma than CNN went through. They decided not to report. I decided to report as much as I possibly could, and I think I was successful. I don't agree with what CNN did, but I have sympathy for the problem of being a high-profile organization that is on satellite and seen in real time. I would question whether it was worth staying under those conditions. Did I pay the exorbitant fees the Iraqis demanded [for visas and satellite phone licenses]? Yes. Did it affect how I reported? No."

Garrels was amazed that her equipment managed to function throughout her time in Baghdad. "I had a laptop, a sat phone, a tape recorder, and a Codeq [a piece of equipment that improves the voice quality on a recording]. There would be these sweeps, and I would try to hide everything. They were all put together with duct tape. It all worked, but I don't know how."

Garrels has been in radio since 1988. She grew up overseas and began her career in television as a foreign correspondent. "I obviously and specifically made the decision to leave television to go to NPR. I found I was not watching NBC and ABC, for whom I worked, and I was listening to NPR." She said that NPR is the best of all broadcast worlds. It is a combination of real writing with broadcast. She is allowed to introduce nuance and is given time to really explore the story.

# Competition and Complaints

# THE "MOST" WAR

When Tom Brokaw proclaimed that Operation Iraqi Freedom would be the most televised war in history, he was correct. But he neglected to mention that it was also an Internet war, a digital camera war, a satellite phone war, and an Arab media war. In short, it was the most covered war in real time in history, with significant advances in technology and increases in media competition.

While a worldwide audience was shown the American military in swift action and the aftermath of war for the Iraqi people, media competition to provide the "fastest" and "best" coverage proved controversial in many aspects. Competition for *the* story lies at the heart of every incident that ran the gamut from simply ignoring the rules to questioning some basic tenets of journalism.

## THE CHANGING COMPETITION

In 1991, CNN established itself as the first global media company. A mere decade later, CNN was fighting an uphill battle against MSNBC and FOX. Once the dust settled, FOX had the highest ratings, in spite of serious, sometimes flagrant, disregard of journalistic ethics. Ethical breaches included Geraldo Rivera's revelations about troop locations, a producer who was caught trying to smuggle artworks out of Iraq, and an apparent tendency to slant the news more often than any other network.

Researchers from the Program on International Policy Attitudes and Knowledge Networks tracked the public's misperceptions of three major news events.[1] First, 48 percent incorrectly believed that evidence of links between Iraq and al Qaeda had been found. Second, 22 percent believed that weapons of mass destruction had been found in Iraq. Third, 25 percent believed that world public opinion favored the United States' going to war with Iraq. Overall, 60 percent of those polled had at least one of these three misperceptions.

In a report released in October 2003, the researchers concluded that the frequency of these misperceptions varied significantly according to individuals' primary source of news.[2] Those who primarily watched FOX News were significantly more likely to have misperceptions, whereas those who primarily listened to NPR or watched PBS were significantly less likely. Of all FOX viewers, 80 percent had at least one misperception, compared with 71 percent of those watching CBS; 61 percent, ABC; 55 percent, NBC; and 55 percent, CNN. Of those who depended on a print source, 47 percent had misperceptions, whereas only 23 percent of those dependent on NPR or PBS had misperceptions. The researchers also concluded that misperceptions were also highly related to support for the war. Among those who held none of the three misperceptions, only 23 percent supported the war. However, 86 percent of those with all three misperceptions supported the war.

Before the first anniversary of the invasion of Iraq, there was a major shake-up in leadership at CNN, primarily because of FOX's stronger ratings. CNN had seen the domestic market fragmented with more news organizations willing to commit resources to twenty-four-hour coverage. The Internet, especially online newspapers, had further fragmented the audience, with on-demand coverage of President Clinton's impeachment and the September 11 terrorist attacks. The Associated Press had also expanded its television services. In short, the stage was set for a strongly competitive environment in which the pressure to be first could easily eclipse the need to be accurate.

Long before the war started, competition pushed major media companies to "compromise," or risk being shut out of the action. A case in point is CNN executive Eason Jordan's *New York Times* op-ed piece in which he described some of the actions CNN took to remain in Baghdad while trying to provide honest coverage of Saddam Hussein's regime. The industry's reaction to the piece was negative, and CNN was accused of withholding information to remain in a competitive position.

Jordan counters the criticism by saying, "The op-ed piece speaks for itself. What I think was not understood unfortunately, and I blame myself, was the fact that CNN had done a lot of tough reporting on the Saddam Hussein regime, and I just sort of expected people to start from that point when they read the op-ed, but I think that a lot of people came away with the mistaken impression that CNN pulled its punches in reporting on the regime in an effort to maintain a CNN presence in Iraq, and that just couldn't be further from the truth. We got thrown out of Iraq time and time and time again. I had an extremely difficult relationship myself with leadership figures in the regime, and Saddam Hussein's cronies despised CNN, so if we were looking to make nice with Saddam, I don't think any of those things would be the case. Nobody is going to be able to look at the reporting we did out of Iraq and say we pulled our punches, because we can prove otherwise."

CNN was criticized in 1991 for revealing too much military information to Saddam Hussein, who was said to be monitoring CNN reports. Jordan agrees that Saddam was monitoring the network. "But it's only part of the story," he said. "The U.S. was using the media, too. The U.S. was using the news media to send messages to Saddam Hussein. The news media are used every day. Certainly, CNN is used by the good guys, and CNN is used by the bad guys. It doesn't matter which side of the fence you are sitting on. I don't think anyone is going to argue that point. The news media are manipulated to the extent that governments and organizations and individuals can get away with it. It's happening every day."

From the first night of the Iraq War, there were questions about the media's and the military's potential spin and manipulation. The media labeled the first action of the war the "Shock and Awe" campaign. It was presented as the military name for the operation, as "Desert Storm" had been in 1991. However, Major Pete Mitchell of the U.S. Marines Public Affairs–U.S. Central Command said that the military never intended for that label to be publicly applied to the campaign. "That phrase came from military circles. It's military jargon that the media picked up and ran with—much to the consternation of the CENTCOM staff. We knew the 'shock and awe' phase wasn't going to be as shocking and awesome as the media were intimating. We had 'select' targets we were prepared to hit, but we knew the impact wasn't necessarily going to fit the definition of the phrase."

Although the embed program was considered successful by both the media and the military, the relationship between the two groups was far from perfect. Several breaches of military rules and journalism ethics occurred.

## REPORTERS WHO DIDN'T ABIDE BY THE RULES

Toward the end of March 2003, three journalists were asked to leave Iraq because they talked too much. The first man to find himself out of a job was veteran reporter Peter Arnett, who was making a comeback of sorts with *National Geographic Explorer* and NBC/MSNBC. Arnett, who won a Pulitzer Prize for his reporting on the Vietnam War, was among the CNN reporters who reported on bombs falling on Baghdad during the 1991 Gulf War. Ironically, *TV Guide* magazine had devoted an article to his "comeback," and NBC anchor Tom Brokaw praised Arnett's live reports once the bombing of Baghdad began this time around. On March 20, Arnett said that he wanted to stay in Iraq because "I just want to see how this regime reacts to . . . invasion. There's only one place you can see that, and it's right here in Baghdad. History is turning on this attack. I think there should be eyewitnesses."

Possibly hoping he would be rewarded with an interview with Saddam Hussein, Arnett agreed to be interviewed by Iraqi Television and uttered three sentences that derailed his career in America: "The first war plan has failed because of Iraqi resistance. Now they are trying to write another war plan. Clearly, the

American war planners misjudged the determination of the Iraqi forces." Both the National Geographic Society and NBC reacted quickly. The society released a statement that read:

> National Geographic has terminated the service of Peter Arnett. The Society did not authorize or have any prior knowledge of Arnett's television interview with Iraqi Television, and had we been consulted, would not have allowed it. His decision to grant an interview and express his personal views on state-controlled Iraqi Television, especially during a time of war, was a serious error in judgment and wrong.

NBC News president Neal Shapiro also issued a statement, published on MSNBC.com:

> It was wrong for Mr. Arnett to grant an interview to state-controlled Iraqi TV especially at a time of war and it was wrong for him to discuss his personal observations and opinions in that interview. Therefore, Peter Arnett will no longer be reporting for NBC News and MSNBC.

Arnett made his apologies for the interview on NBC's *Today* on March 31:

> I want to apologize to NBC, MSNBC, *National Geographic Explorer* and the American people for clearly making a misjudgment by giving the interview to Iraqi Television. Clearly by giving that interview I created a firestorm in the United States, and for that I'm truly sorry.

Pentagon officials were satisfied with the networks' response and took no official action against Arnett. Reporters were shaking their heads that a veteran of this caliber could make such a mistake. He immediately accepted a post reporting for Britain's *Daily Mirror*.

Freelance journalist Philip Smucker, who was working for the *Christian Science Monitor* and the *Daily Telegraph* of London, was the only reporter who was officially escorted from Iraq to Kuwait. On March 26, the Pentagon insisted that he leave following a live interview on CNN. The Pentagon concluded that Smucker, who was not embedded but had been traveling with U.S. troops as they entered Iraq, provided too much information about troop positions. A veteran journalist, Smucker was held incommunicado in military custody for a couple of days before being escorted back to Kuwait. Bryan Whitman, deputy assistant secretary of defense for public affairs, said:

> My understanding of the facts at this point from the commander on the ground is that this reporter was reporting, in real time, positions, locations, and activi-

ties of units engaged in combat. The commander felt it was necessary and appropriate to remove [Smucker] from his immediate battle space in order not to compromise his mission or endanger personnel of his unit.

*Christian Science Monitor* editor Paul Van Slambrouck disagreed with this assessment and publicly supported Smucker. In an editorial published in the *Monitor*, he wrote:

We have read the transcript of the CNN interview and it does not appear to us that he disclosed anything that wasn't already widely available in maps and in US and British radio, newspaper, and television reports in that same news cycle.

Smucker, an American who was based in Cairo for the *Monitor*, had covered conflicts in Afghanistan, Kosovo, Bosnia, and Cambodia. He was reassigned within the Gulf Region.

There was perhaps less surprise and considerably more media focus, often of a gloating nature, when controversial FOX correspondent Geraldo Rivera received an official reprimand for drawing a map in the sand that showed the approximate location of the army's 101st Airborne Division. Previously, in Afghanistan, Rivera had suggested that he was close to the front, with bullets coming very close. He later admitted that he was nowhere near the front line, where the shooting was occurring. So there was little forgiveness from either the Pentagon or his media colleagues when, during a live broadcast, Rivera drew an outline of Iraq in the sand and showed where the 101st Airborne was located relative to Baghdad. To make matters worse, he then indicated where the 101st Airborne was headed next. This was in direct violation of the Pentagon's edict: Do not give away troop location.

Some media reports indicated that Rivera was embedded, whereas others said that he was merely traveling with the division unofficially. Pentagon sources said that he was not embedded and that plans were underway to escort him out of Iraq. But his exit didn't happen that way. Apparently, FOX News executives reached an agreement with the Pentagon that resulted in Rivera's voluntary exit to Kuwait. FOX stood behind him and accused other networks of making too much of the incident. Rivera kept his job.

A fourth reporter, Brett Lieberman of the Harrisburg, Pennsylvania, *Patriot-News*, was asked to leave his posting with the Second Battalion, Twenty-fifth Marines, in late April 2003. According to an article posted on the newspaper's website, PennLive.com, Lieberman and Lieutenant Colonel Robert C. Murphy, the unit's commanding officer, disagreed over an April 25 story that described the unit's mission of patrolling An Nasiriyah after the departure of the Fifteenth Marine Expeditionary Unit. Murphy apparently thought that Lieberman's story included too much military detail. According to the *Patriot-News*, other officers, both in Iraq and in the United States, thought the story was fine and presented no safety hazard to the troops.

Pentagon embed rules gave Murphy the right to ask Lieberman to leave the unit, although Lieberman should have been allowed to appeal the decision up the chain of command, to the Office of the Assistant Secretary of Defense for Public Affairs. Lieberman was never given the opportunity to do so. *Patriot-News* executive editor David Newhouse defended Lieberman, saying in the article: "We were disappointed that Brett's assignment ended this way. During this conflict, outstanding cooperation by the U.S. military has allowed reporters like Brett to bring the everyday experiences of our troops to millions of readers. It has truly been a win-win-win situation for the military, the press and, most importantly, the American people. This seems to have been a disagreement with one or two officers. We are confident, based upon our conversations with other officers, that Brett's story in no way jeopardized our servicemen and women."

## QUESTIONABLE IMAGES

There were several controversies sparked by media images during the course of the major military action. Some involved still photographs, whereas others involved video. Violations of Pentagon rules and the graphic nature of some images certainly propelled some debate, but it was misuse of technology that caused the first dismissal of a photographer.

### The *Los Angeles Times* Case

On March 31, 2003, the *Los Angeles Times* ran a front-page photo that showed a British soldier directing Iraqi civilians to take cover from incoming Iraqi fire outside Basra. The soldier, his left hand gesturing toward the crowd seated on the ground, appeared to be pointing the machine gun in his right hand in the direction of a standing father holding his young child. Two days later, an editor's note posted on the *Times*'s website indicated that the photo was actually a composite of two pictures taken a few minutes apart. Three photos were displayed: the composite photograph and each of the two pictures that had been electronically combined to form it. The editor explained that the fraudulent photo had been uncovered when it was noticed that some of the people sitting on the left side of the shot appeared twice. Photographer Brian Walski, contacted in southern Iraq, admitted he had used his computer to improve the composition.

In the first photo, the soldier has his hand up and his gun pointed in the general direction of the crowd, but the man and child are not prominent. In the second photo, the soldier is in a relaxed posture, his left hand at his side and his gun pointed more toward the ground. The man and child are moving upright, toward the soldier. The composite photograph definitely makes the soldier appear more threatening, especially toward the man and child.

The *Times* has a strict policy against altering news photos. The photographer was dismissed from the staff. Although the action seems drastic—the photographer was likely more interested in improving the image rather than deceiving the audience—it is a matter of trust. In the age of Adobe Photoshop and other software, altering photos is easily done and often cannot be detected visually. Consequently, news organizations such as the Associated Press, the *Times*, and many other print publications support such strict guidelines. Asked when it was permissible for an AP photographer to alter a photo, the swift and emphatic response was "Never!"

### Al Jazeera and American Soldiers

The new kid on the war coverage block, Al Jazeera—the Arabic-language satellite television network—initially received some support from the U.S. news media outlets, many of whom were relying on the Arabic-language satellite network to provide images that were unavailable to them directly. Headquartered in Qatar, where the U.S. CENTCOM was located during the invasion, the network was praised for showing a side of the war that U.S. journalists were not able to provide.

However, the network soon began to face difficulties in America as well as in the Middle East. The network launched an English-language website in March 2003, pushing ahead its planned start-up to provide war coverage. The site became popular very quickly, but almost immediately the site was hacked, and the homepage was replaced by an American flag (see below). The network also had difficulty establishing its Washington bureau because of a general reluctance from U.S. property management companies to rent space for the operation.

Once the war started, Al Jazeera got off on the wrong foot with U.S. commanders when they released footage of dead American soldiers from the 507th Maintenance Unit. At a March 23 briefing at CENTCOM headquarters in Doha, Qatar, Lieutenant General John Abizaid identified an Al Jazeera reporter and publicly chastised him for the release of the footage. "I'm very disappointed that you would portray those pictures of our servicemen. I saw that, and I would ask others not to do that," he said. When pressed by another reporter about his reaction to the footage, Abizaid replied, "I wouldn't want to comment on that. I would say the pictures are disgusting."

Al Jazeera had some embed slots with the U.S. military, with at least one reporter assigned to CENTCOM. Major Tim Blair, who was running the embed program in the Pentagon, said that the network was not given as many slots as most U.S. news organizations believed. Some embedded American journalists said that they had little contact with Al Jazeera's journalists; they suspected the Arab network's journalists were controlled more and given less access than their American counterparts.

Blair remembers very well the day that Al Jazeera released the video footage of the American POWs. "I remember that day because Pentagon correspondents from one of the networks came to us as soon as they got the feed from Al Jazeera and said, 'We want to show you something that we just pulled down. We want to get your views on it.'" He was assured that the network didn't want to run the video because of the sensitivities involved. Blair reviewed the footage, which violated the military's notification policies and likely the Geneva Convention's prohibition on showing prisoners of war—alive or dead. The images were graphic and would likely be offensive to American viewers and enlisted personnel. "I really appreciated their attention to our concerns for the families of these service members, but still, being in a competitive market they had to say, 'If some of the other networks run with this, then we actually would have to run something on this, too.' Within a matter of hours one of the other networks was running some of these pictures and some of the footage," Blair said. "My hypothesis is that there is a lot more journalism integrity in the American media compared with some of the international media markets."

Eason Jordan, who was responsible for CNN's war coverage, would like to agree, but for him, this was a tough call. "You're torn in these situations because, in the one sense, war is hell and you want to demonstrate the horrors of that, and you certainly have pictures to do it; and in another sense, you don't need to be grotesque about it," he says. "War is an awful thing, and some people don't really appreciate how bad it is. But there were certain things that we were not going to show."

He said that portions of the video had extreme close-ups of the wounds and revealed that some of the men had been castrated. "In the videotape you didn't see the actual act happening, but you could tell that's what had happened. We just weren't going to show close-ups of people with bullets in their heads; we weren't going to show people who had been castrated—even if they are not recognizable. But we're torn. We do believe in showing the horrors of war, and we don't believe in sanitizing it or sugarcoating it; but there are limits to what we feel is appropriate to show." CNN did show a small portion of the video, as did their competitors.

Another sensitive issue involved Al Jazeera's footage of the interrogation of American POWs. "I think there was some frustration [from the Pentagon] that we showed the POWs kept alive. We showed them identifying themselves on the air. For the families, it was a godsend that they could see their loved ones, even if they were in custody. I couldn't imagine not showing them," Jordan says. "There was a family here in Atlanta whose son flew an Apache that got shot down. We took the video out and showed them. They knew he was missing, but until we showed them the video, they didn't know he was alive; they had no clue. They were grateful to us for that. So at all times we believe in trying to do the right thing, to be responsible. At times the Pentagon supported our decisions, and at times they disagreed with them; but we always did what was best for us and what was best for family members and U.S. consumers and consumers around the world."

Jordan admits to having a "difficult relationship" with Al Jazeera. "Al Jazeera did not exist in 1991. Al Jazeera had special access ongoing in Iraq, and it's understandable to a degree since the head of Al Jazeera was in Baghdad literally hugging and kissing Saddam Hussein. We are just not doing that. So, Al Jazeera had some access that we didn't have, but I think that Al Jazeera found itself in a bit of a CNN position as well. The expectations for Al Jazeera were very high. And all of a sudden there is a lot of competition. Some people have argued that Abudabi TV really had better coverage out of Iraq during the war than Al Jazeera did. There are a number of Arabic-language broadcasters now who compete tenaciously with Al Jazeera. I don't think it's just an Al Jazeera game any more. There used to be a CNN effect, and there used to be an Al Jazeera effect. Now there are a lot of other broadcasters out there."

Jordan believes that Arab journalists and American journalists bring very different perspectives to the table. "Al Jazeera goes out of its way to be provocative, in my opinion, sometimes at the expense of reporting accurately and fairly and responsibly. I would love to see Al Jazeera improve its journalistic standards. I think it is trying to a degree, but it's in a competitive situation where being inflammatory and provocative is actually a good thing, at least in their mind. But none of that excuses the fact that the U.S. found a way, I think unintentionally in both cases, but I think almost recklessly so, to bomb the headquarters of Al Jazeera, not only in Baghdad, but also in Kabul during the war. There is no doubt that U.S. officials knew the precise whereabouts and coordinates of those Al Jazeera offices and those bombings took place regardless. Now, I don't sign up for what a lot of people suggest, that the U.S. intentionally bombed those facilities knowing they were Al Jazeera facilities, but I think the U.S. could have tried harder to keep that from happening. For whatever reasons those bombings took place regardless."

Bruce Conover, CNN's senior international editor, says that the relationship between Al Jazeera and CNN still exists, in that material is occasionally exchanged. "But since Al Jazeera has become quite controversial for their tendency to politicize their reporting in Iraq and elsewhere, our relationship has become somewhat more distant because we are often not able to trust their sourcing of video material and information."

Al Jazeera's credibility problems were compounded in September 2003 by the arrest in Spain of one of its reporters, Tayseer Allouni, who was accused of collaborating with a man considered to be an al Qaeda ringleader in Spain. Allouni had interviewed Osama bin Laden in October 2001. In addition, Al Jazeera investigated whether Iraqi agents infiltrated its staff in an attempt to "subvert its coverage," as the British *Sunday Times* reported. Citing documents found after Saddam Hussein was ousted, the newspaper reported that three Iraqi intelligence agents had infiltrated Al Jazeera. However, Jihad Ballout, a spokesman, said that there is no evidence that the allegations made in the *Sunday Times* report were true. "The network is unaware of any member of Al Jazeera who is working for any foreign intelligence organization," Ballout said. "We are still in the realm of allegations now. We were told that there were documents; we were presented with documents; but we have not ascertained their authenticity."

Adding to the network's woes, the U.S.-backed Iraqi Governing Council temporarily banned both Al Jazeera and Al Arabiyya from government buildings and news conferences in September 2003, saying that the networks promote violence. In an interview on CNN, anchor Kyra Phillips asked Ballout to respond to the Iraqi Governing Council's claim that Al Jazeera had promoted political violence; had advocated the killing of members of the Governing Council and the coalition; and had aired video of "terrorists terrorizing Iraqis." Ballout responded that "basically Al Jazeera is a news organization. We don't deal in politics. We try to be as balanced as possible. There's a situation, and a serious situation in Iraq as well, that seems to bring about various points of view, and we are doing our duty as journalists and trying to tell our viewers out there exactly what's happening."

Al Jazeera is not universally loved in the Middle East either. NPR correspondent Ivan Watson said that the Kurds in northern Iraq hated Al Jazeera because its reporters did not seem to be paying attention to Kurdish issues and were viewed as pandering to Saddam. He witnessed one of the Kurdish commanders come to blows with an Al Jazeera correspondent over the lack of coverage of the car bombing that had killed members of an Australian television crew and Kurds. Major Blair also was aware that embedded Al Jazeera journalists were not welcome in some areas.

### The Deaths of Qusay and Uday

On July 22, 2003, the U.S. military conducted a raid on a house near the northern Iraqi city of Mosul that resulted in a fatal shootout with Saddam Hussein's sons, Qusay and Uday. On July 24, U.S. secretary of defense Donald Rumsfeld and U.S. administrator for Iraq L. Paul Bremer held a joint press briefing in the Pentagon to explain to the press corps why graphic photos and videotape of Qusay and Uday's bullet-riddled bodies were being released to the American media.

Before Rumsfeld and Bremer's entrance into the press briefing room, a FOX Television technician at the back of the room asked the journalists present if any of them had seen the images that were just then appearing on his screen that was, of course, tuned to the FOX network. Audible gasps erupted across the room as these seasoned reporters saw the graphic images for the first time.

Rumsfeld and Bremer then entered the room and began ticking off what had so far been accomplished in Iraq and what the plans were to improve the infrastructure. Rumsfeld then explained his reasons for releasing the images and responded to questions from the press corps. Rumsfeld assured them that this had not been "a snap decision." "I thought it through very carefully," he said. He evoked a parallel between the current situation and that of Romanian dictator Nicolae Ceaucescu, who was executed in 1989. "Not until people saw his body did they believe he was gone." Rumsfeld similarly believed that showing the bodies to the Iraqis was necessary "to bring closure and so the Iraqis could believe that these two vicious members of that regime are, in fact, dead."

Rumsfeld clearly hoped that if the Iraqis believed the two were dead, they would believe that the regime was truly gone and that violence toward the military would decrease. "If it saves American lives, then I'm confident I made the right decision. It wasn't a close call for me," he said.

Showing the images was a close call for American media. The day before the press briefing, a discussion was taking place in the AP's photo division offices. Managers had gotten the word that Rumsfeld was going to release the pictures, and they knew that they would be graphic. Administrative Director of AP Photos Lew Wheaton said that the AP would have to send the photos out to their members but that it would then be up to them to decide whether and how to use them. The discussions indicated that not everyone in the office thought Rumsfeld should release the photos but that if he did, competition among media outlets would ensure thorough distribution.

As it turned out, the AP offered an alternative to publications with editors who thought the photos were too graphic to run. The same day that they sent the photos of Qusay and Uday they offered a photograph of Iraqis clustered around a television screen that was showing the photos. The screen image was very small, and the focus was on the Iraqis. This was the photo that was displayed most prominently in most newspapers.

Another alternative was to put the photos on affiliated websites. Chris Kelley, of Belo Interactive, says that the *Dallas Morning News* editors decided to put the photos on their website. The viewer had to follow two links to get to the photos. "The first link said, 'View photos.' The second link included a warning that the photos were graphic. Only about half of those who clicked on the first link actually clicked the second link to view the photos," he says.

The following day, the Department of Defense authorized the release of video footage of the cleaned-up bodies of Qusay and Uday. The American networks showed clips all day long and included them in the nightly newscasts. Now, television news directors across the country had to decide whether to show the video on their local news programs. Some, such as WUSA-TV in Washington, D.C., announced that they would not show them. Others warned audiences that children should not view the photographs. ABC was criticized for not warning viewers about them, and NBC revealed the photos before the warning was finished, precluding an opportunity for the viewers to look away or switch channels.

Clearly, countering Iraqi propaganda with an American perspective has been a major part of the Bush administration's foreign policy. One of Bremer's first actions in Baghdad was to establish American-backed media: a sixty-thousand-circulation newspaper, a television network (the Middle East Television Network), and a radio station. The Bush administration reportedly provided $30 million to establish and support these media. In testimony before the Senate Foreign Relations Committee's Broadcasting Board of Governors (BBG), head Kenneth Tomlinson said that the venture was "the most important public-diplomacy initiative of our time. . . . Al Jazeera should not go unanswered in the Middle East." The BBG manages nonmilitary international U.S. broadcasting including Voice of America. The new funds will pay for remaining start-up costs and the network's first year of operations.

However, in short order, the civilian journalists who were put in charge of running these media were complaining about pressure to report only the U.S. side of the story. The first director of the television network resigned in protest. Then Don North, an independent producer and journalist, accepted a position with the defense contractor Science Applications International in January 2003 and arrived in Baghdad April 20 as senior television adviser and trainer for the American-backed Iraq Media Network (IMN). He left Baghdad on July 24, explaining his disillusionment in an article he wrote for *TelevisionWeek*:

> I joined a small group of American and Iraqi expatriate journalists who signed on to bring honest and professional radio and TV to Iraq after the fall of Baghdad. The Iraq Media Network went on the air with radio April 10 and television May 13. It was greeted with great anticipation by Iraqis, who expected that after 35 years of Saddam Hussein's self-serving propaganda, a new free and democratic media would be created that would make the new governing elements transparent and accountable and generate credible debate on the reconstruction of Iraq. . . . Now seven months later, like so many of the goals and hopes for the new Iraq, a credible media has not been realized. The failure to establish television "accountable to the society" is strongly felt. Instead, IMN has become an irrelevant mouthpiece for Coalition Provisional Authority propaganda, managed news and mediocre programs.

Further evidence of Bremer's commitment to promoting the American viewpoint came on March 28, 2004, when U.S. troops sealed the offices of the Baghdad weekly *Al-Hawza*, which is affiliated with radical Shiite cleric Moktada al-Sadr, and ordered the paper closed for sixty days. A letter signed by Coalition Provisional Authority (CPA) administrator L. Paul Bremer was delivered to the paper's staff, which claimed that the publication had violated a CPA decree promulgated in June 2003 that prohibits "incitement" in the media. Specifically, the letter said that the paper had published "many articles" containing false information and had intended to "disturb public order and incite violence against the coalition forces and the employees of the CPA."

According to the Committee to Protect Journalists, the letter specifically mentioned a February 26 *Al-Hawza* article about a deadly car bomb in a Shiite city south of Baghdad, which the article said was actually a rocket fired by a U.S. Apache helicopter. It also cited an article in the same paper's edition, titled "Bremer Follows the Steps of Saddam," which alleged that the CPA was "implementing a policy of starving the Iraqi public." The letter also stated past examples of what the CPA says was the paper's false reporting in two articles from August 2003. One article accused the United States of waging a war on Islam, and the other said the United States wanted to steal Iraqi oil rather than depose Saddam Hussein.

This action received more play in the U.S. media than had the previous resignations of the journalists involved with the U.S. established media in Iraq. Because of their commitment to the First Amendment right to freedom of the press, news organizations generally protest the closing of newspapers, regardless of the politics involved.

### Fallujah Ambush of Civilians

The American news media were tested again when on March 31, 2004, a mob of Iraqis ambushed an SUV, killing four American civilian contractors in Fallujah, a city about thirty-five miles west of Baghdad. Located in the so-called Sunni Triangle, Fallujah remained the scene of violence and resistance against the occupation. The escalating violence was at least partially in response to the American shutdown of *Al-Hawza* and the attempts to arrest publisher al-Sadr. The mob dragged the burned and mutilated bodies of the Americans through the streets and then strung two of them up from a bridge.

Immediately, television cameramen and still photographers arrived on the scene and began capturing images of Iraqi men hurling rocks at the blazing vehicle, the bodies of the men visible through the flames. Then additional footage showed the remains being pulled from the SUV, dragged, and then suspended.

The Associated Press moved eight photographs of the attack, including the mutilated bodies being dragged through the streets and suspended from a bridge, with an advisory to editors to "note graphic content."

In what may have been the most gruesome image published since the September 11 attacks, the *New York Times* carried a large photo of the suspended remains on the front page of the April 1 edition. Across the country, editors and news directors were once again trying to decide whether or how to use the images. For many, the images were reminiscent of the scene in Mogadishu, Somalia, when a mob dragged the body of an American soldier through the streets. However, this time there seemed to be little discussion about the fact that these men were civilians, not soldiers. There were discussions, however, about whether the need to show the horror of war outweighed concern for the family members who had to witness the media use of the visuals.

The *Dallas Morning News* encapsulated the debate going on in newsrooms across the country in the editorial headline "Gruesome Images: Does Taste Trump Newsworthiness?" For its front page, the paper's editors had chosen a photograph of cheering Iraqis around a burning SUV; on an inside page was a black-and-white photo of the bodies strung from bridge girders. President and editor Robert W. Mong Jr. indicated that the goal was to "convey the power of major events" without unnecessarily traumatizing readers.

The *Washington Post*, however, picked a more graphic image for the front page. An Iraqi youth was pummeling one of the charred bodies with a slipper (the same kind of disrespect shown to Saddam Hussein's posters and statues early in the war). The point was to show the reality of war.

The decision was perhaps even harder for the television networks that were getting the images from the Associated Press television division. They were more cautious in their approach. The predominant broadcast image was video of the burning SUV, although the images were handled differently in some cases. For *World News Tonight*, for example, ABC chose to pixilate (blur) the front window of the burning vehicle, a body being dragged out of the SUV and beaten, and the bodies hanging from the bridge girders. On its *Evening News,* CBS ran some graphic footage but blurred images of the bodies. Anchor Dan Rather warned the audience that the images were "too gruesome even for grown-up eyes."

CNN blurred some shots, such as the bodies burning inside the car, but the evening newscast showed the hanging bodies without pixilation. The network did distort other shots, including a scene of the bodies burning inside the car. CNN said that it waited until the U.S. government had time to notify the families of the men before airing the images, although there was an Internet rumor that the wife of one of the slain men learned about her husband's death when she received a call from a journalist in Iraq.

The bottom line was that anyone who wanted to see the most graphic versions of the still photos and videos could easily obtain them, whereas those who might want to avoid them had less opportunity to do so than when the graphic photographs of Saddam's sons were released.

Furthermore, images released during April and May 2004—during the most deadly period for the American military since Baghdad fell—eroded public support for President Bush and the Iraq War. For instance, Tami Silicio was fired from her job with Maytag Aircraft after military officials raised "very specific concerns" about a photo published in the *Seattle Times* of twenty flag-drapped coffins containing the bodies of soldiers who were killed in Iraq. The photo was taken in Kuwait aboard a transport plane. The Pentagon apparently viewed publishing the photo as an antiwar statement, but Silicio indicated she merely wanted the families of the dead soldiers to see the care and respect shown their loved ones. Meanwhile, after filing a Freedom of Information Act requesting photographs, First Amendment activist Russ Kick published on his website more than 350 photographs of American war dead arriving at the nation's largest military mortuary. The Defense Department subsequently denied further release of the photographs to media outlets.

On May 11, sickening video of the decapitation of American civilian Nicholas Berg was posted on a website linked to al Qaeda. Berg identifies himself as he sits in front of five armed, hooded men. A hooded man standing directly behind Berg reads a statement identifying himself, and then Berg is pushed to the floor. Berg is heard screaming as his throat is cut. One of the captors then holds up his severed head. The media reported that the four men who decapitated Berg and videotaped it were members of Saddam Hussein's Fedayeen paramilitary organization. Most U.S. newspapers ran a still photo on the front page that was pulled from the video seconds before the beheading, and television networks ran a video clip that did not show the beheading. The full video can be found on news organizations' websites, including CNN's website.

Perhaps the most damaging blow to the American image abroad, and certainly in the Arab world, was photos depicting American soldiers abusing Iraqi prisoners from October until December 2003 at Abu Ghraib prison. The prison was notorious as a place of torture during Saddam Hussein's reign. CBS was the first media outlet to air the photos, on April 28, 2004, after withholding them at the military's request for about ten days. According to his aides, President Bush learned about these photos from the television report. Soon, a number of photos showing U.S. military prison guards sexually humiliating naked Iraqi prisoners was widely circulated in the media. The international protest that erupted with the publication resulted in courts-martial for seven soldiers, questions about the conduct of civilian contractors who interrogated prisoners, and calls for the ousting of Donald Rumsfeld as secretary of defense. Congressional hearings determined that there were still worse scenes depicted than the ones already in circulation, prompting questions about whether all the photos should be released to the media or whether enough was enough. Polls taken during and after the photos first began to circulate indicated that Bush's approval ratings had fallen below 50 percent for the first time during the war. The media generally blurred the images of the Iraqi prisoners to avoid showing genitalia, but the American soldiers involved, including some women, were shown smiling and pointing to the prisoners. The most ubiquitous image showed Private First Class Lynndie England holding a leash attached to a prisoner's neck. The Arab media were quick to point out the hypocrisy in the American actions and apparent violations of the Geneva Convention, while the American media focused on public disgust. The soldiers' defense was that they were following orders to "soften up" the prisoners for interrogation.

From the time that the Department of Defense released the photos of Saddam Hussein's dead sons through the Abu Ghraib prison scandal, the American public has been subjected to the most graphic images the news media have ever made public. This is a trend that media managers and journalists should question and debate.

## THE FACE OF THE WAR: JESSICA LYNCH

On March 23, 2003, the 507th Maintenance Company took a wrong turn. Eleven soldiers were killed; six were taken prisoner in An Nasiriyah, Iraq; and sixteen soldiers were able to rejoin friendly forces. According to the U.S. Army's official report on the incident, the unit's captain made a "single navigational error" that led the company deep inside enemy territory. As he attempted to retrace his route and rejoin the Third Infantry Division, the company was ambushed. When the 507th tried to fight off the attackers, many of its weapons jammed because of poor maintenance in the sandy conditions. The report concluded:

> Soldiers fight as they are trained to fight. Once engaged in battle, the Soldiers of the 507th Maintenance Company fought hard. They fought the best they could until there was no longer a means to resist. They defeated ambushes, overcame hastily-prepared enemy obstacles, defended one another, provided life-saving aid, and inflicted casualties on the enemy. The Soldiers of the 507th upheld the Code of Conduct and followed the Law of War.

Other than serving as an excellent example of American soldiers' bravery under fire, that might have been the extent of the story except that one of the soldiers who was presumed captured was a young, blonde private first class named Jessica Lynch. Lynch was not the only woman in the company to be taken prisoner. Private First Class Lori Piestewa died in captivity, of injuries she received in the ambush. Specialist Shoshana Johnson was captured and later released along with the male soldiers.

From the beginning, Lynch became the icon for the "new" U.S. Army—the face of the war, as CNN would later label her. Initially, there appeared to be good reason to focus on Lynch and make this the most covered story of the war. The *Washington Post* quoted an official saying that Lynch was "fighting to the death" when she was captured. The media quickly ran with the story, widely reporting that she had emptied her gun in defense of herself and her fellow soldiers. Some accounts indicated that she had received gunshot wounds. CBS News eventually interviewed Iraqi medical personnel at the hospital, who insisted Lynch had not been shot, although she was injured in the Humvee crash. They also questioned the bravado involved in the rescue, saying that Iraqi soldiers had withdrawn from the hospital before the Americans arrived. The Pentagon warned that the matter was under investigation and that reports of Lynch's bravery could be premature. How-

ever, after somewhat recovering from her serious battlefield injuries, Lynch se-
cured an honorable discharge, a book deal, and a made-for-television movie deal
about her exploits.

Journalism.org posted an insightful chronology of how the coverage developed, titled "Jessica Lynch: Media Myth-Making in the Iraq War":

> In the early evening of April 1, the night of the rescue, the 24-hour news net-
> works broke in with a briefing from US CENTCOM in which it was revealed
> that the military had rescued a "U.S. Army prisoner of war held captive in Iraq."
> In the days and weeks following Lynch's rescue, stories about how she was cap-
> tured and what happened after her capture began to circulate. The day after the
> rescue, April 2, the Associated Press quoted "officials who spoke on the condi-
> tion of anonymity" who said Lynch had "at least one gunshot wound." That
> same day the *New York Times* cited "an Army official" as saying that Lynch "had
> been shot multiple times." On April 3, a front-page story in *The Washington Post*
> cited unnamed U.S. officials and said that Lynch "fought fiercely" and that she
> sustained gunshot and stab wounds. "She was fighting to the death," the official
> was quoted as saying in the story. "She did not want to be taken alive."[3]

Bryan Whitman, deputy assistant secretary for media operations, denies that any
"military spin" was involved, but he understands the media's fascination with Lynch.
"America loves its heroes, and America needs its heroes. And so, sometimes, unlikely
individuals become heroes," he said. "I don't think she was the 'face of the war,' as
some of the media characterized her. She went through a very difficult situation, being a prisoner of war and being pretty severely injured. She was the first U.S. soldier
to be rescued from captivity during combat since I don't know when—maybe since
World War II. So, that was a significant event. I think that a dramatic rescue like that,
had it been a male, it would have been covered largely the same way."

Still, there was a lot of misinformation disseminated about Lynch during the
early days of her ordeal, and the coverage was definitely "feminine" in tone. The
initial reports that she emptied her gun trying to defend herself and her fellow soldiers was corrected to indicate that Lynch's gun was jammed and that she was un-
conscious when she was pulled from the truck. She was described in terms of her
height (five feet three) and weight ("a wispy 100 pounds") and handwriting
("neat, girlish"). The American audience was told about her childhood in the West
Virginia hollows, her love of softball, her Miss Congeniality title at a local county
fair. Male soldiers, even the ones captured with Lynch, were never described in
such flowery and personal ways. Her homecoming several weeks after her rescue
was reported live by the major television news networks.

Lynch's coverage also raised questions about racial bias in the media. Fellow female captive Shoshana Johnson, an African American, was described as the daughter

of a Persian Gulf War veteran, the mother of a two-year-old girl, and a cook or chef. When a television reporter interviewed Johnson's mother before her daughter's release, the clip used quoted her as saying that she hoped her daughter was being treated "like a lady." Johnson received no book deal, no movie, and no homecoming televised live. In fact, her family learned that Johnson was a POW when they saw video of her being broadcast by Spanish-language television network Telemundo, before the Pentagon notified them that she was missing.

In interviews and in her book about her ordeal, *I'm a Soldier, Too* (written with former *New York Times* reporter Rick Bragg), Lynch credits Iraqi medical personnel with saving her life in the hospital. Although reports indicate that she was sexually molested while there, she retains no memory of it. Some of the details will likely remain in dispute, but there is one undisputed fact: American soldiers mounted a successful operation to rescue her, and the army captured the moment on videotape, portions of which were later released to the media.

"This certainly was an important story, and news media and news organizations wanted to tell it. And some news organizations got out ahead of the facts," Whitman says. "If you go back and check the record and look at everything that the Defense Department said, nothing was ever embellished. But there were stories, no doubt, that if you take a look at them in retrospect were way ahead of the facts and were way ahead of what we had said. Ultimately, some of them were proven wrong."

## THE PALESTINE HOTEL: PREVENTABLE TRAGEDY
Just before noon on April 8, 2003, an extremely divisive event occurred. Journalists covering the battle of Baghdad from the balconies of the Palestine Hotel looked on in disbelief as the turret of a U.S. M1A1 Abrams tank positioned about three-quarters of a mile away on the Al Jumhuriya Bridge turned toward them and unleashed a single round. The shell struck a fifteenth-floor balcony of the hotel, fatally wounding veteran Reuters cameraman Taras Protsyuk and Spanish cameraman José Couso of Telecinco. Three other journalists were wounded in the attack.

The hotel was well known as the headquarters of about one hundred American and international journalists who had remained in Baghdad throughout the American military's push to Baghdad. It was clearly marked, and none of the journalists there believed that fire directed toward American soldiers had come from the hotel. They simply could not understand why the marines had fired on them.

Both the military and the Committee to Protect Journalists (CPJ) investigated the shelling. Based on interviews with about a dozen reporters who were at the scene, including two embedded journalists who monitored the military radio traffic before and after the shelling occurred, CPJ concluded that that attack on the journalists, while not deliberate, was avoidable. CPJ learned that Pentagon officials, as well as commanders on the ground in Baghdad, knew that the Palestine

Hotel was full of international journalists and were intent on not hitting it How-ever, these senior officers apparently failed to convey their concern to the tank commander who fired on the hotel.

According to CPJ's report on the incident, Chris Tomlinson, an AP reporter embedded with an infantry company assigned to the Third Infantry Division's Fourth Battalion, Sixty-fourth Armor Regiment, arrived in central Baghdad on April 7. He reported that in the midst of skirmishes, snipers on tall buildings aimed at the hatches of the tanks, eventually wounding two members of Captain Philip Wolford's battalion. According to Tomlinson, the tanks were on the receiv-ing end of rocket-propelled grenades, sniper shots, and mortar fire.

CPJ reported that, at midmorning on April 8, two M1A1 Abrams tanks from the Alpha Division moved onto the Al Jumhuriya Bridge, which spans the Tigris River. A videotape, shot by a French television crew on the fourteenth floor of the Palestine Hotel, showed that on the east side of the river, tanks were firing several rounds into a building with satellite dishes on the roof. The turret of one tank was raised, then lowered. A third tank ventured a short distance onto the bridge. Ac-cording to Tomlinson, who was continuing to monitor radio communication, the tanks were frantically searching for a spotter (enemy observer/sniper).

Another U.S. reporter, Jules Crittenden of the *Boston Herald*, who was embed-ded with the Alpha Company of the Fourth Battalion, Sixty-fourth Armor Regi-ment, confirmed Tomlinson's account for CPJ. Crittenden arrived near the battle scene in an armored personnel carrier. He is quoted as saying, "There was a tremendous degree of concern because everybody was looking, trying to figure out where this observer was—in fact, we were doing it, too. We were all concerned that we were about to get an artillery barrage, which we didn't want to happen for obvious reasons."

Tomlinson told CPJ that he attempted to relay a message to the journalists in-side the Palestine Hotel asking them to hang bed sheets out the window to make the building more easily identifiable to U.S. forces. But as Tomlinson was trying to locate the Palestine Hotel in the late morning, one of the tank officers on the Al Jumhuriya Bridge who was looking for the spotter radioed that he had located a person with binoculars in a building on the east side of the river.

CPJ said that in an interview with the French weekly *Le Nouvel Observateur*, Captain Wolford hinted that he gave an immediate order to fire. However, in an interview with Belgium's RTBF television news that aired in May, Shawn Gibson, the tank's sergeant, said that after he spotted someone talking and pointing with binoculars, he reported it to his commanders but did not receive an order to fire for about ten minutes. Crittenden, who was located on the west side of the river with U.S. forces at that point, also recalls troops at the very least discussing the target. "I was aware that they had spotted someone with binoculars and they were getting ready to fire," Crittenden says. "This was being discussed on the radio."

According to Tomlinson, the round that was fired was a heat round, an incendiary shell that is intended to kill people and not destroy buildings.

The CPJ investigation ended with a blunt statement and a question:

> There is simply no evidence to support the official U.S. position that U.S. forces were returning hostile fire from the Palestine Hotel. It conflicts with the eyewitness testimony of numerous journalists in the hotel. While all indications are that the tank round was directed at what was believed to be an Iraqi spotter, other questions emerge. For example, how is it possible for a tank officer to observe a person or persons with binoculars, wait 10 minutes for authorization to fire, according to the tank sergeant, and, during that interval, not notice journalists with cameras and tripods located on other balconies, or the large, English-language sign reading "Hotel Palestine"?

Speaking about two months after the shelling, Bryan Whitman said that, based on the initial reports, he had nothing to contradict the simple fact that U.S. forces received fire and returned fire from those locations. "If the investigation bears out something different, then clearly we will amend the record," he said. "That was the report from the ground and how we have characterized it. U.S. forces are always going to retain the right to self-defense."

The Department of Defense released a CENTCOM report on August 13, 2003, that concluded that the U.S. unit "had positive intelligence that they were under direct observation from an enemy hunter/killer team" and that "the activities on the balcony of the Palestine Hotel were consistent with that of an enemy combatant." It further stated that it was only "some time after the incident" that the American unit became aware that the structure hit by the tank round was the Palestine Hotel, and the Americans didn't know until later that two television cameramen had been killed by the tank round.

## SADDAM TOPPLES

While Jessica Lynch was perhaps the most recognizable "face" of the war, another image will likely be more memorable. On April 9, 2003, with live coverage during the networks' morning shows and numerous photojournalists on the scene, a small drama played itself out and marked the psychological end of the Iraq War for many Americans. As several eyewitnesses reported, a small band of Iraqis began the process of pulling down a large statue of Saddam Hussein. The statue, which had been erected the previous year to mark Saddam's sixty-fifth birthday, was approximately twenty feet tall. Several such statues had already fallen around the city and throughout the country, but this one was different. First, the statue was located close to the Palestine Hotel, where all the foreign journalists who had been covering the war were headquartered. Second, on this day,

U.S. Army and Marine troops moved into Baghdad. Third, Iraqi civilians were feeling safe enough to launch these small celebrations to mark the end of the Saddam Hussein regime, even though he would not be captured for several more months.

The event proved to be a microcosm of the relationship between America and Iraq. During the 1991 Gulf War, President George H. W. Bush called on the Iraqi people to pull down Saddam themselves. That didn't happen, and many of those who had supported U.S. efforts were then killed or severely punished once the U.S. presence was gone; so, twelve years later, the United States completed the task itself. On this April day, a small group of Iraqis tried to pull down Saddam's statue. But, in spite of their efforts, Saddam didn't budge. Then, in a scene reminiscent of old Westerns, when the cavalry arrives to save the day, American soldiers of the Third Battalion, Fourth Marines Regiment rolled up in an M88 tank recovery vehicle. The image of Corporal Edward Chin, twenty-three, attaching a rope around the statue's neck, briefly wrapping Saddam's face in an American flag and then an Iraqi flag, and then pulling the statue to the ground was broadcast on television screens around the world. The following morning, virtually every major newspaper in the country featured a large photo of the event on the front page.

The statue broke first above the boots, leaving Saddam's feet still planted on the base. That evening, French broadcasters interpreted the scene as one that showed how difficult it was for the Americans to remove Saddam's presence from Iraq. But the American audience saw it as an act of patriotism and the fulfillment of a promise to remove Saddam from power.

Was the event carefully staged, or did serendipity dictate conditions that resulted in such a memorable symbol? Bryan Whitman discounts any military spin. "The statue came down. There was no spin in that. Perhaps it was covered only because the journalists were there. The Iraqis instigated the event. If you watch the event unfold, the U.S. military after several hours, said, 'It looks like you need some help here,' and they went over and helped them."

Broadcasting live on NBC's *Today Show,* Katie Couric noted that draping the American flag across the statue was an "in your face" gesture. American soldiers, indeed, had been directed not to display the American flag as a symbol of conquest. Was draping the U.S. flag across the statue's face an issue? "The Defense Department is a big department, and I'm sure there were some people who saw that in many different ways," Whitman says. "The fact of the matter is that these were soldiers who had just fought in a hard-fought battle into the capital of the opposing force. It was a celebration by both the Iraqi people who were on the ground as well as the Americans. To be honest, I didn't even know the Palestine Hotel was in that vicinity. That could very well be why it was covered. I would imagine that there were statues coming down all over Baghdad. But that's the one that the world knew because the media were there to bring it to everybody."

In fact, most of the journalists who were there thought the incident received far more play than it deserved. Both NPR's Anne Garrels and AP's Jerome Delay said it was remarkable only in that it was close to a large group of journalists with cameras.

There was concern that it in fact gave the American people the incorrect impression that the war was over. "Certainly I think it might have heightened expectations that turned out to be wrong. Anybody who saw that as the end of the war would be sadly mistaken," says CNN's Eason Jordan. "There is really only one reason why you saw that in such a big way. And that was that the Baghdad press corps was set up in the hotel across the street from the statue. That's why it became such a big thing. There were statues all over the country being pulled down, but you saw very few of them happening. When the press corps is all in one building and something happens across the street, it is very convenient. So, it was showcased in a way that, while I think it got undue attention, it didn't make it any less riveting from a TV perspective. It was wrong to think that it was the end of the war, but that is certainly the one picture we will take away from the war."

## NOTES

1. The Program on International Policy Attitudes is a joint program of the Center on Policy Attitudes and the Center for International and Security Studies at Maryland, School of Public Affairs, University of Maryland. Knowledge Networks is a consumer-information company.

2. The report can be found at www.pipa.org/OnlineReports/Iraq/Media_10_02_03 _Report.pdf.

3. Available at www.journalism.org/resources/research/reports/war/postwar/lynch. asp.

# Conclusion

## EMBEDS VERSUS UNILATERALS

A great deal of this book has been devoted to describing and comparing the embed and unilateral experiences. The Pentagon began the embed program to make sure American and international journalists were on hand to counter Iraqi propaganda and to show the skill of the U.S. military. In addition, given a military operation of this kind, more than nine hundred journalists were planning to cover the action. Clearly, having journalists rove the battlefield was an undesirable option, not only for a military that was moving at lightning speed, but also for the journalists who could end up as unprotected, inadvertent targets. So, from the military's point of view, providing a protected "structure" for journalists made sense. To its credit, the military also realized that trying to control what journalists produced would not achieve the desired ends; thus, a strategy of unfettered coverage was adopted. An important benefit of this approach was a new and better understanding of the life of the American soldier.

The media still had a long way to go before they were satisfied that the military meant what it said about unrestricted access, especially to the front lines of combat. As noted, some veteran reporters simply refused to become a part of the program, because of their previous unsatisfactory working relationship with the military. Others went along expecting to face censorship and restrictions. In the end, however, both sides agreed that in this kind of military operation, embedding worked to the mutual benefit of the media and the military.

Embedded journalists quickly came to understand that, although they had few rules and no censorship, there were limitations. Numerous embedded journalists point out that they saw only a small slice of the war. Those who were not "lucky" ended up with units that saw little or no action. Those who were lucky saw what their particular units encountered, often with little knowledge of what was happening elsewhere. This situation is exactly what prompted unilaterals. In theory, unilaterals would go where the embeds could not. They could get the "big picture" and counter any potential censorship that might restrict the embeds. Many tried to do just that. But in the end, they had the same problem as the embeds. They often had to stay near the military, not only to get the story, but also to avoid becoming targets. They also were either lucky or unlucky in terms of being in the right place at the right time.

As Bryan Whitman said, ultimately the media themselves have to determine whether the information they got from their unilaterals justified the great risk involved. Clearly, both those who were embedded and those who were unilaterals believed they made a contribution, and media managers believed that they needed both types of journalists in the field to provide the best coverage and meet or beat the competition.

The journalists did represent two major problems for the military that could have affected the outcome of the war. First, there were concerns that the Thuraya satellite phones that most journalists were using could give away troop position. The global positioning function could—in reality or in theory—let technically sophisticated enemies zero in on the phone's signal and permit a military unit to be targeted with missiles and possibly biological or chemical agents. The second concern regarded the media's civilian vehicles. Although most were labeled "television" vehicles, they still added a dimension of confusion and potential hazard to the battlefield. They became "soft targets" that were the object of friendly fire mostly because Iraqis were using similar vehicles for suicide bombing missions. Such vehicles also posed the danger of breaking down, thereby holding up a convoy and delaying the arrival of troops and supplies. The military tried to keep these vehicles off the battlefield by offering embedded journalists free use of their batteries and electrical supplies, but numerous unilaterals and some embeds had nonmilitary transportation, especially television crews who had to drag along satellite dishes as well as backup cameras and recording equipment. They traveled fast, but they didn't travel light.

Additional tensions included those between the embeds and the unilaterals. The embeds—who in most cases had undergone military training and established trust with their assigned units' commanding officers and soldiers—were none too pleased when competition in the form of unilaterals arrived and wanted the same access that the embeds had established. That resentment created a dilemma for the military, also. The Pentagon had gone to great lengths to make the allotting of slots fair and equitable. Officials there didn't want unilaterals upsetting the carefully established allocation of slots—especially since each unit had the maximum number of journalists that it could presumably protect and accommodate.

Although one of the main pre-war concerns about the embed program—censorship—did not materialize, another concern did. Objectivity was feared to be the first causality of war. In fact, the majority of the embeds said that they could not maintain objectivity. They were, after all, eating, sleeping, riding—and in a couple of cases dying—with the soldiers they were accompanying. Soldiers weren't "subjects" in the sense that the journalists interviewed them and then never saw them again. In fact, the journalists saw some of them wounded and dead. The embeds had learned about the soldiers' lives outside the military—the children who were born, the marriages that disintegrated, the relatives who would not be there when the soldiers returned home. The journalists loaned the soldiers sat phones, e-mailed the soldiers' parents and spouses, and wrote stories about them that their families and friends would be able to embrace as proof that, for one day at least, their sons and daughters, husbands and wives, and mothers and fathers were safe. The embeds, however, were keenly aware that they owed their lives to the soldiers surrounding them. That was strong impetus to follow the rules—that is, not give away troop positions—and to perhaps self-censor to avoid irking commanding officers who could make life tougher for them. Regardless, no evidence suggests that any coverage was impaired in any way by this system. Several stories, in fact, might not otherwise have been reported.

On March 24, 2003, an American soldier was arrested for lobbing a grenade into the tent of some of his fellow soldiers, killing one and injuring up to fifteen others. Whether this story would have received the attention it did without the embeds is open to speculation. Similarly, the deaths of Iraqi civilians also might not have received coverage. However, the American media continued to provide details about the lives of Iraqis, both during and after the major military action of the war. Another question that has not been asked is whether the media could have remained more involved in covering the occupation. Would the abuses at Abu Ghraib have occurred had the media been watching more closely?

The media still need to face the ethics of covering war in a more concrete way. For example, there were rumors that some journalists were armed with rifles or grenades when they were in battle zones. Whether carrying arms pushes journalists across the line from noncombatant to combatant simply was not discussed openly during the war. Likewise, the problem of media vehicles' joining, and presumably endangering, military convoys was also dismissed without much thoughtful discussion.

Some journalists crossed lines in other ways. Jim Landers, reporting for the *Dallas Morning News,* said that he considered the ramifications before he stepped forward and took over holding an IV bag to relieve a soldier who was assisting a medic working on a wounded Iraqi. Landers decided that it would not compromise his covering the war if he held the bag so that the American soldier would be free to go on with his unit. CNN correspondent Sanjay Gupta, a physician, performed brain surgery on at least five people, some of whom were Iraqis, while he was embedded with the U.S. Navy's "Devil Docs" unit. These doctors are navy personnel who work for the Marine Corps. Although Gupta reported on the activities of the Devil Docs, he did not report on his personal medical-related activities.

The embeds in general did not seem to consider such involvement unethical as long as their reporting efforts were not compromised.

Also deserving of more open discussion is the conduct of journalists who were willing to release information, either publicly or privately, to government and military officials to gain access and get the "scoop" before their competitors.

The question remains: as a result of the embed program, have the media and the military forged a new relationship that will stand the test of continued military action in Iraq and Afghanistan or other foreign locations? In evaluating the experience, Byron Harris, WFAA-TV, found both good and bad. "The good side of embedding was unfettered access to the troops, who were free in discussing their opinions with us, and unrestrained access to the battlefield as it unfolded in front of us. The embedding process was necessary from a military standpoint because without it, reporters would have become hindrances to the battle. Most reporters have little or no knowledge of the military and would have been most likely killed by friendly fire. I appreciate the military's practical necessity of managing this problem," he said. "The bad side is that the restrictions of the embedding process obviously gave the military a tremendous opportunity to manage the news. We were tethered to them for transportation. We couldn't break away. If our unit was moving, we had to move with them and could only rarely stop to talk to Iraqis."

Clearly, a new respect—if not admiration—has developed between the two groups. Although each side is likely to continue participating in manipulation, perhaps each side will more readily recognize it when it occurs. It is unlikely that embedding will be used in every military operation—especially smaller Special Forces operations. It is even more unlikely that the military will be effective in the future in preventing real-time coverage of major operations. The military received too much benefit from the up-close coverage, while a new generation of journalists now knows what it means to cover war. They now know the uncomfortable, often-harsh conditions and physical demands that soldiers face. They now know what it is to leave loved ones behind for an undetermined amount of time. And they now know what is like to watch comrades die. Was it worth it? You decide.

# Appendices

# APPENDIX A
## RULES AND REGULATIONS

Although there were several versions of the rules and regulations for embeds, this example (provided by Robert Riggs, KTVT-11) includes the basic guidelines. The Pentagon developed a version that was sent to each company, but at that point, the company could supply additional requirements.

Department of the Army
Headquarters US Army Air Defense Artillery Center
Fort Bliss, Texas 79934
Invitational Travel Order No. 2-94
Date: 24 February 2003
NAME: Riggs, Robert Stanley (Member of the Media; KTVT Channel 11–Dallas CBS affiliate)

1. The news media representative (NMR) listed above is on Secretary of the Army/Navy/Air Force and Office of the Assistant Secretary of Defense approved media travel and may use AMC or AMC-gained aircraft to fly from Fort Bliss, TX on or about 24 February 2003 to Kuwait, with return to Fort Bliss, TX on or about 31 March 2003. Purpose of the media travel is to gather material, film/video coverage of the Department of Defense's mission, aircraft, aircrews and support personnel in support of Operation Enduring Freedom to Kuwait. Travel authorized per DOD 4515.13 and AFI 35-206. Variations in itinerary authorized while under public affairs escort. NMRs are not allowed to remain in AOR without public affairs escort and OASD(PA) approval. While on any AMC or AMC-gained aircraft, NMRs will fasten seatbelts during takeoffs, landings, and when instructed by aircrew member or public affairs escort(s).

NMRs will also observe all safety regulations and follow the directions of the flight crew at all times. NMRs will be advised that the possibility exists that the aircraft may be diverted to another location if unexpected mission requirements develop. In this case, NMRs may be required to provide their own transportation to a final destination. Travel is on a non-interference-with-mission basis. Authorization to travel does not authorize displacement of duty passengers or cargo displacement of duty passengers or cargo, however, media is authorized access to aircrew and flight deck. Use of electronic recording equipment is granted at the discretion of the aircraft commander. Such equipment will be turned off if so directed. Aircraft commander will not expend additional fuel. NMRs are not to have access to any classified information or materials. Designated public affairs escort must advise the aircraft commander of the contents of this order. NMRs will be accorded all the courtesies and privileges at equivalent grade of GS-12, rank of O-4, for billeting, exchange privileges, dining facilities, official transportation and open mess (when available) while under public affairs escort. NMRs are authorized excess baggage.

2. The travel authorized herein has been determined to be in the public interest.
3. Address any inquiries regarding this travel order to Commander, US Army Army Air Defense Artillery Center, ATTN: ATZB-DHR-AG, 500 Shannon Road, Bldg 500, Fort Bliss, TX 79916-6812.

## CFLCC GROUND RULES AGREEMENT

Ground rules. For the safety and security of U.S. forces and media, media will adhere to established ground rules. Ground rules will be agreed to in advance and signed by media prior to embedding. Violation of the ground rules may result in the immediate termination of the embed and removal from the AOR. These ground rules recognize the right of the media to cover military operations and are in no way intended to prevent release of derogatory, embarrassing, negative or uncomplimentary information.

Standard ground rules are:

1. All interviews with service members will be on the record. Security at the source is the policy. Interviews with pilots and aircrew members are authorized upon completion of missions; however, release of information must conform to these media ground rules.
2. Print or broadcast stories will be datelined according to local ground rules. Local ground rules will be coordinated through command channels with CENTCOM.
3. Media embedded with U.S. forces are not permitted to carry personal firearms.
4. Media will not possess or consume alcoholic beverages or possess pornographic materials while embedded with coalition forces.

5. Light discipline restrictions will be followed. Visible light sources, including flash or television lights, flash cameras will not be used when operating with forces at night unless specifically approved in advance by the on-scene commander.
6. Embargoes may be imposed to protect operational security. Embargoes will only be used for operational security and will be lifted as soon as the operational security issue has passed.
7. The following categories of information are releasable.
8. Approximate friendly force strength figures.
9. Approximate friendly casualty figures by service. Embedded media may, within OPSEC limits, confirm unit casualties they have witnessed.
10. Confirmed figures of enemy personnel detained or captured.
11. Size of friendly force participating in an action or operation can be disclosed using approximate terms. Specific force or unit identification may be released when it no longer warrants security protection.
12. Information and location of military targets and objectives previously under attack.
13. Generic description of origin of air operations, such as "land-based."
14. Date, time or location of previous conventional military missions and actions, as well as mission results are releasable only if described in general terms.
15. Types of ordnance expended in general terms.
16. Number of aerial combat or reconnaissance missions or sorties flown in CENTCOM's area of operation.
17. Type of forces involved (e.g., air defense, infantry, armor, Marines).
18. Allied participation by type of operation (ships, aircraft, ground units, etc.) after approval of the allied unit commander.
19. Operation code names.
20. Names and hometowns of U.S. military units.
21. Service members' names and home towns with the individuals' consent.
22. The following categories of information are not releasable since their publication or broadcast could jeopardize operations and endanger lives.
23. Specific number of troops in units below Corps/MEF level.
24. Specific number of aircraft in units at or below the Air Expeditionary Wing level.
25. Specific numbers regarding other equipment or critical supplies (e.g. artillery, tanks, landing craft, radars, trucks, water, etc.).
26. Specific numbers of ships in units below the carrier battle group level.
27. Names of military installations or specific geographic locations of military units in the CENTCOM area of responsibility, unless specifically released by the Department of Defense or authorized by the CENTCOM commander. News and imagery products that identify or include identifiable features of these locations are not authorized for release.

28. Information regarding future operations.
29. Information regarding force protection measures at military installations or encampments (except those which are visible or readily apparent).
30. Photography showing level of security at military installations or encampments.
31. Rules of engagement.
32. Information on intelligence collection activities compromising tactics, techniques or procedures.
33. Extra precautions in reporting will be required at the commencement of hostilities to maximize operational surprise. Live broadcasts from airfields, on the ground or afloat, by embedded media are prohibited until the safe return of the initial strike package or until authorized by the unit commander.
34. During an operation, specific information on friendly force troop movements, tactical deployments, and dispositions that would jeopardize operational security or lives. Information on on-going engagements will not be released unless authorized for release by on-scene commander.
35. Information on special operations units, unique operations methodology or tactics, for example, air operations, angles of attack, and speeds; naval tactical or evasive maneuvers, etc. General terms such as "low" or "fast" may be used.
36. Information on effectiveness of enemy electronic warfare.
37. Information identifying postponed or canceled operations.
38. Information on missing or downed aircraft or missing vessels while search and rescue and recovery operations are being planned or underway.
39. Information on effectiveness of enemy camouflage, cover, deception, targeting, direct and indirect fire, intelligence collection, or security measures.
40. No photographs or other visual media showing an enemy prisoner of war or detainee's recognizable face, nametag or other identifying feature or item may be taken. No interviews with detainees will be granted.
41. Still or video imagery of custody operations or interviews with persons under custody.
42. Media representatives will not release names of service members killed, missing or injured until next of kin [NOK] notification is completed.
43. Although images of casualties are authorized to show the horrors of war, no photographs or other visual media showing a deceased service member's recognizable face, nametag or other identifying feature or item may be taken.
44. Media visits to medical facilities will be in accordance with applicable regulations, standard operating procedures, operations orders and instructions by attending physicians. If approved, service or medical facility personnel must escort media at all times.
45. Patient welfare, patient privacy, and next of kin/family considerations are the governing concerns about news media coverage of wounded, injured, and ill

personnel in medical treatment facilities or other casualty collection and treatment locations.

46. Media visits are authorized to medical care facilities, but must be approved by the medical facility commander and attending physician and must not interfere with medical treatment. Requests to visit medical care facilities outside the continental United States will be coordinated by the unified command PA.

47. Reporters may visit those areas designated by the facility commander, but will not be allowed in operating rooms during operating procedures.

48. Permission to interview or photograph a patient will be granted only with the consent of the attending physician or facility commander and with the patient's informed consent, witnessed by the escort.

49. "Informed consent" means the patient understands his or her picture and comments are being collected for news media purposes and they may appear nationwide in news media reports.

50. The attending physician or escort should advise the service member if NOK have been notified.

I, (insert name) _____, am (insert job description) _____, an employee of _____ (insert news organization), have read the aforementioned media ground rules and agree, with my signature, to abide by them. I also understand that violation of these ground rules is cause for the revocation of my media accreditation with CFLCC.

_____

Signature, Date

_____

Printed Name, Affiliate, Address & Phone Number

_____

Witness Signature, Date

_____

Witness Printed Name, Rank & Organization

# APPENDIX B
## "GEARING UP" FOR WAR

At the time the war began, it was believed that Saddam Hussein had nuclear, chemical, and/or biological weapons in his arsenal and that he would be willing to use them in the war. So the journalists embedded with the troops had to prepare for such an attack—the same as the soldiers—as well as for more conventional attacks involving weapons, land mines, and heavy ordnance. The weather would be extremely hot in the daytime and cold in the nighttime. Showers, supplies, and equipment repair shops would be unavailable to many, if not most, of the reporters and photographers.

Clearly, this assignment of covering troops and enemy action within a war zone called for specialized clothing and equipment. Many of the journalists who covered the action in Iraq, as embeds or as unilaterals, carried with them or wore equipment and clothing totaling several thousands of dollars. They needed two sets of specialized equipment: one with which to live and one with which to work. The reporters and photographers basically had to take everything the soldiers took—except the weapons, which the journalists were forbidden to have—plus all of their electronic news-gathering gear.

The military issued a list of items that it recommended journalists take with them. Reading it is a chilling reminder of the danger they were putting themselves in: they were to put their identification card in their left breast pocket and mark their left boot with their blood type and social security number.

To live, they needed equipment to protect their head and face. This included a combat helmet, a ski cap to wear under the helmet, a gas mask and air canteen, goggles, a sun hat, sunglasses, and a neckerchief that could serve as both a sweatband and a head cover. To protect and care for their body, they needed a flak jacket, chemical suit, camouflage pants and jacket, cotton T-shirts, and underwear.

To protect their feet, they needed socks and steel-toed combat boots. They also carried a money belt, backpack, first-aid kit, assorted medicines and antidotes, sunscreen, lip balm, bug repellent, and a shaving razor. To clean up, they carried baby wipes and travel-size detergent packets. To sleep, they carried a sleeping bag, ground pad, and tent. To eat and drink, they carried MREs, a water canteen, and hydration pack. The MREs were self-contained units—no cooking or eating utensils necessary.

To work, they took pens and paper, a videophone or satellite phone with requisite battery pack, travel charger, software, and cables. They carried a laptop computer and a battery charger, a mobile antenna, a digital video camera with tapes, a digital audio recorder with tapes, a shortwave radio, adapter plugs, a flashlight and/or a headlamp, and extension cords. They carried resealable bags to protect their gear from the ever-present sand and dust. And to relax and pass the time they took books, CDs, and magazines.

The military provided the gas masks, chemical suits, boots, and related gear—two sets of everything but the mask. The journalists were issued the same things that the soldiers were issued. And the journalists were expected to carry their gear wherever they went. For the television people, that was often impossible, at least in one trip. They had to rely on Humvees to get some of their gear around, or they had to take two trips carrying stuff back and forth. The full bulletproof-vest units were expensive. One reporter remembers, "We went with the cheaper flak jackets, but if I had it to do over again, I would have insisted on the bulletproof plating. I think those ran over a thousand bucks a piece. I know, with all our gear, we spent several thousand dollars over and above the TV equipment—on helmets, canteens, sleeping bags, and the like."

This assignment would be a life-changing experience for many of the journalists. They would be working in an environment more extreme than many could have imagined. Day to day, the working conditions were exhausting, unrelenting, dangerous, overwhelming, confusing, and uncertain. The reporters and photographers worked quite a few stress-filled twenty-four-hour days.

## APPENDIX C
PACKED FOR WAR

Here is a list of items that the military strongly recommended the embeds take with them for living in the field.

**ITEMS IN BACKPACK**

1 trousers/shirt set, muted desert colors w/cargo pockets

1 belt (as applies)

3 undershirts

3 underwear

5 pair socks, cushion sole

1 pair polypro long underwear (top and bottom)

1 knit watch cap

1 towel, small

1 bath sponge

1 soap, antibacterial (w/plastic container)

1 can shaving cream

1 razor

10 disposable blades

1 package baby wipes

1 bottle hand sanitizer

1 qt. Ziploc bag laundry detergent powder

1 waterproof bag

2 trash bags

1 pair shower shoes (aka flip-flops)

1 sewing kit

1 foot powder

1 toothpaste, full tube

1 toothbrush

1 field mirror

1 nail clipper

1 pair extra eyeglasses (as required)

1 pair of gloves

1 sleeping bag with bivy sack

1 entrenching tool (shovel) w/ carrier

1 CamelBack

1 funnel (for water)

1 per 4 personnel sleeping pad/isoporo mat

1 pair earplugs w/case

1 set extra bootlaces

1 sunscreen

1 insect repellent

1 goggles/sunglasses

1 Gore-Tex jacket/trousers

1 2-person shelter (tent) (optional)

prescription medicine (must have prescription)

90-day supply doxycycline, cipro

2 rolls toilet paper

1 neck scarf/bandanna

1 small daypack

## ITEMS TO BE WORN

1 Kevlar helmet w/chin strap

1 mopp suit (w/gloves carried in cargo pocket)

1 undershirt

1 skivvies

1 pair of shorts

1 ID (in left breast pocket)

1 set socks, cushion sole

1 pair boots (mark left boot with blood type/SSN)

1 pair NBC booties worn over field boots

1 M-40 series field protective mask w/filter

1 NBC meds atropine and 2 pamcl (in M-40 carrier)

1 m 291 chemical decon kit in M-40 carrier

1 armor body upper torso (mark w/name and blood type)

2 canteens w/covers and NBC caps

1 first aid kit

1 wristwatch

1 desert floppy cover (hat)

## PROHIBITED ITEMS (CENTCOM GENERAL ORDER 1A)

No pornography or sexually explicit material

No drug other than prescribed medications which must be accompanied by the original prescription

No alcoholic beverages

No firearms, ammunition, explosives

No bright colored/multicolored bags—please use a black, tan, olive green, or woodland/desert camouflage bag

## APPENDIX D

THE MEDIA AND THE MILITARY MEET TO PLAN THE EMBED PROGRAM

At least three meetings regarding the rules and regulations for journalists participating in the embed program were held in Washington, D.C., during the fall of 2002. Pentagon officials invited representatives of the Washington bureaus to participate in the meetings. Although it is likely that a smaller number of news organizations were informally contacted before these larger meetings, no one in either the Pentagon or the news organizations contacted would confirm who participated or the extent to which they were advising the Pentagon in the early stages. However, transcripts of the three formal meetings are available on the Defense Department's website at www.defenselink.mil/news/Nov2002/t11012002 _t1030sd.html, www.defenselink.mil/news/Jan2003/t01152003_t0114bc.html, and www.defenselink.mil/news/Feb2003/t02282003_t0227bc.html.

News media representatives and their organizations introduced at those meetings were Mark Stern, Copley News Service; Francis Kohn, Agence France-Presse; Robin Doherty, Reuters; George Tamerlani, Reuters Television; Tim Aubry, Reuters Pictures; Richard Ellis, Getty Images; Clark Hoyt, Knight Ridder Newspapers; Richard Sisk, *New York Daily News*; Jack Payton, Voice of America; Merrilee Cox, ABC Radio News; John Henry, *Houston Chronicle*; Chuck Lewis, Hearst Newspapers; Steve Geimann, Bloomberg News; Tobin Beck, United Press International; Wendy Wilkinson, NBC; Jill Abramson, *New York Times*; Robin Sproul, ABC News; David Cook, *Christian Science Monitor*; John Hall, Associated Press Photos; Jim Michaels, *USA Today*; Tom Mattesky, CBS; Kim Hume, FOX News; Laura Myers, AP; Sandy Johnson, AP; Carl Leubsdorf, *Dallas Morning News*; Dave Wood, Newhouse News Service; Peter Copeland, Scripps Howard; Andy Alexander, Cox Newspapers; Cathy Abbott, deputy director, Press Office; Vickie Walton-James, *Chicago Tribune*; Bob Timberg, *Baltimore Sun*; Bruce Auster, *US News*;

Matt Vita, *Washington Post*; Tom McCarthy, *Los Angeles Times*; Deborah Howell, Newhouse News Service; Harry Walker, Knight Ridder Tribune Photos; David Sweeney, NPR News; Craig Gilbert, *Milwaukee Journal Sentinel*; Steve Redisch, CNN; Bill Gertz, *Washington Times*; Gerald Seib, *Wall Street Journal*; David Cook, *Boston Globe*; Thelma Lebrecht, AP Radio; Denise Vance, AP Television.

Defense Department officials introduced were Victoria Clarke, assistant secretary of defense for public affairs; Bryan Whitman, deputy assistant secretary of defense for public affairs; Jay DeFrank, director of press operations; T. McCreary, Joint Chiefs of Staff Public Affairs; Drew Davis, Marines; Steve Pietropaoli, Navy Public Affairs; Larry Gottardi, Army Public Affairs.

Steve Geimann, co-leader of the policy team at Bloomberg News, Washington bureau, and a member of the Sigma Delta Chi Foundation Board, says that the meetings between the Washington bureau chiefs and Pentagon officials allowed journalists to provide input to the Pentagon about the embed program, although he thinks that the input was limited. "It appeared to me, and to others who were at this larger meeting—with fifty-plus news executives—that it was designed to outline what the Pentagon had decided, after talking to some members of the media. These people were never identified, and to my knowledge, there was never any 'pool' arrangement in which a handful of people were designated to represent the other bureau chiefs during this process," he says. "It did appear that the Pentagon had worked out whatever kinks they felt were present with the smaller group. Media input by the time we were called to the meetings appeared to be limited."

The meetings were also used for organization purposes, and the participants were encouraged to have likely embed reporters sign up for military training in Quantico or at another U.S. base. However, meeting participants were told that having someone go through training was no guarantee that a journalist would be selected for an embed position.

"The Pentagon officials, mostly Victoria Clarke and Bryan Whitman, sought to allay all the concerns and issues for the bureau chiefs," Geimann says. "On the surface, the embed plan was magnificent. The media were getting access right alongside the grunts, officers, and other uniformed officers. After the failed/flawed 'national media pool' set up after Grenada and Panama, this idea of letting at least one reporter tag along with a unit was like opening a sliding glass door as far as it would go."

Geimann recalls that many of the bureau chiefs seemed surprised that as a condition of winning a spot as an embed, the media organization pledged to keep the reporter with the group indefinitely. "We were told that the slot was being awarded to a reporter/journalist, not to a media organization. A newspaper, wire service, or TV channel that wanted to replace that person was out of luck."

Whether the embed program was a success depends on whom you ask, Geimann says. "I think for those news organizations that had the resources to have multiple embeds, the system worked well. Reporters and camera crews had up-front access to fighting and often were ahead of the official spokesmen in detailing success and failure on the ground or in the air. The embed also took some of the heat off the briefers in Doha and at the Pentagon. They often ducked confirming news reported by AP, Reuters, CNN, or NBC, until their channels had confirmed the details."

Geimann is uncertain about whether the embed approach helped the public's understanding of the battle. "The ground level coverage was interesting and riveting, in some respects," he says. "I think fewer people got a good sense of how the military was progressing, overall, because too much time was spent on small details and few people were doing the larger, overall story."

# APPENDIX E

ASSOCIATED PRESS PHOTO POLICY

 **Associated Press**

To the AP Photo Staff:

The following statement of our policy on electronic handling of photos was issued in 1990, the infancy of high-speed photo transmission and digital picture handling. It is as valid today as it was then.

Electronic imaging raised new questions about what is ethical in the process of editing photographs. The question may have been new, but the answers all come from old values.

Simply put, The Associated Press does not alter photographs. Our pictures must always tell the truth.

The computer has become a highly sophisticated photo editing tool. It has taken us out of a chemical darkroom where subtle printing techniques, such as burning and dodging, have long been accepted as journalistically sound. Today these terms are replaced by "image manipulation" and "enhancement". In a time when such broad terms could be misconstrued, we need to set limits and restate some basic tenets.

The content of a photograph will NEVER be changed or manipulated in any way.

Only the established norms of standard photo printing methods such as burning, dodging, toning and cropping are acceptable. Retouching is limited to removal of normal scratches and dust spots.

Serious consideration must always be given in correcting color to ensure honest reproduction of the original. Cases of abnormal color or tonality will be clearly stated in the caption. Color adjustment should always be minimal.

In any instance where a question arises about such issues, consult a senior editor immediately.

The integrity of the AP's photo report is our highest priority. Nothing takes precedence over its credibility.

Thank you,
Vin Alabiso

# APPENDIX F

The Committee to Protect Journalists tracks threats to journalists around the world and investigates the circumstances of their deaths or injuries. As of April 2004, CPJ lists twenty-four journalists who were killed while covering the Iraq War: thirteen in 2003 and eleven in the first three months of 2004.

## 2003

### Terry Lloyd, ITV News, March 22, 2003, near Al-Zubayr

Lloyd, a veteran correspondent with ITV News, was confirmed dead on March 23 by the British TV network ITN, which produces ITV News. The previous day, he had disappeared after coming under fire while driving to the southern Iraqi city of Basra.

Two others disappeared with Lloyd, cameraman Fred Nerac and translator Hussein Othman. They remain missing.

The three men, along with cameraman Daniel Demoustier, were traveling in two marked press vehicles in the town of Iman Anas, near Al-Zubayr, when they came under fire, ITN reported. According to Demoustier, the car he and Lloyd had been driving had been pursued by Iraqi troops who may have been attempting to surrender to the journalists. Demoustier reported that the incoming fire to their vehicles likely came from U.S. or British forces in the area.

Demoustier, who was injured when the car he was driving crashed into a ditch and caught fire, managed to escape. He said he did not see what happened to Lloyd, who was seated next to him, or to the other crew members. Lloyd's body was recovered in a hospital in Basra days later.

An investigative article published in the *Wall Street Journal* in May indicated that Lloyd's SUV and another vehicle belonging to his colleagues came under fire from U.S. Marines. The article cited accounts from U.S. troops who recalled opening fire on cars marked "TV." Soldiers also said they believed that Iraqi suicide bombers were using the cars to attack U.S. troops.

The *Journal* article cited a report from a British security firm commissioned by ITN to investigate the incident saying that Lloyd's car was hit by both coalition and Iraqi fire; the latter most likely came from behind the car, possibly after the vehicle had crashed.

The report concluded that "[t]he Iraqis no doubt mounted an attack using the ITN crew as cover, or perhaps stumbled into the U.S. forces whilst attempting to detain the ITN crew." The report also speculated that the missing men—Nerac and Othman, who were last seen by Demoustier in another car being stopped by Iraqi forces—might have been pulled out of their car before it came under fire from coalition forces, and then Iraqi forces used the SUV to attack the coalition forces.

In April, Nerac's wife approached U.S. Secretary of State Colin Powell at a NATO press conference, and he promised to do everything in his power to find out what had happened to the missing men. In late May, CENTCOM said that it was investigating the incident, while the British Ministry of Defense promised to open an inquiry. Neither had made public any results as of October.

In September, London's *Daily Mirror* newspaper reported the testimony of an Iraqi man named Hamid Aglan who had allegedly tried to rescue the wounded Lloyd in a civilian minibus. Aglan told the newspaper that he had picked up a lightly wounded Lloyd, who had suffered only a shoulder injury, and attempted to take him to a hospital in Basra when the minibus came under fire from a U.S. helicopter, killing Lloyd. The paper reported that the bus was also carrying wounded Iraqi soldiers.

An ITN spokesperson told CPJ that a number of elements of Aglan's story are not consistent with ITN's own investigation. She said an autopsy revealed that Lloyd had suffered two serious wounds that likely resulted from Iraqi and U.S. fire. She said that after he was wounded, an Iraqi civilian in a minibus had picked up Lloyd and tried to take him to a hospital in Basra. The minibus later came under U.S. attack. "It was a gunshot to the bus and [Terry] was probably in the bus," she said. ITN investigators believe that either wound that Lloyd sustained before the bus attack would have been fatal.

### Paul Moran, freelance, March 22, 2003, Gerdigo

Moran, a freelance cameraman on assignment for the Australian Broadcasting Corporation, was killed in a suicide bombing when a man detonated a car at a checkpoint in northeastern Iraq. Another Australian Broadcasting Corporation journalist, correspondent Eric Campbell, was injured in the incident.

Michael Ware, *Time* magazine's northern Iraq correspondent and a witness to the incident, told his editor, Howard Chua-Eoan, that several foreign journalists were standing outside a checkpoint on the edge of Gerdigo, a town in northern Iraq near Halabja, interviewing people who were leaving the town in the wake of a U.S. cruise missile bombardment that began on March 21 and continued until the next day.

U.S. missiles were targeting strongholds of Ansar al-Islam, a militant group that the United States designates as a terrorist organization. The area where the journalists were conducting interviews was reportedly under the control of the Patriotic Union of Kurdistan (PUK), a rival of Ansar al-Islam that had just taken over the area.

At around 3 P.M., a taxi drove to the checkpoint near PUK soldiers and Moran, and the driver then detonated his vehicle. Most of the other journalists had just left the scene. Moran, who was filming at the time, was standing only a few feet from the checkpoint and was killed immediately. Campbell was injured by shrapnel.

Chua-Eoan said it appeared that the bomber was targeting the PUK soldiers, not the journalists. According to the Associated Press, at least four other people were killed in the bombing. Militants from Ansar al-Islam are believed to be responsible for the attack.

Chua-Eoan told CPJ that foreign journalists in northern Iraq had recently received warnings from U.S. State Department and Kurdish intelligence officials that Ansar al-Islam may target members of the media, as well as the hotel where most journalists are staying, the Sulaymaniyeh Palace.

### Kaveh Golestan, freelance, April 2, 2003, Kifri

Golestan, an Iranian freelance cameraman on assignment for the BBC, was killed in northern Iraq after stepping on a land mine, the BBC confirmed.

Golestan accidentally detonated the mine when he exited his car near the town of Kifri, John Morrissey of the BBC's foreign desk told CPJ. The cameraman was traveling as part of a four-person BBC crew that included Tehran, Iran, bureau chief Jim Muir, producer Stuart Hughes, and translator Rabeen Azad. Hughes's foot was injured and later treated by U.S. military medics. Muir and the translator suffered light cuts, Morrissey said.

Golestan, who was also a well-known still photographer, had worked frequently with the BBC out of its Tehran bureau.

### Michael Kelly, *Atlantic Monthly* and the *Washington Post*, April 3, 2003, outside Baghdad

Kelly, editor at large of the *Atlantic Monthly* and a columnist with the *Washington Post*, was killed while traveling with the U.S. Army's Third Infantry Division just south of the Baghdad airport, according to a statement from the *Washington Post*.

According to press reports, when the Humvee in which Kelly was riding came under Iraqi fire, the soldier driving the vehicle tried to evade the attack, and the jeep ran off the road and rolled into a canal. Both Kelly and the driver drowned.

Kelly, who had previously served as the editor of the *New Republic* and the *National Journal*, was the first U.S. journalist killed while covering the war.

### Christian Liebig, *Focus*, April 7, 2003, outside Baghdad

Liebig, a reporter for the German weekly magazine *Focus*, died in an Iraqi missile attack while accompanying the U.S. Army's Third Infantry Division south of the capital, Baghdad. Both Liebig and Julio Anguita Parrado, a Spanish journalist also killed in the incident, were embedded with the division, according to Agence France-Presse.

According to *Focus* editor in chief Helmut Markwort, the two men had decided not to travel with the unit to Baghdad, believing they would be safer at the base. Two U.S. soldiers were also killed during the attack, and fifteen were injured.

Liebig, thirty-five, had worked for *Focus* since 1999.

### Julio Anguita Parrado, *El Mundo*, April 7, 2003, outside Baghdad

Parrado, a correspondent for the Spanish daily *El Mundo*, died in an Iraqi missile attack while accompanying the U.S. Army's Third Infantry Division south of the capital, Baghdad. Both Parrado and Christian Liebig, a German journalist for *Focus* magazine who was also killed in the incident, were embedded with the division, according to Agence France-Presse.

According to *Focus* editor in chief Helmut Markwort, the two men had decided not to travel with the unit to Baghdad, believing they would be safer at the base. Two U.S. soldiers were also killed during the attack, and fifteen were injured. Parrado was the second *El Mundo* correspondent to have been killed in conflict in less than two years: Correspondent Julio Fuentes died after gunmen ambushed his convoy in Afghanistan in 2001.

### Tareq Ayyoub, Al Jazeera, April 8, 2003, Baghdad

Ayyoub, a Jordanian national working with the Qatar-based satellite channel Al Jazeera, was killed when a U.S. missile struck the station's Baghdad bureau, which was located in a two-story villa in a residential area near the Iraqi Information Ministry and the former presidential palace compound of Saddam Hussein. Al Jazeera assistant cameraman Zouhair Nadhim, who was outside on the building's roof with Ayyoub, was injured in the blast, which targeted a small electric generator outside the building.

CENTCOM maintains that U.S. forces were responding to enemy fire in the area and that the Al Jazeera journalists were caught in the crossfire. Al Jazeera correspondents deny that any fire came from their building.

The attack occurred during heavy fighting around the bureau in an area that housed government buildings targeted by U.S. and coalition forces. Al Jazeera officials pointed out that the U.S. military had been given the bureau's exact coordinates weeks before the war began.

In an April 8 letter to U.S. defense secretary Donald Rumsfeld, CPJ protested the bombing and called for an immediate investigation. In October, a CENT-COM spokesman confirmed to CPJ that no investigation into the incident has been conducted.

The incident occurred around dawn, after intense anti-aircraft fire began in the area. Talk show host and producer Maher Abdullah, a five-year Al Jazeera veteran who had been in Baghdad for two weeks at the time, told CPJ that planes began flying low in the area at around 6 A.M.

The crew went up to the roof of the building to report but retreated because they deemed it unsafe. According to Abdullah, the crew realized moments later that their still camera had been knocked out of position and now faced the Ministry of Information building, which Iraqi authorities had explicitly warned the crew not to film. Assistant cameraman Zouhair Nadhim returned to the roof with Ayyoub to adjust the camera.

When Ayyoub and Nadhim went upstairs, Abdullah heard a plane fly so low it sounded like it was going to crash into the building. At that point, a missile struck Al Jazeera's small generator, which was located outside the building at ground level just below where Ayyoub was believed to have been at the time. Two Al Jazeera correspondents said that while they suspect that the strike caused his death, he could have been killed by other ordnance.

Another plane passed low about fifteen minutes later and fired another missile, which struck across the road about fifty feet (fifteen meters) from the front door, blowing it off the hinges, according to Abdullah.

Raed Khattar, a cameraman for Abu Dhabi TV who, at the time, was outside on the nearby roof of Abu Dhabi TV's office, saw what was likely the first missile because his office was between the plane and Al Jazeera's office, he told CPJ.

Moments later, Abu Dhabi TV staff on the roof came under machine-gun fire from a U.S. tank on the nearby Jumhuriyya Bridge, and one of their three unmanned cameras was struck by a shell, staff told CPJ. The three-story building was marked with a large banner labeled "Abu Dhabi TV."

In a statement issued hours after the incident, CENTCOM in Doha, Qatar, said, "According to commanders on the ground, Coalition forces came under significant enemy fire from the building where the Al Jazeera journalists were working and consistent with the right of self-defense, Coalition forces returned fire. Sadly an Al Jazeera correspondent was killed in this exchange."

Abdullah noted that until that morning anti-aircraft fire in the area had been sporadic. Days before April 8, Abdullah saw manned Iraqi anti-aircraft positions in the general vicinity—some 220 yards (200 meters) away on the opposite side of the generator, but not immediately near the office. However, on April 11, he discovered one abandoned anti-aircraft gun about 44 yards (40 meters) away from the bureau. Journalists from Abu Dhabi TV told CPJ that Al Jazeera's bureau was located near a villa used by former Iraqi information minister Mohammed Saeed al-Sahaf.

Just before the war, CPJ obtained a copy of the February 24, 2003, letter that then Al Jazeera managing director Mohammed Jasem al-Ali had sent to the Pentagon spokeswoman Victoria Clarke specifying the coordinates of the bureau.

Al Jazeera also maintains that the night before the strike, al-Ali had received explicit assurances from U.S. State Department official Nabeel Khoury in Doha, Qatar, that the bureau was safe and would not be targeted. Abdullah told CPJ, "The coordinates were actually given four months in advance to the Pentagon, and we were assured that we would not be hit under any circumstances. . . . We would never be targeted, that was the assurance."

In an e-mail reply to CPJ, Khoury, who said he did not recall the exact date of his meeting with Al Jazeera, said, "I doubt very much that I assured anybody's safety in a war zone." He added that he did tell the station "what we had been telling all diplomats and civilians, that whereas our troops would do their utmost not to hurt civilians, there was no way to guarantee anyone's safety in a war zone."

In its April 8 letter to U.S. secretary of defense Donald Rumsfeld, CPJ also noted that "the attack against Al Jazeera is of particular concern since the stations' offices were also hit in Kabul, Afghanistan, in November 2001. The Pentagon asserted, without providing additional detail, that the office was a 'known Al-Qaeda facility,' and that the U.S. military did not know the space was being used by Al Jazeera."

CPJ is still waiting for the Defense Department to fulfill a Freedom of Information Act request related to the incident that CPJ filed in May.

### José Couso, Telecinco, April 8, 2003, Baghdad

Couso, a cameraman for the Spanish television station Telecinco, died after a U.S. tank fired a shell at the Palestine Hotel in Baghdad, Iraq's capital, where most journalists in the city were based during the war. At around 12 noon, a shell hit two hotel balconies where several journalists were monitoring a battle in the vicinity. Taras Protsyuk, a Ukrainian cameraman for Reuters, was also killed in the attack.

Agence France-Presse reported that Couso was hit in his jaw and right leg. He was taken to Saint Raphael Hospital, where he died during surgery. Couso was married with two children.

Directly after the attack, Maj. Gen. Buford Blount, commander of the U.S. Army's Third Infantry Division, confirmed that a single shell had been fired at the hotel from a tank in response to what he said was rocket and small arms fire from the building. Journalists at the hotel denied that any gunfire had emanated from the building.

A CPJ report concluded that the shelling of the hotel, while not deliberate, was avoidable since U.S. commanders knew that journalists were present in the hotel and were intent on not hitting it. The report called on the Pentagon to conduct a thorough and public investigation into the incident.

On August 12, U.S. Central Command issued a news release summarizing the results of its investigation into the incident. The report concluded that the tank

unit that opened fire on the hotel did so "in a proportionate and justifiably measured response." It called the shelling "fully in accordance with the Rules of Engagement."

CENTCOM offered some detail—consistent with CPJ's investigation—that
the tank opened fire at what it believed was an Iraqi "spotter" directing enemy fire
at U.S. troops. The release also explained that "one 120mm tank round was fired
at the suspected enemy observer position. . . . It was only some time after the incident that A Company became aware of the fact that the building they fired on
was the Palestine Hotel and that journalists at the hotel had been killed or injured
as a result."

However, the news release failed to address one of the conclusions in CPJ's report: that U.S. commanders knew that journalists were in the Palestine Hotel but
failed to convey this knowledge to forces on the ground.

CENTCOM's results, which were summarized in the release, appeared to back
away from earlier charges by U.S. military officials that the tank unit was responding to hostile fire emanating from the hotel. Yet, despite considerable testimony to
the contrary from several journalists in the hotel, CENTCOM maintains "that the
enemy used portions of the hotel as a base of operations and that heavy enemy activity was occurring in those areas in and immediately around the hotel."

In addition, the news release failed to provide other specific information, such
as how the decision to target the hotel was made.

CPJ has urged CENTCOM to make the full report available, but a CENTCOM
spokesperson told CPJ the report is classified. CPJ is still waiting for the Defense
Department to fulfill a Freedom of Information Act request related to the incident
that CPJ filed in May.

### Taras Protsyuk, Reuters, April 8, 2003, Baghdad

Protsyuk, a Ukrainian cameraman for Reuters, died after a U.S. tank fired a
shell at the Palestine Hotel in Baghdad, Iraq's capital, where most journalists in the
city were based during the war. At around 12 noon, a shell hit two hotel balconies
where several journalists were monitoring a battle in the vicinity. José Couso, a
cameraman for the Spanish television station Telecinco, also died in the attack.

Agence France-Presse reported that Protsyuk died of wounds to his head and
stomach. He had worked for Reuters since 1993, covering conflicts in Bosnia,
Kosovo, Chechnya, and Afghanistan. He was married with an eight-year-old son.

Directly after the attack, Maj. Gen. Buford Blount, commander of the U.S.
Army's Third Infantry Division, confirmed that a single shell had been fired at the
hotel from a tank in response to what he said was rocket and small arms fire from
the building. Journalists at the hotel denied that any gunfire had emanated from
the building.

On August 12, U.S. Central Command issued a news release summarizing the results of its investigation into the incident. The report concluded that the tank unit that opened fire on the hotel did so "in a proportionate and justifiably measured response." It called the shelling "fully in accordance with the Rules of Engagement."

CENTCOM offered some detail—consistent with CPJ's investigation—that the tank opened fire at what it believed was an Iraqi "spotter" directing enemy fire at U.S. troops. The release also explained that "one 120mm tank round was fired at the suspected enemy observer position. . . . It was only some time after the incident that A Company became aware of the fact that the building they fired on was the Palestine Hotel and that journalists at the hotel had been killed or injured as a result."

However, the news release failed to address one of the conclusions in CPJ's report: that U.S. commanders knew that journalists were in the Palestine Hotel but failed to convey this knowledge to forces on the ground.

CENTCOM's results, which were summarized in the release, appeared to back away from earlier charges by U.S. military officials that the tank unit was responding to hostile fire emanating from the hotel. Yet, despite considerable testimony to the contrary from several journalists in the hotel, CENTCOM maintains "that the enemy used portions of the hotel as a base of operations and that heavy enemy activity was occurring in those areas in and immediately around the hotel."

In addition, the news release failed to provide other specific information, such as how the decision to target the hotel was made.

CPJ has urged CENTCOM to make the full report available, but a CENTCOM spokesperson told CPJ the report is classified. CPJ is still waiting for the Defense Department to fulfill a Freedom of Information Act request related to the incident that CPJ filed in May.

### Richard Wild, freelance, July 5, 2003, Baghdad

Wild, a twenty-four-year-old British freelance cameraman who was working in Baghdad, died after an unidentified assailant approached him and shot him in the head at close range on a street near the city's Natural History Museum.

Wild, who had previously worked at Britain's ITN as a picture researcher, went to Iraq with aspirations of being a war reporter. Some press reports stated that Wild was not carrying a camera or wearing any clothing that would have identified him as a journalist at the time of the shooting. One of Wild's colleagues in Baghdad, British TV producer Michael Burke, told newspapers that Wild was working on a story about looting at the museum. While some speculated that he may have been mistaken for a member of the U.S. military, the motive for the murder remains unclear. CPJ considers that Wild was killed in action while working.

### Jeremy Little, NBC News, July 6, 2003, Fallujah

Little, an Australian freelance soundman working for the U.S.-based television network NBC, was injured in a grenade attack in the Iraqi town of Fallujah on June 29 while embedded with U.S. troops. He died of "post-operative complications," according to a statement from NBC News. Little, twenty-seven, was embedded with the U.S. Third Infantry Division for NBC News and had been receiving treatment at a military hospital in Germany.

### Mazen Dana, Reuters, August 17, 2003, outside Baghdad

Dana, a veteran conflict cameraman for Reuters news agency, was killed by machine-gun fire from a U.S. tank near the capital, Baghdad. Dana was struck in the torso while filming near Abu Ghraib prison, outside Baghdad, in the afternoon. He had been reporting with a colleague near the prison after a mortar attack had killed six Iraqis there the previous night. The soldier in the tank who fired on Dana did so without warning, while the journalist filmed the vehicle approaching him from about fifty-five yards (fifty meters).

U.S. military officials said the soldier who opened fire mistook Dana's camera for a rocket-propelled grenade launcher. There was no fighting taking place in the area, and the journalists had been operating in the vicinity of the prison with the knowledge of U.S. troops near the prison gates.

In an August 18 letter to U.S. secretary of defense Donald H. Rumsfeld, CPJ protested the shooting, stating that it raised "serious questions about the conduct of U.S. troops and their rules of engagement."

On September 22, the U.S. military announced that it had concluded its investigation into the incident. A spokesman for U.S. CENTCOM in Iraq told CPJ that while Dana's killing was "regrettable," the soldier "acted within the rules of engagement." No further details were provided. The results of the investigation have not been made public. A CENTCOM spokesman said other details of the report are classified.

Dana's soundman, Nael Shyioukhi, who witnessed the incident, told CPJ that he and Dana arrived at the prison with their driver, Munzer Abbas, in the late afternoon. According to Shyioukhi, several journalists were also in the area. Shyioukhi said that after a short while Dana suggested that they approach the prison gates to begin filming. At one point, Dana identified himself to a U.S. soldier as a journalist from Reuters and asked if a spokesman was available to comment on camera about the attack the previous night. The soldier replied that he could not comment, and no spokesmen were available. Dana then asked the soldier if he and Shyioukhi could film the prison from a nearby bridge. According to Shyioukhi, the soldier politely told them they were welcome to do so.

After filming from the bridge, located between 330 and 660 yards (300 and 600 meters) from the prison, Dana and Shyioukhi, who were wearing jeans and T-shirts, packed their equipment in their car and began to head off for the Reuters office. As they approached the main road to the prison, Dana noticed a convoy of tanks approaching and told Abbas to stop so he could film it. According to Shyioukhi, he and Dana were not apprehensive, because the area was calm, and it was apparent that U.S. troops were in complete control. Neither Dana nor Shyioukhi were wearing flak jackets, and their car was not marked as press.

Dana exited the car and set up his blue, canvas-encased camera with a white microphone facing the tanks while Shyioukhi lit a cigarette. Shyioukhi said Dana filmed for about ten seconds, when suddenly, without warning, several shots rang out from the lead tank, which was approximately fifty-five yards (fifty meters) away.

Shyioukhi ducked for cover, then heard Dana scream and place his hand on his stomach, which was bleeding profusely. He said that within moments of the shooting, approximately six U.S. soldiers, including the one who had shot Dana, surrounded them. Shyioukhi recounted that the soldier who had shot Dana screamed at Shyioukhi to "stand back."

A doctor arrived on an armored personnel carrier after about ten minutes and tried to stop the bleeding. The APC took Dana back to the prison complex for treatment and to get him evacuated to a hospital.

U.S. military spokesman Col. Guy Shields called Dana's death a "tragic incident" and promised to do everything possible to avoid a similar incident in the future. When questioned by London's *Independent* about the rules of engagement for U.S. troops, Shields said, "I can't give you details on the rules of engagement, but the enemy is not in formations, they are not wearing uniforms. During wartime firing a warning shot is not a necessity. There is no time for a warning shot if there is potential for an ambush."

Some journalists at the scene questioned how troops could mistake the camera for a weapon. And according to experts who train war correspondents, although one might easily mistake a camera for an RPG launcher at a distance, a camera would be clearly visible from 55 to 110 yards (50 to 100 meters)—the distance at which Dana was hit.

In December 2003, CPJ received an update to a Freedom of Information Act request filed about the incident with the Defense Department. In the update, CENTCOM said it was preparing a response in Baghdad, which would include a "redacted copy" of the classified report written about Dana's death. CENTCOM said it expects the redaction process to take "at least two months."

### Ahmed Shawkat, *Bilah Ittijah*, October 28, 2003, Mosul

Shawkat, editor of the weekly *Bilah Ittijah* (Without Direction), was shot and killed by one or more gunmen at his office in Mosul. According to press reports, a gunman and an accomplice followed the journalist to the roof of his office in the afternoon. One local journalist told CPJ that Shawkat was on the roof making a call from his satellite telephone when he was shot.

CPJ continues to investigate the case for more details, but based on current research, CPJ believes that Shawkat was killed for his work as a journalist.

Sources report that Shawkat's writing often criticized Islamists, Islam, the former regime of Saddam Hussein, and the U.S-led occupation. According to one local journalist who has followed the case, Shawkat had recently written a piece that questioned whether or not Arabic was the language of heaven.

Shawkat's daughter, Roaa, who also works at *Bilah Ittijah*, told CPJ in an e-mail that her father had received several verbal threats warning him to close the newspaper, as well as one written threat a few months before his death. The *Washington Post* reported on November 16 that Shawkat's son, Sindbad, said that the written threat accused Shawkat of being a Zionist guilty of colluding with infidels. The *Post* reported that Sindbad had warned his father not to write about foreign Islamist extremists in Iraq.

According to the local journalist, Shawkat was confronted in his office a few days prior to his shooting by several men with long beards—sometimes a sign of religiosity in Muslim countries. The journalist told CPJ that a man who has an office in the same building as the paper told investigators that he saw the same bearded men fleeing the scene after Shawkat was shot. The journalist said that both local and regional police were investigating the case, but that the regional police has ended its investigations and closed the case file for lack of evidence. The journalist said that an employee of the paper, whom Roaa also mentioned in her e-mail to CPJ as being a suspect in the case, was released by police, also for lack of evidence.

## 2004

### Duraid Isa Mohammed, CNN, January 27, 2004, outside Baghdad

Mohammed, a producer working for the U.S. cable news network CNN and his driver, Yasser Khatab, were killed in an ambush on the outskirts of the capital, Baghdad, CNN reported.

The network said that Mohammed, who also acts as a translator, and Khatab died of multiple gunshot wounds in the afternoon after the two-car convoy they were traveling in came under fire by unidentified assailants. Cameraman Scott McWhinnie, who was traveling in the second vehicle, was grazed in the head by a bullet, CNN said, but the remaining members of the convoy—two CNN journalists, a security adviser, and the second driver—were unharmed. McWhinnie was treated at a nearby military base.

According to CNN, the vehicles were headed north toward Baghdad when a rust-colored Opel approached from behind. A single gunman with an AK-47, positioned through the sunroof, opened fire on one of the vehicles. CNN's vice president for international public relations, Nigel Pritchard, told CPJ that both CNN cars were unmarked and the attackers may not have been aware they were journalists.

### Safir Nader, Qulan TV, February 1, 2004, Arbil

Nader, a cameraman with Qulan TV, which is run by the Kurdistan Democratic Party (KDP), was killed when the offices of the Patriotic Union of Kurdistan (PUK) and the KDP were attacked in twin suicide bombings at about 10:45 A.M. while the two Kurdish political groups hosted guests to commemorate the first day of the Muslim holiday Eid. More than one hundred people, including several senior leaders in both parties, were killed in the attacks.

According to Qulan's station manager Mafouz Mayi, Nader and another cameraman for the station, Haymin Mohamed Salih, were on assignment covering the festivities when they were killed.

Kurdish groups blamed the attack on Islamist extremist groups based in northern Iraq who oppose the secular Kurdish political groups.

### Abdel Sattar Abdel Karim, *Al Ta'akhy*, February 1, 2004, Arbil

Karim, a freelance photographer for the Arabic-language daily *Al-Ta'akhy*, was killed when the offices of the PUK and KDP were attacked in twin suicide bombings at about 10:45 A.M. while the two Kurdish political groups hosted guests to commemorate the first day of the Muslim holiday Eid. More than one hundred people, including several senior leaders in both parties, were killed in the attacks.

One local journalist who knew Abdel Karim said the journalist was covering the festivities at the time of his death.

Kurdish groups blamed the attack on Islamist extremist groups based in northern Iraq who oppose the secular Kurdish political groups.

### Ayoub Mohamed, Kurdistan TV, February 1, 2004, Arbil

Mohamed, a freelance cameraman for the Kurdistan TV, which is run by the KDP, was killed when the offices of the PUK and the KDP were attacked in twin suicide bombings at about 10:45 A.M. while the two Kurdish political groups hosted guests to commemorate the first day of the Muslim holiday Eid. More than one hundred people, including several senior leaders in both parties, were killed in the attacks.

According to a local journalist, Mohamed was working at the time of his death.

Kurdish groups blamed the attack on Islamist extremist groups based in northern Iraq who oppose the secular Kurdish political groups.

### Haymin Mohamed Salih, Qulan TV, February 1, 2004, Arbil

Salih, a cameraman with Qulan TV, which is run by the KDP, was killed when the offices of the PUK and the KDP were attacked in twin suicide bombings at about 10:45 A.M. while the two Kurdish political groups hosted guests to commemorate the first day of the Muslim holiday Eid. More than one hundred people, including several senior leaders in both parties, were killed in the attacks.

According to Qulan's station manager Mafouz Mayi, Haymin Mohamed Salih was on assignment covering the festivities when he was killed. Fellow Qulan TV cameraman Safir Nader was also killed.

Kurdish groups blamed the attack on Islamist extremist groups based in northern Iraq who oppose the secular Kurdish political groups.

### Gharib Mohamed Salih, Kurdistan TV, February 1, 2004, Arbil

Salih, a freelance cameraman for the Kurdistan TV, which is run by the KDP, was killed when the offices of the PUK and the KDP were attacked in twin suicide bombings at about 10:45 A.M. while the two Kurdish political groups hosted guests to commemorate the first day of the Muslim holiday Eid. More than one hundred people, including several senior leaders in both parties, were killed in the attacks.

According to a local journalist, Gharib Mohamed Salih was working at the time of his death.

Kurdish groups blamed the attack on Islamist extremist groups based in northern Iraq who oppose the secular Kurdish political groups.

### Semko Karim Mohyideen, freelance, February 1, 2004, Arbil

Mohyideen, a freelance cameraman hired by the KDP, was killed when the offices of the PUK and the KDP were attacked in twin suicide bombings at about 10:45 A.M. while the two Kurdish political groups hosted guests to commemorate the first day of the Muslim holiday Eid. More than one hundred people, including several senior leaders in both parties, were killed in the attacks.

The KDP had hired Mohyideen to film the event.

Kurdish groups blamed the attack on Islamist extremist groups based in northern Iraq who oppose the secular Kurdish political groups.

### Nadia Nasrat, Iraq Media Network/Diyala TV, March 18, 2004, Baqouba

Nasrat, a news anchor working for the Coalition Provisional Authority's Iraq Media Network, was killed in the town of Baqouba when unidentified armed assailants opened fire on a bus carrying several employees of the IMN's Diyala Media Centre.

Diyala Media Centre produces the IMN's Diyala TV, a local television station.

Technician Najeed Rashid and security guard Muhammad Ahmad Sarham were also killed in the attack, according to Charlie Reiser, the U.S. Army spokesman in Diyala. Ten others were seriously injured.

The bus was transporting employees to the media centre when a car carrying three men approached and overtook the bus as it approached the station's entry road from the main highway, Reiser said. The assailants then opened fire before fleeing the scene.

Reiser said the employees "were targeted because of their affiliation with the Coalition Forces."

### Ali Abdel Aziz, Al-Arabiyya, March 18, 2004 Baghdad

Abdel Aziz, a cameraman with the United Arab Emirates–based news channel Al-Arabiyya, and reporter Ali al-Khatib were shot near a U.S. military checkpoint in Baghdad.

According to Al-Arabiyya, the two journalists, along with a technician and a driver, had gone that evening to cover the aftermath of a rocket attack against the Burj al-Hayat Hotel. The crew arrived at the scene in two vehicles and parked about 110 to 165 yards (100 to 150 meters) away from the checkpoint, which was situated near the hotel. Abdel Aziz, al-Khatib, and technician Mohamed Abdel Hafez approached the soldiers on foot and spoke with them for a few minutes but were told they could not proceed, according to Abdel Hafez.

As the three men, already in their cars, prepared to depart, Abdel Hafez said that the electricity in the area went out and a car driven by an elderly man approached the U.S. troops, crashing into a small metal barrier near a military vehicle at the checkpoint. Abdel Hafez said that as the crew pulled away from the scene, one of their vehicles was struck by gunfire from the direction of the U.S. troops. Abdel Hafez said he witnessed two or three U.S. soldiers firing but was not sure at whom they were firing. He said there had been no other gunfire in the area at the time.

Apparently, bullets passed through the rear windshield of the car in which Abdel Aziz and al-Khatib were driving. Abdel Aziz died instantly of a bullet wound, or wounds, to the head, while al-Khatib died in a hospital the next day, also due to a bullet wound, or wounds, to the head. CPJ is currently seeking more details about the incident.

According to press reports, the U.S. military commander in Iraq, Lt. Gen. Ricardo S. Sanchez, ordered an "urgent review" of the incident. On March 20, U.S. Brig. Gen. Mark Kimmitt, the deputy director of operations for coalition forces in Iraq, appeared to cast doubt on the assertion that U.S. forces were responsible for the journalists' deaths, citing forensic evidence that showed the number of bullets that U.S. troops fired did not match the number that struck the Al-Arabiyya vehicle, and that the wounds suffered by the Al-Arabiyya journalists were not consistent with those likely to be suffered by passengers in a moving vehicle. According to the *Washington Post*, Kimmitt said that U.S. troops had accounted for all but two bullets fired at the car that crashed into the metal barrier, and those. He pointed out, however, that an autopsy revealed that the Al-Arabiyya journalists were hit by at least five bullets.

### Ali al-Khatib, Al-Arabiyya, March 19, 2004 Baghdad

Al-Khatib, a reporter with the United Arab Emirates–based news channel Al-Arabiyya, and cameraman Abdel Aziz were shot near a U.S. military checkpoint in Baghdad on March 18. Abdel Aziz was killed instantly, and al-Khatib died in a hospital the next day.

According to Al-Arabiyya, the two journalists, along with a technician and a driver, had gone on the evening of March 18 to cover the aftermath of a rocket attack against the Burj al-Hayat Hotel. The crew arrived at the scene in two vehicles and parked about 110 to 165 yards (100 to 150 meters) away from the checkpoint, which was situated near the hotel. Abdel Aziz, al-Khatib, and technician Mohamed Abdel Hafez approached the soldiers on foot and spoke with them for a few minutes but were told they could not proceed, according to Abdel Hafez.

As the three men, already in their cars, prepared to depart, Abdel Hafez said that the electricity in the area went out and a car driven by an elderly man approached the U.S. troops, crashing into a small metal barrier near a military vehicle at the checkpoint. Abdel Hafez said that as the crew pulled away from the scene, one of their vehicles was struck by gunfire from the direction of the U.S. troops. Abdel Hafez said he witnessed two or three U.S. soldiers firing but was not sure at whom they were firing. He said there had been no other gunfire in the area at the time.

Apparently, bullets passed through the rear windshield of the car in which Abdel Aziz and al-Khatib were driving. Abdel Aziz died instantly of a bullet wound, or wounds, to the head, while al-Khatib died in a hospital the next day, also due to a bullet wound, or wounds, to the head. CPJ is currently seeking more details about the incident.

According to press reports, the U.S. military commander in Iraq, Lt. Gen. Ricardo S. Sanchez, ordered an "urgent review" of the incident. On March 20, U.S. Brig. Gen. Mark Kimmitt, the deputy director of operations for coalition forces in Iraq, appeared to cast doubt on the assertion that U.S. forces were responsible for the journalists' deaths, citing forensic evidence that showed the number of bullets that U.S. troops fired did not match the number that struck the Al-Arabiyya vehicle, and that the wounds suffered by the Al-Arabiyya journalists were not consistent with those likely to be suffered by passengers in a moving vehicle. According to the *Washington Post*, Kimmitt said that U.S. troops had accounted for all but two bullets fired at the car that crashed into the metal barrier. He pointed out, however, that an autopsy revealed that the Al-Arabiyya journalists were hit by at least five bullets.

### Burhan Mohamed Mazhour, ABC, March 26, 2004, Fallujah

Mazhour, an Iraqi cameraman freelancing for the U.S.-based television network ABC, was killed in the city of Fallujah, about thirty-five miles (fifty-six kilometers) west of the capital, Baghdad.

The *Washington Post* reported that fifteen Iraqis were killed in Fallujah following a firefight that occurred "as U.S. Marines conducted house-to-house searches" in the city. Agence France-Presse reported that Mazhour, who had been freelancing for ABC for nearly two months, was standing among a group of working journalists "when U.S. troops fired in their direction."

According to ABC News, Mazhour was struck in his head by a single bullet and later died in a hospital. ABC News has asked the U.S. military to conduct an investigation.

In addition the following journalists died in Iraq of causes not related to military action: NBC correspondent David Bloom, who died April 6, 2003, of a pulmonary embolism while traveling with the U.S. Third Army Infantry Division; Elizabeth Neuffer, a veteran foreign correspondent for the *Boston Globe*, and her translator, who were killed May 9, 2003, in a car accident while on assignment in Iraq; veteran *Los Angeles Times* correspondent Mark Fineman, who died September 23, 2003, of an apparent heart attack while on assignment in Iraq's capital, Baghdad.

Four journalists were taken captive on March 24, 2003 and released on April 1, 2003: freelance photographer Molly Bingham; Johan Rydeng Spanner, a freelance photographer with the Danish daily *Jyllands Posten*; and correspondent Matthew McAllester and photographer Moises Saman, both with *Newsday*.

## APPENDIX G

Of the 800 journalists who applied for military training, 232 representatives of all media types were selected. Thirty-nine women (17 percent of the total) underwent training: six in the first training session; eleven in the second; fourteen in the third; and eight in the final.

There were three training sites, but Quantico offered two of the four sessions. The first Quantico training included some time aboard a naval ship. Training was piggybacked with usual military training whenever possible.

The curriculum included several components:

- Basic military skills for people who knew nothing about the military
- First aid
- Protection from nuclear, biological, and chemical weapons
- Behavior under direct and indirect fire
- Exiting from helicopters
- Personal camouflage
- Land navigation
- General information about military rank, sanitation in the field, communications on the battlefield

The news organizations paid for the trainees' meals and lodging when appropriate. There was no evaluation in terms of mastering the training. The journalists participating were asked to give feedback about the training's usefulness. "No one said it was not worthwhile. The journalists all did well," says Lieutenant Colonel Gary L. Keck, who was in charge of the training.

# APPENDIX H

## MAP OF IRAQ

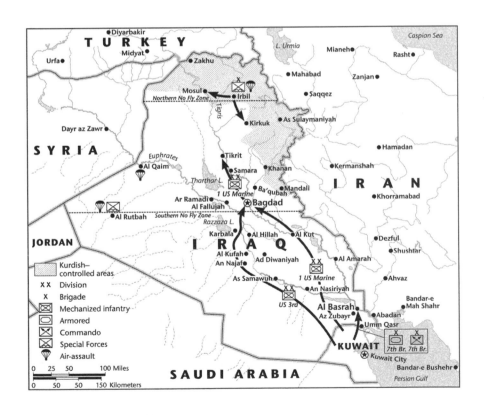

# INDEX

# ABOUT THE AUTHORS

**Judith Sylvester** is associate professor at the Manship School of Mass Communication at Louisiana State University (LSU). She received her doctorate and master of arts (news/editorial) at the University of Missouri, Columbia, and her bachelor of science (English/education) at Southwest Missouri State University. She founded and supervised the Media Research Bureau at the University of Missouri for nine years before joining the faculty at LSU. She served as journalism area head at the Manship School for eight years. She is currently the senior member of the Media Leaders Forum, which regularly conducts surveys of newsroom decision makers and which produces case studies for *Quill* magazine. She teaches media research, ethics, and theory courses. Dr. Sylvester is the author of *Directing Health Care Messages toward African Americans: Attitudes toward Health Care and the Mass Media* (1998), and she is the principal investigator for the LSU–Southern University SmokingWords project.

**Suzanne Huffman** is associate professor of journalism and the broadcast journalism sequence head at Texas Christian University (TCU), in Fort Worth. She was born and raised in east Tennessee. A National Merit Scholar, she earned her bachelor of arts at TCU; her master of arts at the University of Iowa; and her doctorate at the University of Missouri School of Journalism. She has reported, anchored, and produced news at commercial television stations in Tampa, Florida; in Santa Maria, California; and in Cedar Rapids, Iowa. At TCU, Dr. Huffman created SkiffTV (www.skiff.tcu.edu/SkiffTV) and works with faculty colleagues to cross-train students in broadcast, print, and online journalism. Her academic research centers on the practice of broadcast journalism, and her research articles have been published in the *Journal of Broadcasting & Electronic Media* and other academic journals. Dr. Huffman is coauthor, with C. A. Tuggle and Forrest Carr, of *Broadcast News Handbook: Writing, Reporting, and Producing in a Converging Media World* (2000), now in its second edition. She is also a contributing author to *Indelible Images: Women of Local Television* (2001).

Dr. Sylvester and Dr. Huffman coauthored *Women Journalists at Ground Zero: Covering Crisis* (2002). The book contains the stories of twenty-four women who covered the events of September 11, 2001, from New York City, Washington, D.C., and rural Pennsylvania. In 2003, the book won first place in the research division of the National Federation of Press Women's annual contest.